Time Zones,
Containers and
Three Square Meals a Day

Maria Staal

Time Zones, Containers and Three Square Meals a Day

Maria Staal

To my brother Arjen, who accompanied me part of the way
and
Rodel, who became a lifelong friend

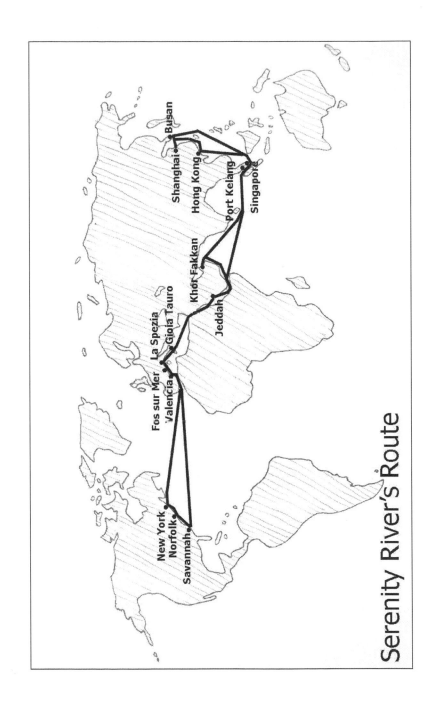

Serenity River's Route

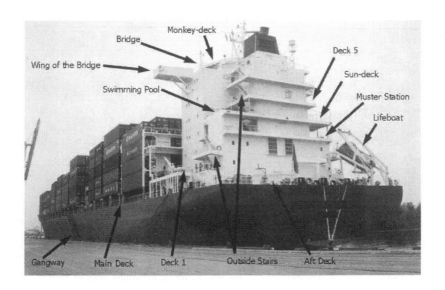

CHAPTER ONE

It was Tuesday afternoon nearly 17.30h and time for the evening meal. I walked down the four flights of stairs from my cabin and turned left into the corridor on deck 1. Normally the corridor would be quiet around this time as the Filipinos were usually having their meal in the crew-mess, but this afternoon a small group of them hovered at the end, some of them peering through the open door of the officers' lounge.

As I looked into the lounge myself, I saw a scattering of books, videotapes and glasses. All the cupboard doors had been left open and the video recorder and dvd-player removed from their respective shelves and placed on the floor.

'What on earth has happened here?' I asked, as I stepped past the Filipinos into the lounge.

'Oh...' Mr Chavira said with a cheeky grin, '...the Russian engineer has done some tidying.'

I looked around more closely. The videotapes were sorted into two piles, English and German. Books the same. All the wires of the dvd-player and video recorder had been rolled up into neat little bundles. The glasses, cups and mugs put in order.

Mr Chavira disappeared in the direction of the crew-mess and Nick, one of the passengers, and I looked at Rodel. The past week-and-a-half on board had taught us that he as steward usually knew what was going on around the ship and we were in need of an explanation, if not some gossip.

'What happened here, Rodel?' Nick asked.

Rodel stepped into the lounge, looking over his shoulder in a conspiratorial way. He leant closer to us and whispered: 'The Russian has gone crazy...'

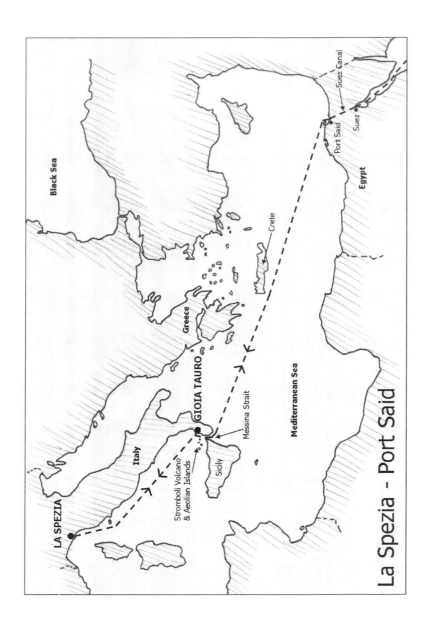

La Spezia - Port Said

CHAPTER TWO

It was a week-and-a-half before the incident in the officers' lounge that I embarked on the *Serenity River* a 225-metre long container ship, which would be my home for the next three months and where I would work for the Ariel Rügen Shipping Company, writing a guide-book for the passengers.

The captain had shrugged his shoulders as his eyes skimmed through the letter from the shipping company that I had handed him, explaining what I was doing on board and said it was all fine with him, as long as I didn't get in anyone's way.

That was why on Sunday afternoon 5th January 2003, Lukas, the tall blonde Swiss passenger, who was in his early 20s, and I, a 33-year old Dutch woman, had a great view as our ship sailed from La Spezia in northern Italy. The bay on which we sailed was enclosed by green hills and in the distance, we could see the snow-capped mountains of the Apennine mountain range.

As the ship left the port several small villages were gliding by, most of them clinging to the steep sides of the hills, their houses painted in bright colours. La Spezia was behind us and as the *Serenity River* turned around the breakwater, we could see the castle of Lerici, high on a hill, protecting the bay. It was sunny and not very cold, but there was a breezy south-westerly wind.

Lukas and I had climbed on to the roof of the bridge, which was the highest point on the ship and commonly known as the monkey-deck. In front of us, the deck of the *Serenity River*, stacked high with containers, stretched out.

After the ship had turned around the breakwater, it suddenly became much colder. Lukas shivered in his thin jacket.

'It's getting a bit cold,' he said. 'I am going back to my cabin.'

'Yeah, no worries,' I said. 'I will see you in the mess shortly.'

It was nearly time for the evening meal, which was good, as I was getting hungry. I enjoyed the view for a little while longer and sniffed the air. Every now and then, I could smell the mixture of metal and heavy fuel oil, a scent I had come to identify with ships and ports. It was really great to be at sea again, I had missed it.

As we sailed out of the bay on to the open Mediterranean Sea, the wind became stronger and the sea choppy. Immediately the ship started moving in an irregular fashion. Not a slow easy rolling on the swell, but an uncomfortable bouncy movement, like a cork on water. Due to the Christmas season, we didn't carry much cargo, and the *Serenity* was riding very high in the water. Without the weight of the cargo, it was easy for the short heavy waves to make the ship move. The deck was bouncing and moving under my feet, and I was able to remain standing only with difficulty.

It didn't take long for a familiar feeling to come up through my stomach. Two years before something similar had happened to me on the *Pegasus Star* when leaving the port of Sydney. But then we had travelled through a tropical cyclone; now there wasn't more than a moderate wind.

'This doesn't feel good,' I mumbled to no one in particular, as I felt more nauseated by the second. 'I'm going to be seasick, and we've only left La Spezia 30 minutes ago...' The popular myth that you only get seasick once and after that never again was clearly not true.

I went inside and to my cabin on deck 5. It was 17.30h, time for the evening meal and I thought it would be a good idea to try to eat at least something. I took off my coat and swallowed a seasickness pill.

4

Descending the stairs on the way to the mess, I tried to act as if nothing was wrong, but I shouldn't have bothered. I didn't bump into anyone.

Rodel was waiting in the mess for the officers and passengers to arrive. With his 25 years, he was the youngest crew-member onboard; medium height and build with the black hair and dark eyes that all Filipinos have.

'Tonight's meal will be rice and goulash,' he said, observing me closely. I knew he could see I was seasick.

'Just some rice and sauce will do me, thanks.'

As Rodel turned around on his way to the kitchen, I could swear I saw a twinkle in his eyes.

I sat down in my regular spot as Lukas walked in. He seemed perfectly fine and I thought to myself that it was very unfair that a landlubber, who had never been at sea before, should be having no problems.

Soon Rodel came in with my plateful of cooked rice and I ate some with difficulty. The ship was still bouncing up and down, causing the cups to rattle around on their saucers. As Rodel brought Lukas his plate of food, one look at it was enough to make me even sicker. I got up.

'I'm sorry, Rodel, but I am not very hungry tonight.'

As fast as I could I walked back up the stairs to my cabin. The only thing I wanted to do was lie down. I hurriedly put my pyjamas on and was fast asleep within five minutes.

When I woke up four-and-a-half hours later, it was only 22.30h. The weird swell had stopped and the ship was gliding quietly through the waves. I could feel the familiar drone of the engines in the distance. The seasickness had nearly gone. I read for a while, but soon fell asleep again.

Waking up the next morning I felt great and at 07.30h went down to the mess for breakfast.

'Good morning, how are you today?' Rodel asked as I walked in.

'Morning, Rodel,' I answered, ignoring his question. 'I'm up for a large breakfast. What's on the menu?'

'Mushroom omelette.'

'Ah, my favourite.'

'Shall I let the cook add extra mushrooms?'

'That would be great, thanks Rodel.'

We grinned at each other as I sat down.

CHAPTER THREE

After leaving La Spezia, our first port of call was Gioia Tauro and it took the *Serenity River* just 24 hours to reach it. The sleepy little village of Gioia Tauro is situated on the top of the toe of Italy in a region that is very rural, so it was a bit surprising to find a large port in this area. On inquiry, I found that it was used as a transhipment port, from where containers were transported from large ships, like the *Serenity*, on to smaller ships, which in turn took them to smaller ports along the Mediterranean coast.

Gioia Tauro's port had a reputation of long waiting periods, and as was predicted by several people beforehand, we had to wait for 36 hours before we could berth. The sea was too deep to anchor, so we just floated around, together with some six or seven other container ships, also waiting for a berth.

As we waited, the crew and passengers walked around with bored faces. *Serenity's* crew complement was 20 people, seven officers, mostly German and 14 crew, mostly Filipino.

***

It was Tuesday 7th January, nearly 20 hours after we first arrived near Gioia Tauro, when at lunchtime in the mess the captain mumbled to Lukas and me that he was getting sick of drifting around.

'After lunch we will set sail for the Aeolian Islands. This will give us something to do,' he said between two puffs on his cigarette.

'Will there be anything interesting to see?' I asked.

'Stromboli Volcano maybe, if we get close enough.'

7

He didn't sound very enthusiastic about it, but we had already discovered that the captain wasn't very enthusiastic about anything. Being in his late 50s, not too tall with a large beer belly and greying dark hair, he seemed to have seen it all before during his lifelong career at sea. He was, however, friendly enough to us.

After lunch, we went on our way to the Aeolian Islands and I found it was nice to be moving again after 20 hours of going nowhere. We moved at the slow speed of 10-15 knots and after a couple of hours Stromboli's distinctive volcano silhouette became visible on the horizon.

As Stromboli drew near, I was standing on the wing of the bridge with Lukas and the second officer. I remembered seeing in an Italian newspaper four days earlier, that the volcano had been erupting.

All three of us were staring through binoculars at the volcano, around which we were making a slow large circle. Even though the eruption had been a week ago, a dense cloud of smoke still rolled down the north side of the volcano into the sea.

'Can you see the little village on the east side?' the second officer asked, pointing at the little white houses visible against the dark green-grey of the mountain.

'Yes. I wouldn't want to live there,' Lukas remarked.

'No, neither would I,' the second officer said. He was a German in his late 20s, tall and thin, with a South African mother. We later discovered that if he spoke Afrikaans and I my native Dutch, we could more or less understand each other.

In the morning, before our outing to the Aeolian Islands, the second officer had taken Lukas and me on our compulsory 'safety walk' around the ship, during which safety and ship rules were explained.

8

The second officer had ticked them off on his outstretched hand. 'No walking forward or aft in heavy weather. No walking forward during the loading of the containers, except to reach the gangway. No hanging around the aft deck or fo'c'sle while berthing. No wandering into the engine-room without an appointment. No entry to the bridge while the pilot is on board. Let the officer-on-watch know you're going on shore leave, and report back in when you return. Keep an eye on the notice board for the announcements of safety drills and changing of the clock.'

He stopped to take a breath and noticed Lukas' slightly stunned look.

'I know it all sounds pretty strict, but it is actually just basic safety,' he said with a smile. 'Now let's go to the muster station.' We went outside to the starboard, or right, side of deck 3. The landing was a bit wider here than on the other outside decks and gave access to the lifeboat.

'This is the muster or assembly station,' the second officer said with a sweep of his arm. 'If the alarm goes off you come here, along with almost everyone else, for a headcount and to receive instructions on what to do. During an emergency we might have to board the lifeboat.' He pointed at the bright orange lifeboat that was hanging at a 45°-angle in its launching contraption on the aft deck. 'So it is important always to come to muster station when the alarm goes off, also during a safety drill.'

Lukas and I nodded with solemn faces.

'That concludes the safety walk. Make sure to remember Ship Rule Number One: "One hand for you and one hand for the ship". This means that, wherever you are on the ship, always make sure you keep one hand free, so you can grab on to something in case you slip, especially outside, as you really don't want to tumble overboard on the high seas.' Again, Lukas and I nodded that we had understood.

Rule Number One actually helped me out one day as I was coming down one of the outside stairs. It had been a bit rainy and halfway down my feet slipped from under me and I half slid, half fell down the stairs on my bottom and managed to stop my descent by grabbing on to the railings. At least there had never been a chance of me falling overboard, but I was sore for days and afterwards moved around with even more care then before...

I watched Stromboli for a while and as it disappeared from sight, I made my way down to my cabin to begin work on the guide-book. I thought it was high time I started earning my keep, as I hadn't done anything so far. The Ariel Rügen Shipping Company wasn't going to give me a free trip for nothing and they were expecting to see a nice informative guide-book at the end of my three months on board.

The next day, Wednesday 8th January, I woke up at 06.00h by an increase in the drone of the engines. The whole night we had continued our slow circle around the Aeolian Islands, and as the ship suddenly started to go full ahead, I, still half asleep, was convinced the captain had given up on a berth at Gioia Tauro and had set sail for the Suez Canal. Obviously, this was not the case and as I went down for breakfast at 07.30h, the port of Gioia Tauro was in sight.

When we finally berthed at 08.00h, I watched the procedure with Rodel from deck 1. He had a rare few minutes of leisure as Lukas and I had already eaten and the rest of the crew were too busy with berthing to think of breakfast.

'Are you planning to go on shore leave?' he asked, as we watched the quay coming closer and closer.

'Yes, I am. I need to find some information about the town to write in the guide-book,' I answered. 'Have you ever been to Gioia Tauro?'

'No, but according to some of the guys, it is very boring.'

'Great...' I said with a bit of a sigh. 'Never mind. I have to visit it any way.'

'Well, enjoy.' With a wave of his hand, Rodel moved to the door to go back to work.

After we had berthed, the loading and off-loading of the containers could begin. Hereto two large gantry cranes, their safety lights flashing and bells ringing, slowly moved towards the ship along the rails that were running parallel to the edge of the quay. The gantries' long arms still pointed up into the sky.

I watched as the cranes manoeuvred themselves into the right spot along our hull and then let their arms down into a horizontal position.

In the meantime, several port workers, or stevedores, had come on board to let the first officer know about the loading schedule. The nerve centre during cargo operations was the ships' office on the main deck. From there also the stability of the ship was monitored, for as containers were taken off and on, the balance of the ship shifted. To avoid capsizing, water was pumped in and out of the ballast tanks to keep it level.

Soon the cranes were off-loading the containers from our deck. One by one, they were lifted and moving through the air on steel cables to be deposited on to the empty trailer of a truck standing on the quay beneath the crane. One truck could in general just carry one container, so as soon as they were loaded they moved off to make way for another empty truck.

Most of the containers were destined for storage first, before being reloaded on to trucks or trains or smaller ships for further transportation. Long rows of stacked containers stood a bit further inland on the quay, waiting to be shipped to their ultimate destination.

Logistically all this had to be a challenge and as I watched the cargo operations I imagined what a nightmare it would be to lose some containers. It probably would be near impossible to find them again in this jungle of steel with all its colourful containers, and where trucks and cranes of all sizes were moving around continuously.

The large gantry cranes that were taking the containers off the *Serenity* were relatively quiet. Just making soft whirring noises every time the grappler moved over the ship. It depended on the skill of the person moving the crane, however, how silent the operation really was. Some crane drivers were very good at aiming the grappler and were able to lock on to the containers with minimal noise. Others were rougher, which resulted in loud banging noises whenever a container was taken up or let down. Often the banging would be accompanied by a slight trembling; making it feel as if a light earthquake was hitting the ship.

Cargo operations went on day and night, and I always hoped they wouldn't do the rows closest to the accommodation at night. I always found it difficult to sleep, with the noise, the trembling and the bright lights that kept moving backwards and forwards all night.

After I had watched all the activity for a while, I went back inside to get ready for shore leave.

It was about 11.00h when Guiseppe, a short stubby Italian with a large black moustache who ran a shuttle bus service, dropped Lukas and me off in the centre of Gioia Tauro. A return ticket from the port to the town, a distance of about seven kilometres, cost eight euros, which seemed reasonable. He was going to pick us up again in three hours, but as soon as he drove off we realised that we probably only needed half that time to explore the town. It had an atmosphere of a seaside town gone out of fashion. Shutters were closed and nobody was about.

'I will have to find a tourist information,' I said looking around the very quiet main square. 'I want to have a map of this place.'

'Okay,' Lukas said. 'I need to find a shop that sells a battery for my watch. I think I saw one from the shuttle bus.' He nodded in the direction we had come.

'Well... good luck with that... I'm going that way.' I pointed to the end of the square, behind which I hoped would be some sort of shopping street.

As I walked off, I looked at the white Mediterranean houses and palm trees that surrounded the square. Reaching the corner, I noticed a small shrine, consisting of a picture of the Virgin Mary and some flowers, located in a niche in the wall of a house.

It turned out that the narrow streets behind the square didn't have any shops. I wandered around; taking a picture here and there, until I spotted what looked like the sign of a travel agent in a side street. In the hope they could at least tell me something about the town I went inside. Talking to the lady behind the desk, a problem soon emerged. She couldn't speak a word of English and I not any Italian. Somehow, she was able to tell me that there was no 'informazione turistiche' in Gioia Tauro and consequently no map of the town existed.

Defeated I walked back to the square to meet up with Lukas. His expedition had been a bit more successful. We discovered a small bakery at the far end of the square and bought some sandwiches, which we ate sitting on a bench in the middle of the square. A lone moped carrying two teenagers without helmets raced by with a lot of noise. Apart from the soft gurgling of the fountain, it was the only sound to be heard.

Guiseppe picked us back up at 13.05h.

Back at the ship, we noticed a man going up the gangway in front of us, carrying a heavy suitcase. He was somewhere in his late forties, tall and broad shouldered. What was left of his hair was blonde.

We soon caught up with him.

'Hi,' I said. 'You must be the new passenger.'

The man balanced his suitcase on one of the steps and put out his hand.

'Yes indeed, I'm Nick. I'm going to Singapore.' He shook our respective hands. 'Are you passengers too?'

'I am,' Lukas nodded. 'I'm going to Singapore as well.'

'I'm not,' I said. 'I'm working for Ariel Rügen, writing a guide-book.'

'Oh...? That sounds interesting. You must tell me more about it later on.' He pointed at his suitcase. 'I better drag this monster up to my cabin and do some unpacking.'

We accompanied Nick further up the gangway.

Once inside the accommodation block, Lukas said he was going to lie down for a bit. I had planned to do some more work on the guide-book, but after the blank I had drawn in Gioia Tauro I didn't feel like it any more.

I went to the officers' lounge instead and poked around in the cupboards for a bit. It didn't reveal much of interest. They mostly contained books in German and a collection of dvds with documentaries about the picturesque Swiss Alps. Then a plastic bag sparked my curiosity. It seemed to contain the pieces of a jigsaw

14

puzzle. The original cardboard box was nowhere to be found however, so I had no idea what the picture was supposed to be.

This was just the challenge I needed and as I waited until it was time for the evening meal, I started piecing together the edge.

CHAPTER FOUR

That evening, after our meal, Nick, Lukas and I retired to the lounge. As I continued with the jigsaw, I half watched Nick trying to get the tv to work. The reception of tv channels on a ship depends completely on the proximity to land. Only close to the coast were we able to get a signal and watch the channels from the countries we were passing.

Nick seemed very much at home on the ship for a newcomer and becoming curious, I asked him, 'have you travelled on a container ship before?'

Nick stopped fiddling with the tv and sat down on a chair near Lukas and me.

'Yes,' he answered. 'I came from Singapore to Europe on this very ship five weeks ago and disembarked in La Spezia. Then while the *Serenity River* did her trip to the United States I travelled through Europe, visiting friends.'

'Ah... that explains it,' I nodded. 'Where did you go in Europe, if I may ask?'

'Germany mostly. I am originally from the UK, but I lived in Germany for quite a few years. I now live in Australia.'

'So you speak German?' Lukas asked. He had been looking through a pile of illegally copied dvds, which were in plastic see-through envelopes, each with its own badly photocopied cover. Unable to find any of interest he dumped the stack on the table.

'Yes, I do. It was handy on the way over to Europe, as most of the German officers on this ship don't speak English very well.' Nick took the stack of dvds from the table and started flicking through it as well.

'Is the crew still the same then?' I asked. I knew some new people had joined in La Spezia, but not exactly how many.

'Mostly, I think. The Filipinos are the same, and the captain, first officer and chief engineer. It's possible that one of the ship-mechanics, the second officer and the third engineer are new.'

After looking through the dvds for a while Nick looked up at me and asked, 'so you said you work for the Ariel Rügen Shipping Company. What is it that you do exactly?'

'I am writing a guide-book for the passengers who travel on this container ship.' I stopped looking at the jigsaw pieces and leant back on the couch.

'Ah... Just this ship?'

'No, the book is meant for this ship and three sister ships that do the same route. But it is not going to be a real book to be published. More like a one-off scrapbook with information about the ship, its route and the different ports that are visited. It will tell the passengers how to get from the ship to the centre of a town, what sights there are to see etcetera.'

Nick nodded and put the dvds on the table. 'That sort of information is often hard to get on a ship. Not every captain is keen to play the tourist guide for passengers.'

'Exactly, I hope that the book will fill the gap by giving practical, local information.'

'Where do you get the information?'

'I have already done some research at home on the specific ports we visit. But I will also try to go ashore in each port and gather information about the port from ship's agents, taxi drivers etcetera. Information about the ship and the routes, I will obviously get on board from the officers and crew.'

'Have you written a guide-book like this before?'

'Yeah, last year. I then did a three-month round trip on the *FTK Kowloon* and wrote a book for that ship and four sister ships, also on the same route.'

Lukas had been listening quietly. He had heard part of the story before, but now he asked, 'how did you get this job? It sounds like an ideal way to travel and see the world.'

'It is ideal,' I smiled. 'I absolutely love it. I guess I was lucky to get this job. Three years ago, I was a passenger on a container ship going from Europe to Australia. I went the same way back and the captain, although he was a nice guy, didn't seem much interested in helping out the passengers.

'So whenever we were in a port, I went to the tourist information and got a whole pile of leaflets about the town and the sights. Back on the ship, I cut out the pictures from the leaflets and arranged them on pieces of paper, together with some information about the town. The first officer loved the idea and gave me a folder for the pages. It formed a one-off scrapbook with information for the passengers, which stayed onboard the ship.

'When the ship reached Rotterdam and I disembarked the captain told me I should send a copy of the scrapbook to Ariel Rügen. He was sure the shipping company would be willing to give me a free trip on another ship, if I made another guide-book for them. I did just that, and here I am.'

'Wow,' Nick said. 'So you invented your own job.'

'Basically, yes,' I nodded. 'I guess I was lucky that I phoned Ariel Rügen just at the time they were already thinking about the possibilities of a guide-book for their ships.'

'So you don't get paid, but instead get a free trip?' Lukas asked.

'Yep.'

'Cool.'

Outside the loading of the containers still continued and every now and then, the ship shook slightly. The loading would be finished soon.

'Isn't it strange to be the only woman on board?' Lukas asked after a short silence in which I had turned my attention back to the jigsaw.

'No, not really,' I answered. 'I originally studied construction engineering. That is also a profession with very few women, so I am used to it. And I must say that I have never felt threatened in any way while on any of the ships. Even in ports I have never had any problems.'

'Talking of ports... what did you guys think of Gioia Tauro?' Nick asked, changing the subject.

'A very quiet town,' Lukas said. 'Not much happening.'

'A bit boring,' I remarked. 'I had trouble finding information about it.'

'I spent three days in Gioia Tauro waiting for the ship to berth,' Nick said.

Lukas stared at him. 'Wow, that must have been horrible...'

Nick smiled.

'It wasn't too bad. Being the only tourist, I was actually invited to the mayor's office. He gave me a map of the town. You can borrow it for your book, if you like. I could point out some of the sights.'

'There were actual sights?' Lukas asked dryly.

'A very pretty cathedral.'

'Ah...'

During the last part of our conversation, the third engineer had wandered into the lounge. In his late 30s, he was short and thin, with dark brown hair and a moustache. He had listened to us for a bit and as our conversation fell silent, he introduced himself as Peter, in very broken English. Would it be okay if he talked to us every now and then, so his English would improve? Of course, we said, no problem.

We left Gioia Tauro at 21.45h that evening for the Suez Canal. I had been hoping to see the ship go through the Messina Strait in daylight, but it was dark again, just as it had been on the *Galactic Star*, the ship I had travelled on as a passenger when I returned to Europe from Australia.

The Messina Strait is the stretch of water between the end of Italy's toe and Sicily, and the most direct route to the Suez Canal from Gioia Tauro. When we went through the Strait on the *Galactic Star* it had been the late evening and the street lights and buildings of Reggio on the main land, and Messina on the Island of Sicily, had been clearly visible on either side of the narrow water.

***

Keeping to our average speed, around 20 knots, it took us about 55 hours to get from Gioia Tauro to the Mediterranean entrance of the Suez Canal at Port Said in Egypt. Not much happened in that time. I continued writing the guide-book, while Nick and Lukas watched movies in the lounge or tried to put pieces in the jigsaw. It was still too cold to be outside much, and the swimming pool outside on deck 4 hadn't been filled up with water yet.

I was lucky to have the owners' cabin, one of the largest on board, which was the corner cabin on the port, or left, side on deck 5. It had windows looking forward as well as to the side. Apart from a large living room, with sitting area and desk, I had a separate bedroom with an en-suite bathroom.

Also on deck 5 was a smaller single cabin, occupied by Lukas, and the captain's office that was only ever really used in a port when the ship's agent or customs & immigration officers came on board.

Nick's cabin was on deck 4.

Routine set in on the ship and I quickly noticed that in addition to the captain, most of the officers were heavy smokers - puffing away in the lounge in the evenings, while watching a movie.

Luckily, only the captain had the annoying habit of smoking in the mess, usually when everyone else was still eating. He always managed to smoke three cigarettes within five minutes after finishing his plate, filling the whole mess with dense smoke. It made me cough and loose my appetite, as I didn't feel like taking in lots of smoke at the same time as whatever food was on my fork. Disgusting!

At one point on our trip to Port Said, we passed some American navy ships. They were also on the way to the Suez Canal. January 2003 was the build up to the American invasion of Iraq and 60,000 American soldiers were on their way to the Gulf.

On Thursday evening as I went back to my cabin from our evening meal in the mess, I came past the notice board in the stairwell on deck 1, where important messages were posted with bright orange and yellow magnets. Two messages were always posted on the board and never seemed to change - a crew-list and the weekly menu of the meals that would be served in the officers' mess. This time a new message had appeared warning us that the clocks had to be put forward one hour that night. It was the first of many occasions during the trip that the clocks needed changing and this time it would take us to Egyptian time.

**

On Saturday morning, 11th January, 06.00h the *Serenity River* joined the second south-bound convoy into the Suez Canal.

Contrary to what many people think, ships can't just go through the Canal by themselves - they have to go in a convoy. Two south-bound convoys leave Port Said every day, the main one at 01.00h, a smaller one at 06.00h.

A north-bound convoy leaves Suez, on the southern end of the Canal, also at 06.00h.

The north-bound and south-bound convoys can't pass each other in the Canal itself, as ships these days are too wide. Instead, the north-bound convoy and main south-bound convoy pass each other in the Bitter Lakes.

The second, smaller, south-bound convoy waits for the north-bound convoy in a side canal.

At 10.30h, our convoy had reached the side canal and the *Serenity* was, along with all the other ships in the convoy, diverted for its wait. Two Egyptians in a little boat caught our lines and fastened them to large concrete bollards situated along the side of the canal. After the ship was secured, the Egyptians' boat was winched up to the height of our main deck, where the two men disembarked.

According to the rules, every ship that traverses the Suez Canal has to have on board at least: a) two pilots b) two mooring men c) an electrician. The mooring men come onboard in case the ship gets engine trouble and needs to be fastened along the Canal. Sandstorms can also stop the convoys, as the Suez Canal cuts through a desert.

On disembarkation from their little boat, the two mooring men subsequently 'set up shop' on our main deck. Like everyone on board, they had to wait until we started moving again, possibly for up to seven hours. In the meantime, no one had much to do and the mooring men saw the wait as an opportunity to make a little bit of money on the side. So they emerged from their little boat laden with boxes full of cheap trinkets.

Our main deck was soon turned into a shop as mats and blankets were rolled out on which were displayed an array of plastic pyramids and sphinxes, fake papyrus roles, bunches of 30-year old postcards, three shoeboxes full of illegally copied cds and dvds, some cans of fizzy drinks and cheap mobile phone covers.

After lunch, I walked down to the main deck with Nick and Lukas and soon we were looking down at everything that was laid out. The mooring men looked up at us with hopeful faces.

After a while Nick said, 'Maybe we could buy a bunch of ten postcards and divide them among us?'

'That's not a bad idea.'

I picked up a bunch of postcards and looked through them. The pictures on the front of the cards were clearly taken many years ago - some were of old-fashioned ships in the Suez Canal, others of buildings along it.

'How much is a bunch of ten postcards?' I asked one of the mooring men.

'Five US dollars.'

I looked at Nick and Lukas and they nodded their assent.

'Done,' I said and gave the man his money.

Some of the Filipinos had come down and were looking through the dvds for movies they hadn't seen yet. We lingered on the main deck a bit longer and looked out on to the island that separated us from the Suez Canal. It was filled with shallow sand dunes.

All the time we were on the main deck, Lukas had been very quiet. He seemed slightly uncomfortable near the Egyptians. At lunchtime he had told us it was his first time outside Europe and said he wasn't sure yet how to interact with non-Western cultures. Soon he went back inside to have a rest in his cabin.

Around 13.00h the north-bound convoy started to go by in the Suez Canal. It was a fascinating sight. The sandy island between the Canal and us made it look as if the ships were floating through the dessert.

It took until 17.00h for the whole north-bound convoy to pass, after which we could finally go on our way.

That evening, after the captain had come down to the mess and manoeuvred his considerable bulk into his usual seat, he casually remarked to us, 'you won't be allowed to go ashore in Jeddah.'

'What...?' Nick and I said in unison.

Jeddah, situated on the Red Sea, in Saudi Arabia was our next port of call and I had really been looking forward to visiting it, mainly because Saudi Arabia was not a country I had been to before.

Nick was also clearly disappointed.

'Why can't we go ashore in Jeddah?' he asked.

'They don't let passengers go on shore leave. As a matter of fact, they don't let any of us off the ship.'

Rodel was hovering near the captain to tell him tonight's menu and the captain agreed to a plate full of potatoes, broccoli and pork.

'If the ship's agent is afraid we will make trouble,' Nick suggested with some desperation, 'maybe he can organise a guided tour for us. That way there is no chance of us getting lost, or being back too late.'

The captain looked sceptical.

'Maybe we can send a fax to the agent in Jeddah? Suggesting a guided tour?' Nick asked.

'You can send a fax all you like, but I am sure it won't do you any good.' The captain started tucking into the plate of food Rodel had brought him and began a conversation in German with the first officer, who had just walked in.

Nick and I started talking about the fax and what to put in it. Then Lukas remarked that he wasn't really interested in going on the guided tour.

'Why not?' Nick asked. 'You might never be able to set foot in Saudi Arabia again.'

'I'm just not interested right now. It's all moving a bit fast for me.'

'Okay, no problem. It's your decision.'

At 22.30h, the three of us stood looking over the city of Suez and the dark bay, as the convoy finally reached the end of the Suez Canal.

'Let's hope the agent will post our cards,' Lukas said as we watched the ship's agent and pilot climbing down to the boat that had come to fetch them.

'I'm sure he will,' Nick said. 'The five US dollars we added will be more than enough for some stamps, so he can put the rest in his pocket.'

Having received the two men safely, the little boat moved away in a slow arc. The *Serenity River* sailed into the Bay of Suez and calmly glided past the ships that, anchored, were waiting for the next day's convoy to start.

The night wasn't cold at all. We had left wintry Europe behind us.

After breakfast, the next morning Nick and the captain went to the bridge to send the fax to the ship's agent in Jeddah.

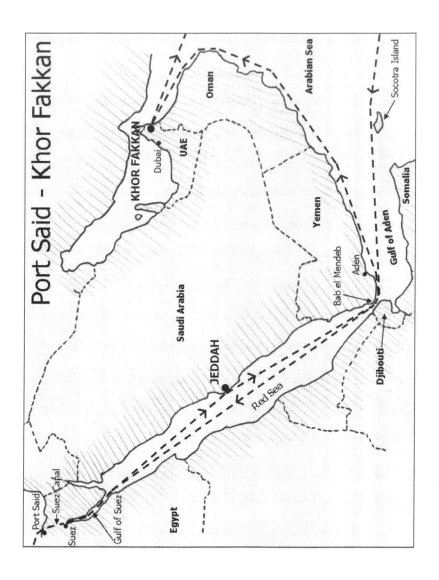

CHAPTER FIVE

As I stepped into the lounge at 11.05h most of the officers were already present. According to a Sunday tradition on many ships, the captain had invited his officers and the passengers for a drink in the lounge before lunch.

I noticed Nick talking to the captain at the end of the bar and Lukas and the second officer standing in a corner, discussing computers.

One of the ship-mechanics was behind the bar and asked me what I wanted to drink.

'Er... an orange juice, please.'

As I waited for my drink, the first officer, who was sitting on a stool, started talking to me. Like the captain, he was in his late 50s with an even larger beer belly. His short hair was totally grey. As long as I had been on the ship, he had never said more than 'good morning' or 'good evening' to me, but now he seemed to have finally lost his shyness. His English was very good, much better than the captain's was.

'So I see you have started a jigsaw,' he said pointing at the table on which the jigsaw lay.

'Yes,' I nodded.

'I noticed that it doesn't grow very fast.'

'Well, that's because it's not easy. The picture is missing and I have no clue what it is supposed to be.' The ship-mechanic handed me my drink and I took a sip.

The first officer smiled. 'I understand you're staying on the ship for three months, so you have more than enough time to finish it.'

'Yes, you're right.'

From the corner of my eye, I saw Nick moving towards me, clutching a piece of paper.

'This telex just came in from the Jeddah agent.' He handed me the piece of paper. It read:

> to: master m/v serenity river
> fm: slc – jeddah
> re: city tour of jeddah for 13/1/03
> dear captain – good morning to you.
> sorry to inform you that passengers are not
> allowed to get transit visa.
> please be guided accordingly.
> b.regards, ship agent

'I assume this means our trip is off?' I remarked.

'Yep, and I don't think we can do anything else about it.'

I handed him the paper back and sighed. 'This is very annoying.'

'I know.'

There weren't many people for lunch that afternoon, as the officers kept on drinking in the lounge. After two glasses of orange juice I had had enough, especially of the too many lungs full of cigarette smoke. Lukas came with me to the mess and not much later Nick walked in. He had been doing some thinking.

'Ship's agents always come to the ship twice when we're in a port, don't they?' he asked.

'Yes,' I said. 'Once soon after we arrive and again just before we leave. Why?'

Nick absentmindedly stirred the vegetable soup that Rodel had put in front of him.

'What if we ask the agent on his first visit to buy us some postcards of Jeddah? He can bring them on his second visit. If we want we can then quickly write them and with some money give them back to the agent to post before he leaves.'

'That's a brilliant plan,' I smiled. 'That way we will at least have something that came from the city.'

'Are you up for that?' Nick asked looking at Lukas.

Lukas nodded. 'But it might be best if we let you do the talking.'

'No worries.'

It was with some mixed feeling that I put my clock forward that evening, to arrive at Saudi time. I had really been looking forward to visiting Saudi Arabia, and now I would not be able to set one foot in it.

***

We arrived in Jeddah early the next day, Monday 13th January. It was very hazy. I had heard that the Saudis don't like people taking pictures of their ports, so as we approached I took some from my cabin window on the sly.

The landscape around Jeddah was very flat. Not much of the city was visible from the ship. Soon we came to the port and sailed slowly past a futuristic looking white tower, probably the port authority building.

As we berthed, the first thing I noticed was that all the workers in the port were Indian.

It took a long time before the agent finally arrived. He was a young man with a short beard, dressed in a traditional Saudi long white robe with a red scarf fastened around his head. After he had finished his business with the captain, Nick approached him about the postcards. They sat down in the captain's office, while I hovered at the open door. I had for the occasion put on a long wide, black tunic over my t-shirt and trousers.

Nick soon realised that the agent spoke very little English. He seemed to think Nick was asking him to be allowed off the ship and kept saying 'No, no, not possible...'

After a fruitless five minutes, Nick gave up. The whole time the agent had ignored me completely.

Thoroughly frustrated we walked down to the main deck to have a look over the railing on to the quay.

'You know,' Nick said to me as we arrived at the main deck, 'maybe we should ask one of the Indian workers to buy us some postcards.'

'Good idea.'

We walked up to an Indian man, holding some rope. After some attempts to ask him about postcards we were both surprised to find that he couldn't speak English either. This was a bit unusual to us, as in our experience Indian people outside their home country usually are able to speak English very well. We weren't very lucky in our quest for postcards. Like the agent before, the man completely ignored me and I started to feel as if I was invisible.

Lukas had joined us on the main deck and as we looked down on to the quay, we noticed a guard standing at the bottom of our gangway, carrying a serious looking gun.

'Is he there to keep us from going off or bad guys coming on?' Nick asked.

As we were taking it all in, we noticed the ship's agent coming out of the accommodation block, on his way to the gangway. As soon as he saw us, he stopped dead in his tracks, stared first at me, then at Nick, turned on his heel and went back inside.

'That's not good,' I mumbled to Nick.

'No, it's not,' he agreed. 'Maybe it's better if you go back inside.'

'My idea exactly.' I quickly made my way up the outside staircase to deck 1. I waited in the lounge a bit nervous that I had messed things up.

Nick and Lukas came walking in after five minutes. Apparently, as soon as I had gone upstairs the agent had come back out with the first officer, and had told Nick that I was not allowed on the landside of the ship. If I wanted to go outside it had to be on the waterside, otherwise I had to stay inside. The agent had explained he was worried the presence of a woman would be a distraction to the workers on the quay.

As there was not much I could do about it, I resigned myself to a boring day. At least I was able to vent some spleen by writing a rather sarcastic little piece for the guide book about Jeddah. That made me feel better.

My worry that I had given some trouble to the first officer by appearing on deck proved unfounded when he walked into the mess at lunchtime. As soon as he spotted me, a big grin appeared on his face. He said he didn't agree with the rules, but that it was better to abide them.

The whole episode had made Lukas really uncomfortable and it was clear he couldn't understand that the first officer, Nick and I were joking about it. Lukas was showing all the symptoms of a culture shock and I hoped he would get over it before we reached Singapore, otherwise he would be in even more trouble.

We sailed away from Jeddah around 00.30h that night and the only interesting thing that happened in the afternoon was the arrival of a bunker barge along side us. 1500m³ of fuel oil was pumped from the barge into our tanks. As this happened on the waterside of the ship, I watched it for a while and chatted with some of the Filipinos, who were keeping an eye on the hoses pumping the oil into our ship. They told me that the crew of the bunker barge was Russian and Filipino.

At one point Peter, the third engineer, came to the main deck to have a look and when he realised some of the people on the barge were Russian, he started talking to them over the railing.

The bunker barge left at 21.00h.

In the evening, I did a bit of the jigsaw, while Nick tried to get some reception on the tv. It wasn't long before he stumbled across a Saudi soap with English subtitles and settled down to watch it. Lukas soon had enough of the soap and instead helped me with the jigsaw. It started to look as if it was depicting some weird flowers.

After about half an hour, I was sick of trying to find pieces that fit and retired to my cabin. With the window open, I sat on the windowsill and watched the loading of the containers for a long time. It was a still and quiet evening and apart from the sounds of the cargo operations in the distance, the only thing I could hear was silence.

I didn't stay up to see us sail away from Jeddah that evening. I actually had had quite enough of it.

CHAPTER SIX

The day after we left Jeddah I met up with the little group of Filipinos, who were curiously staring through the open door of the officers' lounge at the mess Peter, the Russian engineer, had made.

After Rodel had made the remark that Peter had gone crazy, Nick and I followed him to the mess for our evening meal.

I was actually a bit surprised by Rodel's remark, as none of us had noticed anything too weird about Peter. The other officers had ignored him a bit, but we had thought that was because neither Peter's German, nor his English were very good. Only that afternoon I had heard a rumour that Peter didn't get along with the chief engineer and that the captain had decided to send him home in Singapore. Nothing however, had indicated to us that Peter was on the brink of a break down.

As Nick and I sat down for dinner, the captain came in and asked us if we knew who had made the mess in the lounge.

'We were assuming it was Peter,' Nick said.

The captain heaved a big sigh.

'You know...' he said, 'Peter told me two days ago that he couldn't stay on the ship. He said that he had a vision that showed him the work on the ship was wrong for him and that he should go home. I said I had already arranged for him to leave the ship in Singapore.'

Nick and I listened to the captain in silence. We were both slightly stunned as it wasn't normal that the captain of a ship would tell the passengers what went on between the crew. It seemed as if he was glad to be able to get it off his chest. Rodel brought out our meals and the captain continued.

'After my conversation with him, Peter stopped working altogether and just hung around the ship. He has done nothing for the last two days... Apparently, he even asked the Russians on the bunker barge in Jeddah to take him onboard their ship. That's how much he wants to get off.'

Nick and I looked at each other. We had both seen Peter talking to the crew of the barge. The captain hadn't finished his story yet.

'This morning I found Peter in the garbage room,' he continued. 'He had removed his all his clothes, except his underpants, and was in the process of throwing them in the garbage. I stopped him and told him to put his clothes back on. Later he managed to climb on to some of the containers, something that is quite dangerous as you can fall off and break your neck, or fall off into the sea, with little chance of surviving. A few of the Filipinos saw him and got him down.'

The captain took a large fork full of mashed potatoes and peas and as he put it in his mouth, Nick said, 'and in the afternoon Peter hung around in the lounge and tidied up.' The captain nodded.

During the captain's story, some of the officers had come in for their meal. The chief engineer was among them, which was rather unusual as most of the time he ate his meals downstairs in the ship's office on the main deck.

As Nick stopped talking, Peter suddenly appeared in the mess, dressed only in tracksuit pants. Everyone stared at him as he purposefully walked towards his seat, as if planning to sit down for a meal.

The captain stopped him.

'You can't eat like that. Go and dress yourself properly.'

Peter stopped in his tracks and looked as if he hadn't understood the captain. With a 'good evening', he turned on his heels and walked out.

Everybody started talking at random about what had just happened. From across the table Nick remarked, 'it looks like he doesn't know what he is doing. Maybe it would be best if he were locked up.'

I nodded.

At that moment Peter appeared again, still only wearing tracksuit pants.

The captain, obviously very annoyed and sick of having to deal with Peter's shenanigans, all but shouted at him, 'go and put a shirt on.'

'That is not important,' Peter remarked almost casually.

I thought the captain would explode in anger, but he managed to keep it in.

Then Peter walked towards the chief engineer and started mumbling to him. From the corner of my eyes, I saw Nick tensing his muscles, getting ready to jump up and grab Peter, in case the Russian was going to hit the chief. But instead, Peter stopped his mumbling at the chief and turned towards Nick, apologising for not returning the two bottles of water Nick had lent him.

Then Peter turned to me and started apologising as well. I couldn't understand a word he was saying, but told him it was okay.

After that, he turned around and left the mess for a second time.

For a little while no one spoke. The atmosphere had become rather tense and the whole situation made me feel quite uncomfortable.

Nick was the first one to speak.

'Isn't there somewhere on the ship we can lock Peter up?' he asked the captain.

The captain snorted. 'I'm not going to lock him up.'

'Why not?' Nick asked surprised. 'He can't keep wandering around like that.'

'Ah... it will be okay,' the captain said in a dismissive way. 'He's not hurting anyone by walking around half naked.'

At that point, one of the ship-mechanics walked in, reporting he had just spotted Peter in his cabin packing a suitcase. Most of the officers sniggered a bit when they heard this news. Their meals finished, they started to file out of the mess and into the officers' lounge. Nick and I remained on our own in the mess. Lukas joined us. He had only just arrived and had missed everything.

'This can't be right,' Nick said shaking his head. 'The captain is wrong not to lock him up.'

'Yeah, you're right,' I said. 'I must say I feel rather uncomfortable about it all. I don't think I would like to walk to my cabin by myself. I am sure Peter wouldn't harm me, but I don't feel very safe.'

'I can understand that,' Nick said. 'Whenever you want to go up, I will escort you.'

After Lukas had finished his meal, the three of us went into the lounge for a quick look. The captain and the rest of the officers were hanging around the bar, drinking beer and making jokes. It all seemed rather light-hearted, but it had a nervous undertone. The second officer and the ship-mechanics had busied themselves tidying up the mess Peter had left behind.

As the captain seemed to want to ignore the situation, no one really knew what to do. The first officer had poured me a glass of orange juice and handed it to me. I really didn't want to stay long, so I quickly finished it and was soon ready to go up.

Nick walked me to my cabin and on the stairs, we bumped into Rodel.

'He is getting more crazy,' Rodel said, looking over his shoulder as if to check that Peter wasn't around. 'He has washed his tracksuit pants and put them back on soaking wet. Now he's wandering around leaving a trail of water everywhere.'

Nick sighed. 'This is becoming ridiculous. I will try and convince the captain to lock him up.'

The next hour-and-a-half I spent with my cabin door locked, playing minesweeper on my laptop. My mind kept wandering, thinking about what, if anything, was happening downstairs.

At 19.30h, my phone rang. It was Lukas updating me on the situation.

'Peter has tried to launch the lifeboat,' he said 'Apparently to see if it still worked. But the captain still doesn't want to lock him up. The chief engineer and ship-mechanics have gone down to the engine-room. Apparently some alarms have gone off down there.'

'Did they seem worried about that?'

'Yeah.'

'Great... Anyway, thanks for the update.'

I hung up and thought to myself that it was rather stupid of the captain to have let the situation come this far.

Half an hour later Lukas phoned again. Peter had been found and locked up in a small cabin on the aft deck.

As I walked into the lounge three minutes after Lukas' phone call, I could feel the atmosphere was much lighter. I accepted another glass of OJ from the, now smiling, first officer, and joined Nick and

Lukas, who were sitting around the table on which the half finished jigsaw puzzle still lay.

'So... what's the story?' I asked curiously.

'Well, there *was* something wrong in the engine-room,' Lukas said. 'Apparently Peter had propped open a door, which had automatically caused several ventilation vents to close.'

'We understand that it is a normal procedure to have the ventilation vents closed when that particular door opens,' Nick continued, 'but it was not supposed to remain open. Without ventilation the engine could have suddenly stalled, causing enormous damage, leaving the ship floating about unable to move anywhere.'

'And it is certain Peter left that door standing open?'

'Yes,' Nick nodded. 'After this discovery the captain was finally persuaded that Peter had become a danger to the ship and that it was better to lock him up. The captain then ordered the two ship-mechanics to prepare the small cabin on the aft deck. They fiddled with the door lock, so it would only open from the outside and took all loose stuff out of the cabin.'

'I didn't know there was a cabin on the aft deck,' I remarked.

'There is,' Nick said. 'Apparently it is only ever used by the Egyptian mooring men in the Suez Canal. When the mechanics were getting the cabin ready, one of the Filipinos came into the lounge telling us he had seen Peter wandering around on deck 2. The captain asked me to come with him and we found Peter, just wearing his underpants and nothing else. The captain then asked Peter if he would come along with us for a little talk and he followed without problems. We took him to the little cabin. Once inside the captain asked Peter if he would mind staying in the cabin for a while and if he needed any bed sheets. Peter answered he was okay and we locked the door behind him.'

'Wow,' I said, while Nick took two large gulps of his beer. 'So it was that easy?'

'It was. I had the feeling he had no idea what was going on.'

'But what's going to happen now?' Lukas asked. 'I understand that Peter is supposed to leave the ship in Singapore. That's a week-and-a-half away. Surely he can't stay locked up in the cabin that long?'

'I rather think the captain will try to have him fly back from our next port, Khor Fakkan,' Nick answered.

'That's still four days away,' I remarked.

'Yes,' Nick nodded. 'We will have to wait and see.'

CHAPTER SEVEN

The strong wind made it difficult to keep my binoculars steady, but even so, I could clearly see the lighthouse on the small island. As I moved the binoculars down towards the waterline, I spotted a beach and some houses with a 4WD parked near them.

We were sitting on the monkey-deck, above the bridge, from where we had a nice view over Bab el Mendeb, the narrow strait we were traversing.

Bab el Mendeb, 25 kilometres wide, separates the Red Sea from the Gulf of Aden and we could easily see Yemen in Asia, to our left and Djibouti in Africa, to our right. It was not hard to imagine that at this point, 70.000 years ago, early modern humans had left Africa, getting across the water and into Asia, as the first step in their migration across the rest of the world.

It was 11.00h in the morning and while we were looking out over Bab el Mendeb, we were talking about the unusual events of the night before that were still fresh in our minds.

'Isn't it a bit strange that we never noticed anything of Peter's craziness before?' Lukas asked.

'Well,' Nick answered, 'if I were the captain, I would want to keep something like that under wraps from the passengers as well.'

'Yeah, I guess. But he's telling us everything now.'

'He can't hide it anymore,' I said, playing with the strap of my binoculars.' We saw everything happen before our eyes last night.'

'That's true,' Lukas said. 'I wonder why Peter was so obsessed with his clothes.'

'I have a theory about that,' Nick said.

Lukas and I looked at him.

'Rodel told me this morning that Peter has broken the washing machine that the crew use to wash their working clothes. Apparently, he had washed his steel-capped working boots in it to try to get them clean.

'Yesterday morning the captain saw Peter throwing his clothes in the garbage and in the evening he washed his tracksuit pants and put them back on. Looks to me that Peter is obsessed with cleaning his clothes. That's why he washed his shoes and chucked his dirty clothes in the garbage.'

'Yeah,' I nodded. 'That is not a bad theory at all. That would explain why he walked around half-naked last night. He probably thought his clothes were dirty and didn't want to wear them anymore.'

'Now I understand also why one of the crew complained to me that he had to wash his working clothes by hand,' Lukas said. 'Peter had wrecked the washing machine.'

'Luckily for us the one for normal clothes still works,' Nick said.

The Yemeni island had past and the *Serenity River* began a curve to the left, which would take us into the northern part of the Gulf of Aden.

I had to think back to that morning, when the captain and Rodel had brought Peter his breakfast on a tray. Not knowing how Peter would react after a night of solitary confinement, the captain had ordered a fire hose to be rolled out and put under pressure. It was held by one of the Filipinos, who aimed it at the door of the cabin.

A little crowd had gathered on the aft deck. The first officer, two ship-mechanics, four or five more Filipinos, Nick and Lukas all stood and watched as the captain and Rodel walked towards the door.

The captain knocked on the door, shouting that breakfast was coming and turned the lock. He opened the door and stepped inside. Nothing happened. Rodel stepped inside the cabin as well, carrying the tray. Twenty seconds later the captain and Rodel, who was empty handed, returned to the aft deck. The door was closed and locked and the fire hose rolled back up. It was a bit of an anticlimax, but everyone was relieved.

I had followed the whole procedure from deck 1, from where I had been looking over the railing on to the aft deck below. As they walked away, I had seen Nick talking to Rodel.

'So what else did Rodel say to you about Peter this morning?' I asked Nick.

'That Peter was very calm and had told the captain he would like to stay in the cabin to think and order the many things he had going around in his mind.'

'I hope the captain is organising for someone to take him back to Germany.'

'Yes, it's obvious that Peter won't be able to travel on his own back to Europe.'

Lukas got up.

'I'm getting hungry,' he said. 'It must be nearly time for lunch.'

I looked at my watch. It was 11.28h. Lukas was right. Lunchtime on the ship was at the early hour of 11.30h. As we trooped down the outside stairs to deck 1, we noticed that the swimming pool on deck 4 had been filled with nice warm water from the Red Sea. Nick became all-enthusiastic, as he had been waiting a long time for the pool to be filled up for the first time.

'I can't wait to go for a swim after lunch,' he said with a big grin on his face.

'It's not a very large pool,' Lukas remarked. 'You won't be able to swim very far.'

45

'Well, as long as I can get wet,' Nick said, still enthusiastic. 'Are you going to join me?'

'Yeah, of course,' Lukas nodded smiling. He had actually been looking forward to a swim as well.

In the evening, after our meal, we watched as Rodel prepared Peter's meal.

'Isn't it scary to take Peter his meal?' I asked Rodel.

'No, not at all,' Rodel said, as he put a spoon and a fork on the tray. 'He is very calm.'

'You're not going to give him a knife, are you?' Nick asked.

'No...' Rodel turned around and opened a drawer.

'Just this one...' he said as he took out an enormous kitchen knife.

But for the twinkle in his eyes, Rodel's face was completely straight.

We were still laughing as Rodel put the knife back in the drawer, took up the tray and made his way to the aft deck.

Later in the lounge, the captain told us of his talk to Peter that evening.

'I think he is getting better,' the captain said, while pouring himself a beer.

'Oh...?' Nick remarked with a sceptical look on his face.

'Yes. He actually thanked me for locking him up and said he had learned a lot from me.' The captain lit one of his ever-present cigarettes.

'Then I told him he was flying home to Germany from Khor Fakkan and he asked if instead he could stay on board in the cabin on the aft deck.' The captain chuckled a bit at the thought.

The second officer and ship-mechanics walked in and the captain directed his attentions to them.

'Does that sound to you as if Peter is getting better?' I asked Nick quietly.

'No, not all. Sounds to me as if he just wants to stay where he feels safe.'

'Well, in any case... I don't want to think about Peter for the moment,' I said. I turned my attention to the jigsaw. I had managed to do quite a bit of it in the afternoon and was determined to finish it that night. Within half an hour, I put the last piece in its place. It was finished and turned out to be a picture of a flowering cactus.

Nick and Lukas whiled away the evening with two games of backgammon.

***

The next morning, Thursday, we were still sailing past Yemen, on our way to Khor Fakkan in the United Arab Emirates. The coast was clearly visible and it was nice to be sailing in view of land for a change.

We were staying 35 nautical miles out of Yemen's coast to avoid being the target of a terrorist attack. That this was not as unlikely as it sounded became clear during breakfast, when the first officer told us we were sailing at the exact spot where three months earlier a French oil tanker had been severely damaged in a terrorist attack, killing one of its crew.

Most of the day I continued working on the guide-book. Even so, I still managed to spot several large pods of dolphins during the day. One pod came very close to the ship and I looked down on it from the wing of the bridge. The water was very clear and I could see

47

them swimming under water, often jumping playfully out of the water. They had a lot of fun.

But the most remarkable dolphin sighting happened around 11.30h that morning. I was getting ready to go down to lunch, when I saw a pod of dolphins splashing around from my cabin window. I grabbed my binoculars and ran outside for a better view. The dolphins had surrounded a large shoal of fish and were busy feeding on them. Outside the whirling circle of dolphins and fish, some human fishermen were patiently waiting in little boats, probably hoping to catch some of the fish after the dolphins had had enough to eat. It was a fantastic sight.

During the day, the captain took Peter back to his own cabin for a shower and to get dressed. The little cabin on the aft deck had a toilet and sink, but no shower and Peter was still only wearing his underpants. While he dressed he had asked the captain if he could go back to work again. He had clearly no idea of the situation he was in. With his suitcase and some other personal belongings, Peter was locked up again in the small cabin.

While this was going on Nick and Lukas had paid a visit to the engine-room. Nick had already seen it before, but Lukas hadn't really felt like going by himself. They came back with enthusiastic stories.

'I had no idea the engines were so large,' Lukas said during lunch. 'It was most impressive to see. They were the size of two decks!'

I nodded. 'Did you see the desalination machine?'

'Yes, incredible to think they can make drinking water from seawater.' He smiled. 'When I first came on board I thought I would have to shower with seawater, but that is not the case at all.'

'Yeah, I know,' I said. 'I had the same. One of the first things I did on my first ship when I arrived was tasting the water that came out of the shower. It was actually a bit of a relief to find it was fresh water.'

'And the noise and the heat in the engine-room,' Lukas continued. 'Unbelievable. It was good they made us wear ear protection.'

'Yeah, otherwise you couldn't be there,' Nick nodded. 'What I always enjoy seeing is the propeller shaft. The way it spins round. It really gives you a good idea of the power involved to make the ship move.'

'I hope the pictures turned out okay,' Lukas said, 'even though a picture wouldn't be able to capture the size and noise of it.'

'I am going to let Peter out of the cabin for the day,' the captain announced the next morning at breakfast. The first officer, ship-mechanics, Nick, Lukas and I, all stared at the captain with a surprised look on our faces.

'I am convinced Peter is not dangerous anymore, and it will be fine to have him walking around.'

'Do you really think that is a good idea?' the first officer asked.

'Yes,' the captain nodded. 'It will be fine. He will be locked up again tonight.'

Everyone looked very sceptical.

As the officers went to work, we remained in the mess for a bit longer. Rodel came in to clear the tables.

'I think the captain has gone crazy as well,' Lukas remarked.

'No,' Nick said, shaking his head. 'He's afraid that Peter will complain to the ship's agent in Khor Fakkan about his treatment.'

'Peter won't do that,' I said. 'He has no idea what is going on around him. He will not complain.'

'I am sure he won't. Nevertheless the captain thinks he will...'

***

We had left the Yemeni coastline and the Gulf of Aden behind us that night and had entered the Arabian Sea. The hills of Yemen's coast had made way for the lower and flatter coastline of Oman, which was not visible all the time. It was still a long way around the Arabian Peninsula to our destination Khor Fakkan.

I managed to do a lot on the guide-book and in preparation to our visit, read up on the United Arab Emirates and Khor Fakkan.

After the evening meal, the captain took some close-up pictures of Lukas and me with his digital camera. He needed the pictures for the shore leave passes that would get us into Khor Fakkan. Nick had brought some pictures with him. All three of us were looking forward to getting off the ship for a little while. We had not set foot on land since Gioia Tauro, eleven days earlier.

As the sun was setting that evening, we were looking down from deck 1 at Peter, who was still roaming around on the aft deck. The captain had decided not to lock him up again, much to the dismay of his fellow officers and crew.

'I had a conversation with Peter this afternoon,' Nick said.

'Did you?'

'Yes, if you can call it a conversation. He's in a totally different world and has no idea where he is.'

'Why do you think the captain hasn't locked him up again?' Lukas asked. 'It can't just be about Peter complaining to the agent.'

'My guess is that the captain will want everything to look as normal as possible.' Nick's eyes followed Peter as he disappeared from view around the corner. 'If the agent discovers that there is something wrong with Peter, he might not let him off the ship and that would be a huge problem for the captain.'

'But assuming someone will come from Germany to take Peter back,' I said. 'Won't that alert the agent that something is not right?'

'Yeah, it might. I really hope someone does come to take him back. If I go by the conversation I had with him this afternoon, Peter really can't travel by himself.'

'Has the captain said anything about organising for someone to pick him up?' Lukas asked.

'No, he hasn't.'

For a long time we stared silently out at the wake of the ship and the setting sun.

As I went to bed that night, I put my clock forward another hour. We were now on United Arab Emirates time.

CHAPTER EIGHT

'So you are saying that you had to get Peter down from the containers again this afternoon?' I yelled to Mr Morayta, the bosun, as I tried to make myself understood above the noise of Mr Orozco and Mr Garrido singing loudly to music that came out of the karaoke machine.

'Yes,' Mr Morayta yelled back. 'He said he was checking for fire when we took him down.'

'You must be happy he will be gone soon,'

'Absolutely.' Mr Morayta took a gulp from his orange juice. Being somewhere in his late 30s he was dressed in his overalls and had left his day-glow jacket, safety boots and helmet outside the door. As bosun he was the boss of the deck crew and when he smiled bunches of little fine lines appeared in the outer corners of his eyes.

A nice silence came over the crew-lounge as the two men came to the end of their song. It was a special night in the lounge as it was Mr Orozco's 31st birthday and we had been invited to join in the festivities. Like Mr Morayta, more of the Filipinos were dressed in their working clothes, as they were on standby.

The *Serenity River* was waiting to berth at Khor Fakkan, but the wait had been a bit longer than anticipated.

We had arrived near Khor Fakkan around 16.00h that Saturday afternoon 18th January, slowly gliding past dozens and dozens of anchored tankers. We were supposed to have berthed in the early evening, but at 21.00h, we were still waiting for the green light.

'Do you think Peter has packed yet?' Nick asked me smiling. That question had become the standing joke on the ship that day, as the captain had done nothing but try to get Peter ready for his impending departure from the ship. First, the captain had become angry when he discovered that Peter had unpacked his suitcase in the little cabin, putting everything in drawers and cupboards. He had ordered Peter to pack everything back in his suitcase, which Peter had interpreted as take everything back to his old cabin and put everything into drawers and cupboards. When the captain discovered this, he had shouted at Peter to re-pack his suitcase and stop fooling around.

'I have no idea what Peter will do next,' I answered Nick, as the next karaoke song started up. Rodel joined us, handing me a bowl of peanuts.

'Here, take some. Are you going to sing?'

I had dreaded that question ever since the party had started. I smiled at Rodel and said, 'Probably not.'

'Why not? We have some very good songs.'

'Karaoke is not really my thing. Sorry.'

At that moment, Peter walked into the crew-lounge. Everyone stared at him for a bit, until one of the Filipinos broke the ice by handing him a bottle of beer. He sat himself down on one of the couches.

'Can I sing?' Peter asked in his broken English.

'Of course,' Mr Morayta said. 'Just wait till they are finished.'

As Peter started his song a little while later, I thought to myself he looked rather oblivious to the fact he was about to leave the ship.

The phone rang. It was the order the crew had been waiting for. We were going to berth. The lounge soon emptied, but for Rodel, Mr Garrido the electrician, Nick, Lukas, Peter and me. We hung around, eating peanuts, while Peter and Mr Garrido kept singing.

Forty minutes later, we had berthed in Khor Fakkan. Peter was supposed to leave the ship immediately with the agent, but he was still with us in the crew-lounge.

'Peter, have you packed yet?' Nick asked, this time serious.

Peter stood up and walked out of the lounge.

'Do you think he is getting his suitcase?' Lukas asked.

'No idea,' Nick said. 'Let's go outside to see him off.'

Hovering around on the main deck with Rodel and Mr Garrido, we saw the agent walk up the gangway. He was a short, somewhat stocky Indian man in his early 40s, with neatly combed short black hair and a thin moustache. He walked past us as he made his way upstairs to sort out Peter's papers with the captain.

Night had fallen as we were berthing and everything was dark except for parts of the quay, which were lit by large lights. Rows of containers were stacked near the ship, but the loading hadn't started yet. It was warm and I felt that sweat was slowly starting to moisten the back of my t-shirt.

'Didn't the captain say Peter's plane leaves at half past two?' I asked.

Lukas nodded. 'And the drive to the airport in Dubai is two hours.'

Nick looked at his watch.

'It's a quarter to eleven now. They'll have to hurry if they want to make it before the check-in closes...'

'I can't believe Peter is not here,' Lukas said.

'You're right,' Mr Garrido said. 'I will go and have a look for him.'

'I'll come with you.'

'Is there anyone going to escort Peter back?' I asked Nick, as we watched Lukas and Mr Garrido walk up the stairs.

'I don't think so.'

'I can't believe the captain is letting him travel by himself.'

'He just doesn't want the agent to notice anything unusual.'

'Even so...'

'Yeah... I know,' Nick sighed.

The captain and the agent came out as Mr Garrido and Lukas came back down the outside stairs.

'Where is Peter?' the captain asked, angry at not seeing Peter where he had told him to be.

'He was just in the crew-lounge,' Mr Garrido answered. 'Singing karaoke again. He didn't want to come down.'

'Get him here,' the captain said impatiently and Mr Garrido ran back upstairs.

Soon Peter came down the outside stairs, carrying a small bag and a coat.

'Where's your suitcase?' the captain growled.

Peter looked at him with a bemused look on his face.

'Go and get your suitcase. Now,' the captain shouted.

Peter turned around and walked slowly back up the stairs.

The agent had watched all this with some surprise. He didn't say anything, however. To break the tension Nick asked him if we were allowed to go on shore leave the next day.

'Yes, of course,' the agent answered with a strong Indian accent. 'As long as you are back at eleven o'clock.'

'We better leave right after breakfast, then,' I said, and Nick nodded.

The captain meanwhile had checked his watch every two seconds and now looked impatiently up at the stairs on which Peter had disappeared.

'Where is that man?' he asked.

'I think I will give the airport a call to let them know the passenger is on his way,' the agent said, pulling out his mobile. 'Hopefully they will keep check-in open for him.'

Still Peter didn't come down and as the agent wandered off to make the call, the captain really exploded.

'How long does it take to get a suitcase,' he shouted. 'I will go and look for him myself.'

He disappeared up the stairs.

The agent had finished his call and rejoined us. We didn't really know what to say, so we looked at him with silly grins on our faces.

Then Peter came down the stairs, with his suitcase, but without the captain. The agent didn't want to waste any more time and led Peter down the gangway. Looking at the way Peter was carrying his suitcase, I got the distinct feeling it was empty.

As the agent and Peter walked along the quay towards the agent's car, the captain came running down the stairs, breathing so heavily he wasn't able to speak.

We watched from up high as the agent pushed Peter into his car and drove off. Everyone breathed a sigh of relief, specially the captain.

A quick inspection of Peter's cabin that evening by the captain, worked out that all his belongings were still in the drawers and cupboards. He *had* left the ship with an empty suitcase.

CHAPTER NINE

When I woke up the next morning and looked out of the window, I was pleasantly surprised by the breathtaking view that greeted me. The darkness of the night before had completely obscured the orangey hills that surrounded the port on three sides. The town of Khor Fakkan stretched out along a narrow beach, its white houses situated on a strip of land that was hemmed in by the hills on one side and the water of the bay on the other.

I was looking forward to exploring the town. As soon as I was dressed, I went down the stairs for breakfast. It was Sunday, 19th January.

Walking into the mess, I saw the captain and ship's agent having breakfast together. This was rather unusual. After I had said yes to Rodel's question if I wanted pancakes, I sat down and noticed that the captain was actually on the phone to someone.

'No... You must go back to the airport,' he said in German in a very exasperated tone. 'Go back to the airport and buy a new ticket.'

It could only be Peter the captain was talking to. It sounded as if he had managed to miss his flight.

Rodel brought me my pancakes and the agent asked him for a teapot full of hot water and four teabags.

The captain handed the phone back to the agent, who began to talk to someone in English.

'Go back to the airport with him. Then take him inside and get him a new ticket.'

The agent listened as the phone spluttered something at him.

'Yes, I know he wants to come back to Khor Fakkan, but under no circumstance take him here.' The agent started to sound exasperated as well. 'Take him to the airport and buy him a new ticket. We will pay you back later.' He broke the connection.

I tried to act as if I hadn't listened, and chewed away on my pancakes.

'This taxi driver is okay,' the agent said to the captain. 'We always use this firm. He will make it right.'

Rodel brought out a white teapot, four teabags and two cups and saucers. He placed everything on the table in front of the agent.

After the agent had put the four teabags in the pot, he looked at the captain.

'I am beginning to think something is wrong with this man's head,' he remarked casually. The captain was silent.

'The suitcase that he carried off the ship yesterday was empty, you know...'

Still the captain didn't say anything, so the agent looked at me. Again, the only thing I could do was look at him with a silly grin. Luckily, Nick and Lukas arrived at that same moment and sat down at my table.

The agent took his unused knife and stirred the teabags around in the pot.

'Why was that man sent home?' he asked, trying for the third time to get a response from the captain.

The captain meanwhile had been thinking hard and said, 'He was fired because he didn't do his work properly and didn't get along with the rest of the crew.'

It sounded to me like a very favourable description of the situation.

'Ah... I understand now,' the agent said. He peered into the teapot and concluding the tea had the right strength, fished the teabags out with his knife and squeezed them between his thumb and forefinger to get rid of the excess liquid. He then poured two cups of tea, one for himself and one for the captain.

'Oh, by the way,' he suddenly remarked to us. 'You can get your shore leave passes at the gate. Be back here by eleven o'clock, but no later than half past eleven.'

We thanked him and started eating as fast as we could, as we were all eager to be off.

***

It was 08.00h when we met at the top of the gangway and made our way down to the quay. Sticking to the marked walkway, as the agent had told us to do, we set course for the gate. I noticed that, as in Jeddah, all the workmen in the port were Indian.

Within five minutes, we came to a small duty free shop and had a quick look around. It sold the usual stuff, newspapers, magazines, toiletries and international phone cards. A few seamen from other ships were hovering around, trying to find out which phone card would give them the most minutes to call home.

As we didn't have a lot of time, we soon headed for the gate, situated opposite the shop. Arriving there, we were told by two men that our shore leave passes were held at the outer gate, a ten-minute walk away. Having no other choice, we trudged up the road. It went quite steeply up the side of a hill and around in a large curve. Halfway up it went down hill again and at the bottom was a small glass building. It reminded me of a tollbooth. Just past the building, a barrier stretched across the width of the road. It was the outer gate.

Having reached the small building, one of the three men who guarded it started looking through a pile of papers for our shore leave passes. The men wore similar army green uniforms with hats and somehow looked out of place. Then it struck me - they looked out of place because they didn't look Indian or Arab. They looked a bit like Himalayan people, with weathered brown faces and almond shaped eyes.

Nick had also noticed the difference and asked one of the men if he was Ghurkha. Yes, the man said. They were all Ghurkha's. According to him, many ports in the United Arab Emirates used specially trained Ghurkha security forces.

I had never seen a Ghurkha before, but had heard of these soldiers from Nepal, who had for almost two centuries been recruited by the British army. These days the Indian army recruits most of the Ghurkhas, with just a few still serving in the United Kingdom.

Having received our passes, with the picture the captain took neatly stapled to one corner; we walked around the barrier and now officially set foot in the United Arab Emirates. At first glance, it struck us how clean and tidy everything was. The grass was green and neatly mown. There was no graffiti on the walls and no litter being blown about.

As we walked in the direction of the town, we passed the old harbour. Looking across the water, we had a great view of the container port and the *Serenity River*. On the opposite side of the harbour was a mosque. Outside the door, dozens of shoes were lined up, waiting for the people who were worshipping inside.

As we wandered past the mosque, a large Mercedes pulled up next to us. An older man with a grey beard, dressed in a white robe and red headscarf rolled the window down and stuck his head out.

'You have dollars?' he asked, a big smile on his face. 'For dollars I give you lift anywhere.'

We looked at each other feeling slightly uncomfortable. The Filipinos on the ship had warned us against taking lifts in Middle

Eastern countries, as they were sure we looked too American and most likely would be kidnapped.

After weighing the pros and cons, we decided that taking a lift might be handy, as we had little time and no idea where we were going. The man could probably drop us off near the shops and a tourist information.

The man was overjoyed at our decision to accept his offer. As we got in - Nick in the front and Lukas and I on the back seat - we told him that we would like to go to the shops. He started driving at considerable speed and as I didn't feel completely at ease, I kept a sharp eye out for the route we were taking. My unease was not helped by the fact that as soon as we drove off, the man locked all the doors by pressing the lock-all-doors button. As the doors locked with an audible click, I could sense Nick tensing up as well.

The man meanwhile was full of enthusiastic questions. Where were we from? How long were we staying? Did we like it so far? Had we been anywhere else in the UAE? As Nick and I answered him, pretending to be completely relaxed, Lukas was quietly staring out of the window.

At first, the route took us through the outskirts of the town. The houses were mostly single story, painted white with small windows. The streets were narrow. There didn't seem to be many people about. Then as the car turned a corner, we were suddenly on a wide four-lane boulevard with a broad central reservation, covered in grass and palm trees. Shops lined the street on both sides.

As we neared the end of the boulevard, the man slowed down and stopped at the kerb. The doors unlocked with a loud click. He pointed across the street where a building was skirting a roundabout.

'Post office there,' he said. Then nodding towards the shops on our side of the road he said, 'supermarket and money exchange here.'

We thanked him and handed over a five US dollar bill. He took it with a big smile and wished us a good time.

Watching the Mercedes driving away, I couldn't help but feel a sense of relief. As we walked towards the money exchange Nick confessed he had also felt somewhat worried when all the doors had locked. At least our fears had proved unfounded.

The money exchange was still closed, which was not so strange as it was not even 09.00h. We decided to check out the other shops while waiting and came across a travel agent. We went inside and a man behind a desk answered my questions. No, there wasn't a tourist information in Khor Fakkan. And, no, a map of the town didn't exist. It felt like being back in Gioia Tauro, with the difference that the people here could speak English. My eyes fell on an English newspaper that was lying on the man's desk. Where could I buy one? At the supermarket a few doors down.

To the supermarket we went. It turned out there were three English UAE newspapers in existence. I bought a copy of each, to the total amazement of the shopkeeper. While Nick and I hovered around the supermarket waiting for Lukas to do some more shopping, we remarked to each other that at least 80% of the people we had met so far were Indian or Bangladeshi. Khor Fakkan seemed to have a large expat community.

From the supermarket, we made our way back to the money exchange, which by now was open and I changed my unspent Saudi riyals into UAE dinars. As we walked out, I saw a large colourful poster pinned to the wall depicting a birds eye view of Khor Fakkan. I realised that, although it wasn't a proper scale map, it was at least something I could use and I turned around to ask where the poster had come from. It was for sale at the bookshop on the other side of the street.

Leaving La Spezia - the green hills around the bay are dotted with picturesque villages.

The lifeboat hangs in its launching contraption on Serenity's *aft deck. Peter's cabin is just off the picture to the left.*

The eruption of Stromboli Volcano seen from the bridge of the Serenity River.

The mooring men and their little boat are winched up to the main deck after our arrival in the side canal of the Suez Canal.

A ship in the Suez Canal seems to float through the dessert.

Approaching Jeddah's container port.

Khor Fakkan in the morning sun.

A narrow path runs along the ship from the accommodation block to the fo'c'sle.

The fo'c'sle - one of the enormous anchor chains is visible at the bottom right.

Rodel in charge of the barbecue.

The engine is several decks high and extremely powerful. The engine-room itself is the noisiest and hottest place on the ship.

However modern the cargo ship, their interior furnishings always seem rather retro. This is the officers' lounge.

The small Hindu temple sits quietly admits the activity of Port Kelang's Westports container terminal.

A large gantry crane picks up a container from the deck to deliver it on the quay.

Singapore's skyline seen from the bridge of the FTK Kowloon - *the deck of the ship, stacked with containers, stretching out before it.*

Serenity's *gangway.*

We crossed the road and entered the bookshop. I soon spotted a drum full of rolled-up posters. I took one out and bought it. Meanwhile Nick and Lukas were checking out the postcards. All of them were of Mecca. Nevertheless, Nick bought two and said he would like to send them right away.

Off to the post office we went. So far, all the shop owners and assistants had been Indian, but the post office was staffed by Arabs. Nick wrote his two cards and then bought some stamps.

Having seen all the shops we decided to walk to the beach. It was very picturesque. Grass and palm trees lined the beach on one side, making it nice and shady to walk under. The sun had come out and it was suddenly much warmer. Although the UAE are not such a strict Islamic country as Saudi Arabia, I was dressed in my jeans and a sweater with long sleeves. At least in the shade I wasn't too hot.

At the end of the beach in the distance, we could see a large building, which had been pointed out to us as the Oceanic Hotel. Having enough time we slowly made our way towards it. I was hoping the hotel shop would have some postcards of Khor Fakkan, as I wanted to use them in the guide-book.

Halfway to the hotel Lukas suddenly said that he would rather sit in the shade and wait for us to come back. Of course, no problem, we said. He sat down.

It was 10.30h when Nick and I reached the hotel. The hotel shop turned out to be very small. They sold one postcard of Khor Fakkan, a view of the bay, but it was taken 20 years ago, when the container port wasn't there. I bought it anyway.

As we walked back out, we saw Lukas walking towards us. He had realised that it was getting close to 11.00h and didn't want to get back to the ship too late. There wasn't enough time to walk all the way back, so we hailed a taxi to take us to the gate. Looking across the bay from the taxi, we had a nice view of the *Serenity* and we noticed the loading was still going on. This meant the ship wasn't about to depart, but it didn't make Lukas any easier. I reminded him that the agent had told us it would be okay if we came back at 11.30h, so we still had 30 minutes left.

The taxi dropped us at the outer gate. As we got out, we spotted a small teahouse we hadn't noticed before and went in for a quick cuppa. Lukas remained very fidgety and when our tea was finished, he and I went on our way towards the gate. Nick had noticed a small fish market at the old harbour and went for a quick look. He said he would catch up. At the outer gate we had to hand our shore leave passes back in, and I was happy I had made a photocopy of it at the post office as a souvenir.

After another walk up and down the hill, we reached the inner gate and I decided I would have enough time to make a quick phone call to my parents. Lukas continued on to the ship. I went inside the duty free shop and bought a phone card. It gave me 14 minutes of phone time to call the Netherlands.

Back on the ship, I heard that the loading was going to take another 30 minutes, but the stevedores had first gone for lunch. We probably could have stayed ashore a bit longer.

***

At 14.00h, we were standing on the wing of the bridge with the captain and watched as the last container was loaded on board. The captain was very eager to be off and said he hoped the pilot would be on board in five minutes.

Suddenly his mobile phone rang, and he answered it, somewhat surprised.

'Yes?' Listening to the agitated voice on the other side of the line, his face became more and more red and he moved away from us towards the bridge. As he stepped inside, we heard him say, 'no... you're joking...'

Wondering what had happened we hung around on the wing. After five minutes, the captain came back out.

'You're not going to believe this,' he said. 'Peter has walked into the office of the agent in Khor Fakkan. The taxi driver had bought him a new ticket for a flight tomorrow and then checked him in at a hotel. After the taxi driver had gone Peter walked out of the hotel, without his suitcase, passport and ticket. He then managed to take another taxi to the office of the agent.'

We listened to the captain in silence.

'The agent just told me on the phone that we need to take Peter back on board. Well... that's not going to happen. I have phoned Ariel Rügen in Germany and I am waiting for an answer from them.'

Right at that moment, his phone rang and the captain disappeared again inside.

'Great Scott...' I said.

'This is so weird,' Lukas said.

'Unbelievable,' Nick said.

'What on earth is going to happen now?' I asked.

'Who knows?' Nick answered. 'I suppose we won't be going anywhere until they have found a solution.'

We waited.

Ten minutes later the captain came out again.

'The shipping company said we can't take Peter back on board. They are phoning the German consulate in Dubai. The agent has also phoned me again and said that Peter is clearly crazy. He is refusing us a pilot until things are sorted out.'

'So we are stuck here for now?' Nick asked.

The captain nodded and went back inside.

We walked down stairs. On the main deck we found the chief engineer, second engineer and the electrician, hovering near the bottom of the outside stairs. As we joined them Nick said, 'so... we're not going anywhere for now...'

'Yes,' the chief nodded. 'We have to wait for the agent to come on board and talk with the captain.' The chief sat his stocky body down on one of the bollards welded to the deck, his beer belly straining at the zip of his greasy blue overalls.

'This is going to cost Ariel Rügen a lot of money,' Mr Garrido said.

'You think?' Lukas asked.

'Of course,' the chief said. 'Every hour we are berthed longer than necessary will cost a lot.'

A car came driving on to the quay below us. The agent and another man got out. Peter wasn't with them. They walked up the gangway and passed us on their way to the captain's office on deck 5.

'Can they make us take Peter back onboard?' I asked.

'Yes, they can,' the chief answered.

'But I am sure they will try to negotiate a compromise,' Nick said. 'The captain will have to come clean about everything that happened. No more secrets.'

We waited for almost an hour and more of the engine-room crew joined us. At 16.00h the two men finally came back down again.

As they walked past us, the agent said, 'you are allowed to go.' The chief got up and made his way to the engine-room. His crew followed him.

Within ten minutes, the pilot was on board and the lines released. The *Serenity* started drifting away from the quay.

After the pilot had left the ship, we went back upstairs, to the wing of the bridge, curious to find out what had happened. The captain came out and joined us.

'Peter will stay in the UAE for now,' the captain said. 'He will be looked at by a doctor in Khor Fakkan and be kept under supervision. The doctor will try to get him admitted to a mental hospital in Dubai. When he's a bit better, he will fly back to Germany under supervision.'

The captain sighed deeply. 'I will go to my cabin now and rest for bit,' he said, and trudged off.

'Is it me or could this whole situation have been avoided,' I said quietly. 'If Ariel Rügen had sent someone from Germany to take Peter back, they wouldn't have had this problem.'

'Yes,' Nick nodded. 'And the captain should have let one of the crew-members escort Peter to the airport to hand him over. In my opinion everyone underestimated the situation.'

'And now poor Peter ends up in an institution in Dubai,' Lukas said. 'I feel sorry for the poor guy.'

'Yeah, me too,' I said.

We stared out over the water and watched from above as an old-fashioned dhow went past us on its way to Khor Fakkan. These traditional Arab sailing ships used to take cargo along the coast of the Arabian Peninsula, India and East Africa. They are rare these days, so we were lucky to see one.

After it had disappeared, we went down to the lounge to wait for the evening meal.

I never did find out what happened to Peter in the end. I hope he eventually made it back to Germany.

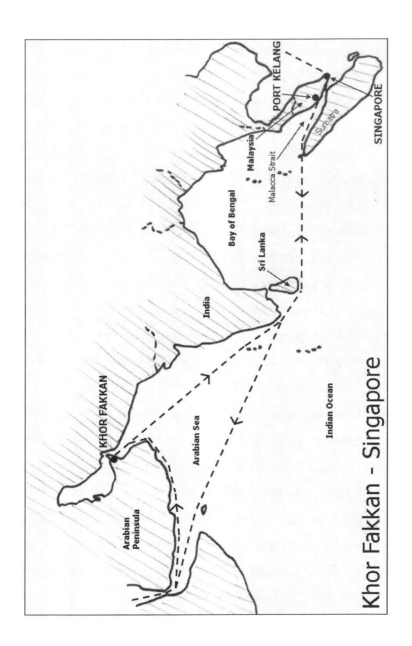

Khor Fakkan - Singapore

CHAPTER TEN

A sense of normality returned to the *Serenity River* after we had left Khor Fakkan. We were on our way to Port Kelang, a growing container port on Malaysia's west coast about 40 kilometres west of the capital Kuala Lumpur. It would take a week to reach Port Kelang, crossing the Arabian Sea, around the southern tip of India and Sri Lanka into the Bay of Bengal until we reached the northern most point of Indonesia's Sumatra Island. Rounding that we would enter the Malacca Strait, one of the busiest shipping routes in the world on which Port Kelang is situated.

I had plenty to do on the guide-book, much of which I wanted to have finished before we reached the Malaysian port.

Outside it was sunny and warm. Nick and Lukas spend most of their time on the sun-deck or hanging around the swimming pool. Inside it was much cooler. The air-conditioning was on at full blast, leaving me no choice but to wear my jeans and fleece while typing away on my laptop.

At lunch the first day after we had left Khor Fakkan, the captain announced he would open the doors of the ships store that evening at 17.00h, for all who wanted to have a look inside.

The ships store, or slop chest, was a sort of mini duty-free shop, selling mostly alcohol, but also chocolate, crisps and toiletries. Normally people would order things from the store by writing whatever they wanted on a piece of paper, and leave it in the officers' mess. The captain, who was the keeper of the store, would then deliver the requested items to the cabins, leaving said items outside the doors.

It seemed that on our trip so far, the captain was thinking that we hadn't bought enough. In my case that was true, as I hadn't bought anything from the ships store. I was still trying to get rid of the sweets I had bought in a supermarket in La Spezia, but I admit that my stash was dwindling.

To induce buying the captain had decided to let us have a look inside the store, in the hope we would be eager to buy if we actually saw the products on offer.

It was a cunning plan. As we came face to face with the items for sale, none of us could resist buying something. I walked away with two cylinders of Pringles sour-cream-and-onion crisps and a large purple tin of Quality Street chocolates. This was opened and tucked into that evening after our meal, as the three of us watched Star Wars The Phantom Menace in the lounge.

We had to cross four time zones to reach local Malaysian time, which meant changing the clocks four out of the seven nights to come. We made a start that evening by putting our clocks forward one hour as we went to bed.

The next day, Tuesday, was another hot day. Again, I didn't notice much of it, as I worked on the guide-book in my cabin, but I did spend an hour on the sun-deck in the afternoon, finishing the three newspapers I had bought in Khor Fakkan. For national UAE newspapers, a lot of the news seemed to focus on India, Bangladesh and the Philippines, another clear sign of the number of expat workers.

Having finished with the papers I took them to the crew-mess, before the evening meal. Mr Morayta had seen me reading the newspapers that afternoon and I had shown him the amount of Filipino news they contained.

'Would you mind if I borrowed the papers after you are finished with them?' he had asked shyly. 'It's difficult for us to get news from home, so we welcome every chance.'

I had said I would gladly drop the papers off in the mess later on.

***

That evening just before sunset, I went down to the fo'c'sle.

It was Alec, the son of the chief engineer on my first ship, the *Colonial Star*, who first told me about the fo'c'sle. According to him, it was the best part of the ship and he wasn't wrong.

We were off the coast of Spain on the Atlantic Ocean and heading for Cape of Good Hope. It was a quiet sunny day and Alec was walking in front of me on the narrow path leading to the front, which ran the length of the ship. A railing was all that kept us from falling into the sea, many meters below.

As we got further away from the gleaming white accommodation block, the constant drone of the engines became less felt. I suddenly noticed the soft hissing sounds of the waves rushing past the hull of the *Colonial Star*. The sound didn't disturb the peaceful silence that had come over this part of the ship.

Having reached the end of the path, Alec led the way up a short stairs. I followed him and going around the corner of the last containers, saw in front of me a large triangular deck.

'This is the fo'c'sle,' Alec said with a wave of his arm, indicating the space.

'Wow,' I said, as I wandered around, looking at the huge anchor chains and bollards. 'I had no idea the front part of the ship would be like this.'

In the middle of the deck, a short white mast pointed towards the sky, just high enough to reach over the top of the front most containers. I had noticed this mast from the bridge. A small building with a door, a bit like a metal shed, was built around the foot of the mast.

'That's the paint store,' Alec said. 'The door leads to a stairs that go down below this deck. All the paint and brushes and other materials for the maintenance of the outside of the ship, are kept in there.'

I focused my attention on the enormous anchor chains that were coiled up on two huge winches. Most of the shackles were painted white, but every now and then, one was red. The chains went down through two holes in the deck, one on each side of the paint store.

'Are the anchors actually fastened to the ends of these chains?' I asked, as I tried to peer down one of the holes.

'Yep,' Alec nodded. 'They hang, one on each side under the hull.'

'It's a pity that the sides are too high to see the water,' I remarked, looking at the grey bulkheads that enclosed the deck on two sides. They came together in a point, where a short metal ladder went up.

'You can do a Titanic there if you want,' Alec said, as he saw where I was looking. 'You know... Like Kate Winslet, stretch out your arms and shout "I'm on top the world" or something like that.'

I smiled at the thought. 'Nice idea, but if I ever did that, I would make sure I was here by myself.'

'You *can* actually look over the sides if you climb up there,' Alec said, as he walked to another metal ladder, situated at the side. It reached up to a platform halfway up the bulkhead. He climbed up it and I followed. The bulkhead now only came waist high. I watched as the sea stretched out in front of me - no land was in sight. In appearance, the water looked the same as it did from the accommodation block, but because of the quiet atmosphere on the fo'c'sle, it felt as if I was in a completely different place. I looked down over the edge of the ship and noticed it dropped away sharply, towards the bulbous nose. The nose was half-visible through the waves that were crashing over it as the ship moved forward. Halfway down the hull I saw one of the anchors. It looked a bit rusty.

I turned around and had a nice view of the fo'c'sle and the sea on the other side. Alec had made himself comfortable and was sitting down on a small ledge, his feet on the railing that protected us from falling on to the deck. I sat down as well.

'I love to sit here,' Alec said. 'Especially on a quiet day like this. It's great to get away from everyone every now and then. There is no noise here. I love listening to the waves going by. It's my favourite place on the ship.'

We listened to the waves for a while in silence.

'But in a storm it is very dangerous to come here,' Alec continued. 'It's difficult to imagine on a quiet day like this, but when it is very windy and the waves are high, they crash across this deck with an enormous force. So you make sure you check it's safe, before you come here.'

'I will. I promise.'

'Good.'

As I sat myself down on a ledge in the bulkhead of *Serenity's* fo'c'sle, I thought back at my conversation with Alec. On all the ships I had travelled, the fo'c'sle had soon become my favourite place. I remembered sitting on the fo'c'sle once when, on a quiet day, the ship was rolling quite a lot. It felt like sitting in a rocking chair. One moment my side would rise high above the rest of the deck, which angled away from me. The next moment everything was reversed and my side would be at the lowest point, the rest of the deck rising above me. It was a very soothing, almost hypnotic, movement.

The fo'c'sle was also the best place from which to see the flying fish. As the ship moved forward, startled flying fish would jump out of the water and with a few vigorous sweeps of their tails gain enough momentum to glide over the waves, away from the ship, stretching out their fins like wings. The bigger flying fish would glide for quite some time before diving, nose first, back into the water. Most of the flying fish I saw were greyish with bright blue stripes along the edge of their 'wings'.

I sat on the fo'c'sle for a while that evening, as the *Serenity River* sailed across the Arabian Sea. I listened to the waves and looked at the flying fish. The sun was slowly setting and as it got dark, I made my way back to the accommodation block and the bustle of the other people.

The clock needed to be put forward again, and I did so, just before I went to bed.

CHAPTER ELEVEN

As I walked toward the mess for breakfast the next day I nearly bumped into Mr Espinosa, the cook, who was carrying a small dead pig, wrapped in a see-through plastic bag.

He smiled as he saw my puzzled face and said, 'for the barbecue, tonight.'

'Ah...' I said. 'And how are you going to prepare it?'

'It's going to be roasted on a spit this afternoon, on the aft deck.'

'Good... I think you are going to be a busy man today, what with all the preparations for tonight.'

'Rodel is helping me. We all want a good party.'

'Yeah,' I nodded. 'We do. I'm looking forward to it.'

The captain had decided that Wednesday night was going to be the best night for a ship barbecue. On many container ships that sail through the warmer climates, it is a tradition to have two barbecue evenings, one on the way over to Asia and one on the way back.

As some windy weather was expected for the latter part of the week, it was thought best that our barbecue was to be held sooner, rather than later.

At the end of the afternoon, I walked down to the aft deck to have a look at the pig being roasted. I am a vegetarian myself, but have no problem with seeing other people prepare or eat meat.

As I arrived on the aft deck, the party already seemed to have started. Most of the Filipino deck crew were hanging around an oil drum that was vertically cut in half, to form a large trough. It was filled with glowing charcoal and an immense heat radiated from it.

The pig was centred above the hot coals on a makeshift spit that was slowly and patiently turned by Mr Salinas.

Most of the Filipinos were drinking beer from bottles, except Rodel, who had just come down from deck 1, to have a look at how the pig was progressing.

'It's going to be finished soon,' Mr Morayta remarked. 'Then we can carry it up to deck 1 and start our barbecue.'

Everyone cheered. The barbecue evenings were a nice change to the otherwise rather monotonous evenings on the ship.

The deck crew that wasn't taking turns in rotating the pig on the aft deck had helped Rodel set up some long tables on deck 1, behind the outside stairs. Another barbecue was set up on which the cook was now grilling some more meat. He had also prepared several different salads and two types of steaming hot rice.

Nick, Lukas and I had chipped in, buying a casket of beer for the crew. Passengers buying the crew beer during a barbecue was a well-appreciated tradition.

Mr Morayta and Mr Salinas carried the pig up from the aft deck on a large stainless steel platter. The captain had the honour of making the first cut. As he did that Mr Orozco manoeuvred some speakers out of the windows of the crew-lounge, and with some help from Mr Garrido, managed to get the music started.

After I had heaped my plate with food, I sat down next to the second officer and we started a conversation in Afrikaans/Dutch. Not having spoken Dutch for some time, it was a bit weird for me to speak my native language again. It was also a bit weird for the second officer, as he was used to speaking German and not Afrikaans. After a while however, we could understand each other well enough.

'I'm hoping to fly home from Singapore,' the second officer said in Afrikaans, as he cut a piece of pork. 'My wife is expecting our first child in about two weeks time, and of course I would like to be there.'

'Yes, I can understand that,' I answered in Dutch. 'It would be nice if you were back home for the birth.'

'The problem is that the captain is not sure yet if Ariel Rügen has found a replacement for me,' he sighed. 'So I have to wait and see.'

'I hope it will work out for you. Fingers crossed.'

'Yeah, fingers crossed.'

As the evening progressed, the darkness set in. I wandered over to the part of the deck where most of the Filipinos were sitting.

'Do you like this music?' Mr Orozco asked, rock music spilling out of the speakers behind him.

'I actually prefer blues, but rock is okay.'

'Have you ever heard of the Vengaboys?' Mr Garrido asked. He and Mr Orozco were the music lovers of the crew, often singing karaoke together in the crew-lounge.

'Yes,' I said with a smile. 'I have heard of the Vengaboys. The Filipinos on the other ships absolutely loved them.'

'We also love the Vengaboys,' Mr Orozco said. 'It's great music for dancing. Do you want to dance? I have a Vengaboys cd. I can put it on.'

'Yeah, I don't mind dancing.'

Mr Orozco went inside to change the cd and crank up the sound. As the first track of the Vengaboys' fast dance music started, the captain looked up with a slight frown, but he didn't say anything.

Nick and the second officer also walked over and watched as Mr Orozco, Mr Garrido and I danced. There wasn't much space, but our dance moves seemed contagious and soon more Filipinos joined us. After half an hour of the Vengaboys, Mr Orozco asked if I had some other cd we could dance to. I ran upstairs to my cabin and got my Blues Brothers cd. On the other ships, the crew had always enjoyed the Blues Brothers and I hoped it wouldn't be any different on the *Serenity*.

Two hours later, we were all completely exhausted. It was nearly 23.00h and most of the Germans had by now gone to their cabins, as had some of the Filipinos who were on night shifts. As the party wound down, those who were left helped Rodel take the plates and glasses inside. The tables would be put away in the morning.

With the music still going round in my head, it took me a long time to get to sleep. At least we didn't need to put the clocks forward that night.

***

The weather changed on Thursday. It was still warm, but it became cloudy and a strong wind came up. The sea was rough, but the ship wasn't rolling. I hoped the containers wouldn't start creaking, as they had done on the *Galactic Star*, two years earlier.

We were then also crossing the Arabian Sea, when a storm came. It had made the sea very restless and the ship pitched and rolled a lot - large waves crashing over the containers in the front. I hadn't been seasick, but it was difficult to sleep at night, due to the constant irregular movements of the ship and the noise of the waves crashing into the hull. On top of all this, some of the containers had started making loud steel-on-steel screeching noises every time the ship rolled. There was no escaping this noise. It sounded as if the ship was being wrenched in half. This situation went on for three days. When we reached the Gulf of Aden, the storm and swell disappeared. By then everyone was cranky and tired.

At least it wasn't that bad this time round in the Arabian Sea, but the waves did crash on to the fo'c'sle every now and then, sending a shudder through the whole ship. It was too windy to be outside much.

During the day, I tried several times to get the Dutch World Service on my little short wave radio. I wasn't able to find the right frequency and ended up listening to the BBC World Service instead. Normally I wouldn't mind, but the day before, on Wednesday, there had been general elections in the Netherlands and I was interested to hear the results.

During the evening meal that night, Lukas told us he had spoken to the captain about leaving the ship in Port Kelang instead of Singapore.

'I have one whole week in Singapore before I fly to New Zealand,' he said. 'I think I might get a bit bored.'

'Yes, you might,' Nick said. 'It's a great city, but a week is very long. Are you planning to travel overland from Port Kelang to Singapore?'

'Yeah.'

'That's a great idea. That way you will see a bit more and kill some time.'

'That's what I thought, but the captain thought it was too dangerous.'

'What?' I said. 'The captain is crazy. I don't think he has ever set foot outside a port at all. He has no idea what he is talking about. What you are planning is not dangerous.'

'She's right,' Nick said. 'Don't listen to the captain. Just go for it. It will be a great experience.'

'I am glad you guys are thinking like that,' Lukas said. 'I am looking forward to it, although I must confess I'm a bit nervous as well.'

'You'll be fine,' Nick reassured him. 'No problem.'

That evening it was, again, time to put our clocks forward one hour.

***

During long sea crossings, everyone always got a bit restless. Especially when there is no land in sight, you could be forgiven for thinking you would never set foot on solid ground again.

The wind had died down in the night and we had sailed around the southern end of Sri Lanka. The *Serenity River* was now in the Bay of Bengal, heading for Indonesia.

Lukas started to sort out his luggage. Nick teased him a bit about this, as we wouldn't be in Port Kelang for another three days.

'I'm just sorting,' Lukas said. 'Not packing...'

I kept busy ticking off things-to-do on my guide-book list and to my delight found that I was on schedule. The latest bit of writing I had finished was a little chapter with do's and don'ts about shore leave, telling passengers they should never leave the ship without the agent's phone number and crew-list to prove they really belonged on the ship.

In the evenings, we discovered an easy way to get rid of the cigarette-smoking officers in the lounge. Whenever we started watching an English movie, the Germans would soon trickle out, leaving us in a smoke-free environment. It wasn't that we hated the company of the officers, but all three of us had problems with the ever-present cloud of dense cigarette smoke, the main producers of which were the captain and first officer.

It worked again that evening as we decided to watch Doc Hollywood. Only the second officer remained and watched for a while until it was time for him to get some sleep. His watch on the bridge would start at midnight and end at 04.00h.

When the movie finished, I went up to my cabin, advanced my clock by one hour (thankfully the last time before Port Kelang) and tried get some sleep. Unfortunately, my body hadn't caught up yet with the ever-changing ships time and I was actually still wide-awake. As I was staring at the ceiling, I remembered that the plastic bag in which I kept my dirty washing had become almost full. I thought I might as well do something useful as I was lying awake and with a sigh, got out of bed, dressed and walked down the stairs with my bag of washing in one hand and a box of detergent in the other.

It was 23.30h when I arrived in the washing room on the second deck down. It was two decks below the main deck, and I found it deserted. I stuffed my clothes in the machine marked 'White or Private Clothes ONLY' and switched it on. A second washing machine, next to the one I was using, has two signs on it. One read 'Working clothes ONLY', the other 'Out of Order'. It was the machine Peter had broken when washing his working shoes.

The washing cycle of my machine would take 40 minutes.

Bored I started reading the notices on the door of the washing room. There was a schedule indicating who could wash his clothes when and a notice saying that an iron and ironing board were available from the steward. According to the washing schedule, the passengers could wash their clothes on Tuesday mornings, Thursday mornings, Friday afternoons, and evenings in general. This meant I wasn't doing anything illegal.

I wandered out of the washing room, into the corridor and had a look inside the sauna room. The small indoor swimming pool took up most of this room. With its four by five metres it was slightly larger than the outdoor swimming pool on deck 4. It was also filled with seawater. The sauna room had no windows and as this whole deck was situated right above the engines, it was hot, stuffy and noisy, the floor vibrating beneath my feet. The outdoor pool, although smaller was much more inviting for a swim.

The sauna took up just a tiny bit of space in a corner of the room. Next to the sauna was a door that led to the sports room. I opened the door and peered through it without much enthusiasm. I saw a table tennis table, two home trainer bikes and a dartboard on a wall. I didn't think anyone ever used any of the equipment.

Suddenly my stomach rumbled. I couldn't believe I was actually hungry at this time of the night. I made my way up the stairs to the officers' mess, where I knew Rodel kept some packets of ryvitas in a drawer. I found them, took a packet out, and slipped on to a bench behind a table. Although all the lights in the accommodation block were on day and night, giving an illusion of activity, there was no one around - everything was quiet.

I nibbled away on some ryvitas and waited for the washing machine to finish its cycle.

CHAPTER TWELVE

Most people know what jet lag is and many know what it feels like to have your body clock out of sync with local time. The only way to get over jet lag quickly is to get along with local time as much as possible, however much the urge to go to bed and sleep. On a ship, this is unfortunately not possible.

A ship is travelling at a much slower pace than an airplane, but it crosses time zones all the same. When it travels from east to west or vice versa, the time zones come by too quickly for the body clock to adjust. As local time keeps changing, the body struggles to keep up and adjust. The result is a severe tiredness during the day and waking up in the middle of the night or wanting to go to bed early in the evening. Another symptom is feeling hungry at odd times of the day.

After five nights in which we had put the clocks forward four times we were all tired and grumpy, our bodies very confused.

On Saturday 25th January, the morning after my midnight washing expedition, I didn't want to go down to breakfast, but instead just stay in bed. After a while however, I noticed I was too hungry and dragged myself out of bed.

In the mess, Nick and Lukas were just finishing their breakfasts. Lukas looked like a zombie, which was just how I felt, but Nick seemed to have fewer problems.

'Aren't you terribly tired?' I asked him, trying to keep the jealousy from my voice.

'No, just a bit,' he said.

'Lucky you,' I mumbled.

Rodel emerged from the pantry carrying a plate full of scrambled eggs, fried mushrooms and grilled tomatoes. I noticed the dark rings under his eyes as he put the plate in front of me.

'At least you will stay on the current time, until well after Singapore,' Nick remarked. 'You'll have time to catch up.'

'Yeah. Thank goodness for that,' I said with a big sigh. 'If there is one thing I don't like about travelling on container ships, it's the ship lag.'

'The what?'

'Ship lag. You know, like jet lag, but then drawn out over days, even weeks.'

Nick smiled and nodded. 'Yes, that's a good name for it.'

'I think I am still on Khor Fakkan time,' I grumbled as I tucked into my eggs. 'I did my washing at midnight and didn't fall asleep until two in the morning. I can handle the time changing when there is a day, or two in between each time. But this number of changes in a row just throws me off completely. I can only imagine how bad the crew must feel. At least I can go for a nap in the afternoon.'

'Actually,' Lukas said after I had finally stopped grumbling. 'I think I might go for a nap right now...'

I nodded with a sigh. 'That sounds very temping.'

Three-and-a-half hours later it was time for lunch. I met Lukas on the stairs and asked if he had actually gone back to bed.

'I did,' he nodded. 'Slept for about an hour-and-a-half. You?'

'Yeah, same...'

As we walked into the mess, I noticed the baskets filled with assorted bread and buns on each table. I groaned as I remembered it was Saturday and we would get 'eintopf' for lunch. I absolutely hated eintopf, but unfortunately, the Germans on the ship seemed to love this Saturday tradition from their homeland. In fact, on all the ships of the Ariel Rügen shipping company, eintopf was eaten every Saturday, just like in many German homes.

Rodel came.

'Do you both want a plate-full of eintopf?' he asked.

Lukas nodded yes.

I shook my head and said, 'No thanks, Rodel. I will just have some bread.'

Rodel left.

'You really don't like the stuff, do you,' Lukas said. 'It's just a thick soup with potatoes and cabbage, you know.'

'Yeah, I know. But on all the ships I sailed, we had it every Saturday. I just can't stand it anymore.'

Rodel brought Lukas his plate.

'Are you sure you don't want anything?' he asked me. There was a bit of worry in his voice. 'Maybe you like something else?'

'It's okay, Rodel. I'm not that hungry anyway. Ship lag, you know...'

'Yeah, I know...' He smiled and walked back to the pantry.

Nick came in and sat down at our table. His face lit up when he saw Lukas' plate.

'Eintopf! Great.'

I glared at him, while Lukas tried to hide a smile.

'One of the Filipinos told me there is going to be a party tonight,' Nick said.

'Really? What's the occasion?' I asked.

'I don't know.'

Rodel came out again, carrying Nick's plate with soup.

'Ah, Rodel,' Nick said. 'Do you know anything about this party tonight?'

'It's just for the engine crew. We're a bit angry that it is not for everyone.' He turned around and walked away.

'Interesting,' Nick said.

'Are we invited?' Lukas asked.

'I'm not sure. Possibly.'

The whole day the rumours about the party continued. In the evening, I asked Rodel again about the party and he said it was held by the engine crew to celebrate them finishing the maintenance of the generator.

'It's the chief engineer's fault,' Rodel whispered. 'He only likes his own crew and therefore he didn't invite anyone else. It's not very good for morale, if you ask me. The captain doesn't like it, but he can't stop the chief throwing some fish on the barbecue on the aft deck.'

After the evening meal, Lukas and I watched another Star Wars movie in the lounge. We had started early and as I came back to my cabin at 20.30h, the phone rang. It was Nick saying that people were looking for me. Apparently, the passengers *had* been invited to the party and they wanted to know where I was.

I didn't feel much like going, but after some persuasion from Nick went down to the aft deck.

A barbecue had been positioned in front of Peter's old cabin. On it were some sizzling fish that were being watched by Mr Orozco. The rest of the engine crew hung around it, some standing some sitting on the bollards that were welded to the deck. Mr Chavira, the second engineer, came to me and handed me a drink.

'What is it?' I asked.

'Bacardi and coke. I am sure you like it,' he said with an engaging smile. He was considerably shorter than I was and quite tubby. I didn't normally drink alcohol, but felt I couldn't really refuse. I took a tentative sip. The liquid burned as it went down.

I cleared my throat and asked, 'So you have finished the maintenance of the generator?'

'Yes, we have worked on it for weeks.'

'Congratulations.'

'Thank you. You must come one day and have a look in the engine-room.'

'Yeah, I will.' I took another sip of my drink.

The party continued and at 22.15h, I excused myself and went back to my cabin. I was completely knackered and fell asleep almost immediately. Unfortunately, I woke up again only a couple of hours later. My body clock still hadn't caught up with real time.

***

'Well, I will show you my uniform, but I won't put it on,' the captain said as he walked to his closet. He opened the door and after some searching pulled out a coat hanger over which was draped a jacket and trousers.

We watched as the captain pulled the jacket off the hanger and held it up in front of him. It looked slightly ridiculous as his legs, bare except for some baggy shorts and bath slippers with socks, stuck out from underneath it.

'You should put it on,' Nick coaxed. 'Otherwise we will never get a good idea what it looks like.'

Nick, Lukas and I had been having a small farewell party for Lukas in the lounge that Sunday afternoon, when the captain had walked in. He had soon asked us to continue our little party upstairs in his cabin. It seemed he wanted some company; so, a bit reluctantly, we walked up with him to his cabin on deck 6.

After some drinks had been poured, the conversation went to the subject of uniforms and why none of the officers on the *Serenity* were wearing them.

'Ach... Ariel Rügen is not that strict about it,' the captain had said. 'And we prefer to wear our own clothes.'

'But you have a uniform, don't you?' Lukas had asked. The captain had nodded.

Now we looked at the captain as he was debating with himself if he should put his jacket on.

'Okay...I will put it on,' he said. 'But only the jacket.' He slid the jacket over the top of his white polo shirt. It was black, double breasted with large gold buttons.

'Maybe we can take a picture of the four of us with the self-timer,' Lukas said.

'Yes, good idea,' the captain said. 'But then I will put this on also.' He went back to the closet and grabbed a white captains hat from a shelf.

'Perfect,' Lukas smiled.

After the picture was taken (Lukas making sure the captain's shorts were in the frame), the captain took off his jacket and hat and put them back in the closet. We sat down again.

'So, we are in the Malacca Strait now,' Nick said to change the subject.

'Yeah, sailed into it last night,' the captain nodded, taking a sip of his drink. 'We're on piracy alert now.'

'Pirates? Really?' Lukas asked.

'Oh yes,' the captain answered. 'The Malacca Strait is a hot spot for pirates unfortunately.'

'What do they do?'

'They usually come at night in a little fast boat and try to board the ship. If they succeed, they might steal equipment or try to break into the accommodation block to steal money from the crew. Sometimes they even hijack a ship and put the crew overboard in a lifeboat.'

Nick and I nodded at the captain's story. We had both heard it before and in fact, when I travelled on the *Galactic Star*, another container ship, sailing about 50 kilometres to our starboard, had been attacked by pirates that night as we were going through the Malacca Strait.

'How do we stop them from boarding?' Lukas asked.

'We've put some strong searchlights on the wings of the bridge and aft deck. Some of the crew will be on watch tonight and search the water with the lights,' the captain answered. 'We have also rolled out the fire hoses, so we can deter them by spraying water, in case they come too close. And all the outside doors of the accommodation block will be locked, so no one can get in.'

'Wow, it all sounds pretty serious.'

'It is,' the captain nodded. 'It's not a joke.'

***

The next day, Monday 27th January, we berthed at Port Kelang's Westports container terminal at 08.00h. No pirates had attacked us that night.

It wasn't the first time I was in Port Kelang. On the *FTK Kowloon,* we also berthed here, and with the two passengers, I had gone into the town for some sightseeing. The actual town of Port Kelang is situated about 12 kilometres from Westports container terminal and it features a ferry terminal, a railway station, a large vegetable and meat market, many smaller shops, teahouses and little restaurants. The town is surrounded by mangrove forests, which skirt the banks of the Kelang River. The mouth of this river forms a small delta, with islands also covered in mangrove forests, although on some islands nature has made way for palm oil plantations.

I stood with Nick and Lukas on deck 1, looking out over the island opposite our berth. It was approaching low tide and a muddy beach was slowly emerging. I heard the sounds of birds in the distance.

'One of the Filipinos on the other ship told me he had seen alligators on that beach,' I said.

'Cool,' Lukas remarked.

We had heard from the captain at breakfast that we would be leaving at 12.00h, so we didn't have enough time to go on shore leave. That was a disappointment as Nick and I had hoped to accompany Lukas to the railway station in Port Kelang.

'So are you ready for your big adventure?' Nick asked Lukas.

'Yep,' Lukas nodded. 'Except that I still need my passport back. The agent has taken it to get it stamped by immigration. He is returning it later.'

'Well, that will give you some time to walk with us to the Hindu temple.'

'What Hindu temple?'

'The one on the quay,' Nick said with a nod towards the other side of the ship. 'Didn't you notice it as we berthed?'

We walked to the other side of the ship and went down the gangway. As I looked down on to the quay, I noticed again what a funny port it was. The containers were stored away from the ship on the other side of a canal. This set up made being berthed at Port Kelang a quiet affair, as the noise of the stacking and re-stacking the containers in storage didn't reach the ship, as it did in other ports.

At regular intervals the canal was spanned by concrete bridges, which had, apart from a two-lane road, a walkway for pedestrians. The walkway and road were separated from each other by large concrete flowerpots, which were filled with colourful flowers and plants. The far side of the canal was lined by grass its entire lenght, in which trees and flowers were planted. On one of these areas of grass was situated a Hindu temple.

Weirdly enough the temple didn't look at all out of place. The roof had blue tiles in the same colour as the gantry cranes that were loading the containers. We walked around the temple and then climbed up the few steps into its inner sanctum. Several colourful statues of deities looked down at us. One was of a woman wearing a blue sarong, holding a bowl. She had a serene smile on her face and a golden tiara adorned her long black hair. A similar statue was situated on the other side and it was as if they were welcoming us inside. Further back two statues were flanking the main shrine. One was of a pink elephant wearing a white dress. He was sitting down under a canopy, which was elaborately decorated. The main shrine held the statue of a man. He was wearing a white skirt and turban, and was holding a flaming gold sword in one hand and a golden club in the other. People had burned incense at his feet.

'I wonder what this deity represents,' Nick said quietly.

'Yes,' I nodded. 'Me too.'

After we had seen the temple, Lukas went back to the *Serenity* to wait for his passport. He didn't want to walk too far away from the ship. He seemed to have recovered from his little bout of culture shock and was now ready to move on.

Nick and I wandered passed the stacked containers to the port authority building, the outside of which was covered in glass with a large staircase in the front. Inside the entrance hall was nice and cool. In the corner, we discovered a newsagent and I bought two Malaysian newspapers.

As we walked back to the ship, we came past a small wooden building. It was open to one side. Inside we could see tables and chairs on which some port workers sat, eating a meal and drinking tea. A counter was situated at the back. Apparently, it was a canteen.

'Shall we go in for a cup of tea?' Nick asked me.

'Do you think we are allowed inside?'

'Why not? We can always ask.'

We went in. Everyone stared.

'Could we buy a cup of tea?' Nick asked the man who was standing behind the counter.

'Yes,' he said. 'Teh tarik?'

'Two please,' Nick answered and the man started to prepare a teapot.

'Now watch how he makes this,' Nick said to me.

The man filled the teapot with some teabags and boiling water. When the tea was strong enough he took the teabags out and added some tablespoons of sugar, and warm milk. Then the man poured the milky tea in a smaller pot. He then poured the tea from the smaller pot back into the teapot, holding the smaller pot high above his head. The tea spilled down like a waterfall, but miraculously it all ended back up in the teapot.

Spellbound I watched as the man repeated the pouring twice more. Again, nothing of the tea was lost. He then poured the tea into two glass mugs. It had become all frothy and was ready to be drunk.

I gave him a big smile.

'That was amazing,' I said. He smiled back.

The tea was strong, but milky and very sweet. Absolutely delicious.

'So this is called teh tarik?' I asked Nick as we sat down at one of the tables.

'Yes,' Nick nodded. 'I think it is a Malayian speciality.'

When our tea was finished, we continued our walk back to the ship. We arrived at 11.30h, just in time for lunch. The agent had not yet come. Lukas had taken down his luggage and sat down with us for the meal.

At 12.00h the agent came. Lukas received his passport and we walked with him to the gangway. The agent offered him a lift to the railway station in Port Kelang. We waved as they drove off.

We left Port Kelang half an hour later. Singapore was ten hours sailing away, but just outside the port, we went for anchor.

'I wonder why we are waiting here.' I asked, as I stood with Nick on the sun-deck looking at other ships also at anchor.

'I think the captain would rather anchor here in daylight, than wait for a berth in Singapore in the dark.'

'Yeah, you're probably right. Singapore anchorage is notorious for its pirate attacks,' I remembered. 'That must be the reason.'

In the evening, as we were still anchored at Port Kelang, we watched Malaysian tv in the lounge. One of the ship-mechanics joined us. After the news in English, it was time for an episode of Farscape, a sci-fi tv-series. It turned out that the ship-mechanic was a sci-fi freak, just like me.

At 22.00h, the anchor was hauled up and we set course for Singapore.

CHAPTER THIRTEEN

Singapore is a city-state situated on an island at the southern tip of the Malay Peninsula. Since its independence from the British Commonwealth, in 1963, Singapore has become an important modern economy. Almost five million people live on the island that measures about 36 kilometres from east to west and about 20 kilometres from north to south. Singapore is highly cosmopolitan with a varied ethnic population. The Chinese with about 75% form the largest ethnic group, followed by nearly 14% Malay and 9% Indians. The Europeans, Arabs and other groups comprise the last 2%.

Four official languages are spoken in Singapore of which English and Mandarin Chinese are the most common. Malay and Tamil are the other two.

Singapore has a very low crime rate - its streets are clean and safe. This sense of security is enforced by a set of very strict rules, which have penalties from very high fines to imprisonment

Singapore is a popular tourist destination, with around 10 million visitors per year. Many tourists come to shop, with the Orchard Road shopping precinct being the most popular. Another reason to visit Singapore is to experience the unique blend of Asian cultures and cuisine in a modern cosmopolitan setting.

***

After an uneventful 10-hours sail from Port Kelang, we berthed at Singapore's PSL International Port on Tuesday 28th January, at 08.15h.

Apart from Nick, the captain and first officer were also disembarking here. At 09.00h the new captain, first officer and third engineer arrived on board.

I saw the new captain briefly as he made his way up the inner stairs. He was a tall, slim man in his early 60s, with short grey hair and glasses. He was obviously much fitter than the old captain was, as he almost ran up the stairs without even once having to rest and catch his breath.

As we were waiting for a stamp in our passports from immigration, Nick had taken his suitcase down from his cabin on deck 4. We were planning to go into Singapore together and do some sightseeing, until it was time for me to go back to the ship. Shore leave was to be until 19.00h.

Our passports arrived at 10.00h and after a brief visit to the ship's office on the main deck to tell the officer-on-watch we were going, we walked down the gangway together.

Singapore's container port is large. A shuttle bus was in service to ferry crew and port workers from the ships to the gate and back. At the bottom of our gangway, we found a small sign screwed to a lamppost, indicating that here was a stop for the shuttle service.

As we waited for the shuttle bus, we saw a taxi drive up and stop at the bottom of the gangway. Not long after it arrived, the old captain and first officer came down dragging along their luggage. We waved goodbye to them as they got in the taxi and drove away.

'It didn't take them long to get off the ship,' I remarked as we watched the taxi disappear around the corner of a stack of containers.

Nick nodded. 'Looks almost as if the captain got off as quickly as he could.'

'Wouldn't surprise me after all that happened. He must be happy to hand over the responsibility to someone else.'

'Still, I thought handing over command would take a bit longer than that.'

'It's a pity for the second officer the company couldn't find a replacement for him in time,' I said after a bit of a silence. 'Now he won't be back in time for the birth of his child.'

'Yeah, that is a pity for him,' Nick said. 'It must be hard for seafarers to miss out on such important things.'

'Yes,' I nodded.

The shuttle bus came and we went onboard. As I sat down on one of the plastic seats, I had to think back to the last time I had boarded one of these shuttle buses at Singapore. I was at the time travelling on the *FTK Kowloon*, and as I boarded the shuttle bus on my way back from shore leave, I noticed that the stevedores already on the bus were staring at me with curious looks on their faces. It seemed they were keen to find out where I was going, because when we reached the ship and I pressed the button to get off, they nudged each other and whispered 'Ah... *Kowloon, Kowloon*'.

After the shuttle bus dropped us off at the gate, we walked to Tanjong Pagar Station. The plan was to let Nick check into his hotel, so that he could drop off his suitcase.

From Tanjong Pagar we took the underground to Bugis, which is situated just a bit north of the Colonial District. Nick's hotel was just around the corner. He checked in, as I waited in the lobby. It was almost lunchtime and after Nick had taken his suitcase up to his room, we found a small Malay restaurant down the road and had a bite to eat.

Our meal finished, we walked out of the restaurant and found a photographer where we both handed in some films for the 3-hour developing service. After a visit to an internet cafe, we wandered around the area for a while, not wanting to walk too far away from the photo shop, and came across a large mosque that was situated in a square. Many tourists hung around, taking pictures and checking out the nearby souvenir shops.

At 14.30h, I phoned my parents. It was only 07.30h in the Netherlands and they had just woken up. I spoke to them for half an hour, while Nick wandered around the shops. Then it was time to go back to the photographers and pick up the pictures.

Flicking through them, I was happy to see they had turned out okay. During our crossing from Khor Fakkan, I had taken a picture of everyone on board and had got double prints of all the portraits.

'Here is yours,' I said to Nick as I handed him his close-up.

'Thanks,' Nick said. He rummaged through his photos. 'As we are swapping pictures you can have this one. I've got two of them.' He handed me a picture he had taken of the pig being roasted on the aft deck. A small group of Filipinos surrounded the spit, smiling into the camera.

Outside the shop we wondered what we could do next.

'The Raffles Hotel is not too far away from here,' Nick suggested. 'From what I hear it's a nice building, well worth a visit.'

'Let's go there then,' I said and we started walking.

The façade of the Raffles Hotel was impressive - three stories high, with lots of round-headed windows and a veranda on the ground floor.

We walked into the hotel and I picked up a small leaflet from a stand. Flicking through it and reading snippets of information, I learned that the Raffles Hotel was the most famous hotel in Asia, built in 1887 in the colonial style. One of the things that made the hotel famous was the Singapore Sling, a cocktail that was invented in 1915 by one of the hotel bartenders. Many tourists came to the hotel especially to have a sip of that famous drink.

Walking through the hotel, we came to a large inner courtyard shaded by huge tropical plants, with a bar in the middle.

'Now that we are here, do you want to try out the Singapore Sling?' Nick asked.

'Why not,' I answered.

'Two Singapore Slings please, ' Nick said to the bartender. As the man turned around to mix the drinks, I thought I could sense a slight disappointment in him that we hadn't ordered something else. He probably did nothing else all day but mixing Singapore Slings.

The drinks were soon ready and put in front of us - a piece of fresh pineapple decorating the rim. The Singapore Sling itself was bright pink and very sweet, but not at all unpleasant. We found a place to sit on the first floor veranda

By now, it was 17.30h and I wondered if I would have enough time for an evening meal, as there was only one-and-a-half-hours of my shore leave left.

'It wouldn't surprise me if the loading had been delayed,' Nick said, while he sipped his Singapore Sling. 'Why don't you give the agent a ring, to find out?'

'That's a good idea, but I haven't got his phone number on me.'

'I have.' Nick rifled through his wallet and found a piece of paper on which was scribbled down the agent's name and phone number.

When our drinks were finished, we went in search of a public phone. I rang the agent and was told that the ship was now due for departure at 22.00h, which meant I would have plenty of time for a meal.

Nick remembered there was a large food court in Little India, and on our way to it, we walked through a street with two large temples, one Hindu and one Chinese where preparations were in full swing for the celebrations of the Chinese New Year, which was in four days time. Even outside the temple, it smelled strongly of incense.

We arrived at the food court and walked past the different stalls to choose what to eat. There were stalls selling Chinese, Indian, Malay, Vietnamese, Thai, Korean and Japanese food. Many people were milling about trying to choose. I decided on some Chinese and ordered vegetarian fried rice and a teh tarik. Nick went for some Malay food and we sat down to eat at a table in the middle of the court.

After the meal, it was time for me to get back to the ship. We walked back to Bugis station and I said goodbye to Nick wishing him a good journey back to Australia. From Bugis I took the underground to Tanjong Pagar Station. The ride didn't take as long as I had anticipated and it was only 19.35h when I arrived back at the station.

Coming out, I noticed it had become dark. Even so, I felt completely safe as I walked the 15 minutes back to the gate.

As I approached the gate, an immigration officer stepped out of his booth. I took my passport out of my bag, ready to show it to him. The shuttle bus that was waiting for customers at its stop opposite the booth would leave in ten minutes. I was nicely on time.

Arriving at the booth, I handed my passport to the immigration officer. He took it and studied my photograph and name. Then he flipped through the pages, looking at the different stamps until he found the right one.

A frown appeared on his forehead.

'You are staying on a ship?' he asked, looking at me closely.

'Yes,' I said. 'The *Serenity River* .'

'You are still staying on that ship? You didn't disembark this morning?'

'No, I didn't disembark. I went on shore leave.'

He looked at the stamp again.

'This stamp indicates you disembarked. It is a 14-day visitor permit to Singapore. It is only given to people who disembark.' He held the passport out for me to see. 'If you are still on the ship, you have got the wrong stamp.'

I blinked at him, feeling slightly uncomfortable. Did this mean I couldn't go back to the ship?

'Did you bring a crew-list with your name on?'

'Er... no.'

'The phone number of the agent?' Blast it; I had given it back to Nick after the phone call.

'No.'

'Did you bring your ticket for passage on the ship?'

'No.'

'The phone number of the captain?'

'No.'

I sighed and thought about the chapter I had not so long before written for the guide-book. I had instructed the passengers never to go on shore leave without the crew-list and the agent's phone number. Had I followed my own advice? No, of course not.

'Have you got any proof on you that you still live on the ship?' the officer continued.

'Well... I have developed some pictures today. I took them on the ship.'

A faint smile showed briefly on the man's otherwise stern face.

'I am sorry, but I can't take that as proof.'

'No, obviously... I understand.' I racked my brain at what could be done. It suddenly felt as if hours had past, and I felt panic rise up inside me. What if the *Serenity* was about to depart? They would leave without me, not knowing I was stuck at the gate!

Suddenly I had an idea.

'Do you have a phonebook?' I asked. 'I phoned the agent earlier today and I can look up his name and number.'

The officer looked at the small desk inside the booth. It was empty but for a small clipboard to which was attached a list.

'I am sorry, but I don't have a phonebook here.' He took the clipboard from the desk. 'What was the name of your ship again?'

'*Serenity River*.'

With the index finger of his right hand, the officer went down the list, checking names. Halfway down he stopped. 'Ah... The *Serenity River* is on this list of ships currently in the port.'

He looked at me with a less stern face.

'I will call a colleague to escort you to the ship, so that he can ask the captain if you indeed belong on it.'

'Okay,' I said somewhat relieved. I hoped the captain would recognise me, as I had only briefly met him that morning on the stairs.

After his phone call, the officer gestured to one of the two chairs that were shoved under the desk in the booth.

'Please, sit down. It might take a little while.'

I pulled out the chair and sat down.

'So you are a passenger on this ship?' the officer asked as he sat down on the other chair.

'Er... no, not really. I am on assignment for the shipping company, writing a guide-book for the passengers.'

'Oh... interesting. And your assignment is how long?'

'Three months. Our next port of call is Busan in South Korea.' I looked at my watch. 'That is... if the ship doesn't leave without me.'

'I am sure it won't.' The officer smiled, his former frigidness gone. 'Where are you from?'

'The Netherlands.'

'Are you coming back to Singapore?'

'Yeah, I think so. In about two weeks time.'

'You better bring the crew-list and agent's phone number next time you go on shore leave.' It wasn't a ticking off, just some friendly advice.

'I will,' I smiled. 'You can be sure of that.'

The officer smiled back and we sat in silence for a bit. From the corner of my eye, I saw some people board the shuttle bus. It drove off on its route across the port.

Then a police car pulled up next to the booth.

'Ah... here they are,' the officer said and stood up. I got up as well.

Three police officers, two men and a woman, climbed out of the car. The officer handed one of the men my passport and explained the situation. Then he showed the driver the quickest way to the ship.

'Thank you, goodbye,' I said to the officer as I sat down on the back seat of the police car. The female police officer joined me in the back.

With blue lights flashing, we drove across the port.

The woman smiled at me. 'I have never been on a container ship before,' she said. I smiled back.

In no time, we pulled up at the bottom of the *Serenity's* gangway. As I got out, I saw the shuttle bus trundling towards us in the distance. It's faster and more exciting to travel by police car, I thought to myself.

I looked up at the ship and saw some of the crew looking down from up high, curious about the flashing blue lights and the police car.

I led the way up the gangway. One of the police officers and the woman followed me. As I reached the main deck, Mr Morayta quietly asked me, 'what happened? You got arrested?'

'Nah,' I answered. 'I've got the wrong stamp in my passport and now they don't believe I belong here.'

'Ah, I see,' he smiled.

I showed the police officers to the ship's office. The new first officer was on duty. I had only seen him very briefly as we checked out that morning when we left.

The police officer asked him if I lived on the ship and I kept my fingers crossed, he would remember me.

'Yes, of course,' the first officer said without hesitation. I could have hugged him.

He got the crew-list out. The police officer checked my name and passport number with the one on the list. When he was satisfied, he gave me back my passport and wished me a good evening. I took the officers back to the main deck and watched as they descended the gangway, got into their car and drove of, blue lights still flashing.

We departed that evening at 23.30h, still later than expected. I wasn't tired yet and walked down to the main deck to see the quay glide away from us. As I waited for departure the Filipino third officer, Mr Adega, walked by with some of the deck crew. They were on their way to the fo'c'sle to release the lines.

'Do you want to come with us, to see us go?' Mr Adega asked.

'Is that allowed?'

'Yeah, why not. It's dark, so no one will notice you.' He walked off. 'Just stick to the sides, out of the way. It's not too dangerous.'

'Okay,' I nodded and followed him.

It wasn't very spectacular. On command of the captain, port workers released our lines from the bollards down below on the quay. The deck crew winched them up and the *Serenity*, with the help of a tug-boat, started to drift away.

For a while, Mr Adega and I watched, as Singapore's twinkling skyline got smaller. Then we walked the long way back to the accommodation block. We were on our way to Busan.

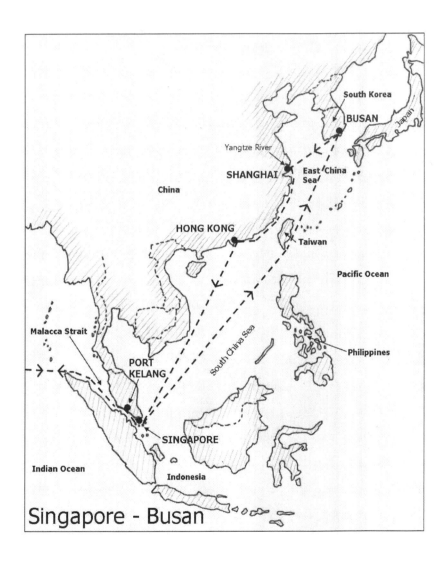

Singapore - Busan

CHAPTER FOURTEEN

The seating arrangements in the mess had been juggled about a bit after Nick and Lukas had left and with the arrival of the new captain. He was a bit more old school than the previous captain and was therefore of the opinion that officers and crew didn't mix during mealtimes, no matter which country they were from.

The new regime started at lunchtime the day after we left Singapore, a Wednesday. As soon as I walked into the officers' mess for lunch I noticed Mr Adega and Mr Chavira, third officer and second engineer respectively, sitting at a table by themselves eating their lunch. The captain and first officer were sitting at another table, on which one place was still empty - that of the chief engineer. I thought to myself that that chair would most likely remain empty, as the chief hardly ever ate with the rest of us.

The captain got up as he saw me come in and indicated to his right, where another table was set with three places.

'I hope you don't mind sitting with the second officer and third engineer for now,' he said. 'It would be a bit strange for you to sit alone, now that the passengers have gone.'

'That is very thoughtful,' I smiled, and sat down in my new place. 'I don't mind sitting with them at all.'

The captain sat down again and said, 'I understand your brother is coming on board in La Spezia.'

'Yes, he's is coming with us from La Spezia to New York. He is looking forward to it.'

'And, I suppose, so are you.'

'Yes, indeed. I am.'

'It's nice to have family on board,' the captain said, pricking some peas with his fork. 'I heard you had a bit of an adventure at the gate last night,'

'Yeah, they wouldn't let me back in, because I had the wrong stamp.'

The captain nodded. 'My wife had that once, as well. She was also taken back to the ship in a police car, same as you. She told me she had quite enjoyed the ride across the port with the flashing blue lights.'

'Yeah, I can imagine that,' I said. During the conversation, I had realised that the two ship-mechanics were not in the mess with us. As they were not officers but crew, I figured they were probably eating their lunch in the crew-mess.

The first officer had listened to the conversation and now asked me which part of the Netherlands I came from.

'Groningen,' I said. 'In the north.'

'Ah, yes,' the first officer nodded. 'I have been there a few times. It is a nice city.' He was a short, stubby man in his late 40s and like the old first officer, had a large beer belly.

'How long will it take us to get to Busan, captain?' I asked.

'Nearly six days,' he answered. 'Best get prepared for a change in the weather. It is freezing up there at the moment.'

The captain had finished his meal and to my great relieve he didn't light a cigarette. I sincerely hoped that the days of a smoke filled mess and lounge were over.

The second officer and new third engineer walked into the mess and sat down at my table. I hadn't met the new third engineer yet, so we shook hands and introduced ourselves. He looked young, in his mid-20s, and had long blond hair that was tied into a ponytail.

'No doubt you have heard that your predecessor went crazy,' I said to him.

'Yes, they told me,' he answered smiling. 'But don't worry; I am not planning to go crazy.'

'Good,' I smiled back.

After lunch, I walked past the pantry and saw Rodel tidying up. I stepped inside and said, 'this is a bit of a change, isn't it, with the ship-mechanics banned from the officers' mess.'

'Yes,' Rodel nodded. 'They weren't too happy about that.' He stacked the plates into the dishwasher. 'And neither were the third officer and second engineer. They would rather eat in the crew-mess with the other Filipinos. But if you ask me it won't be long before the ship-mechanics have their meals with the chief in the ship's office.'

'You think so?'

'Yes,' Rodel said. 'Not because they don't want to sit with the Filipinos, but because the chief will ask them. The chief doesn't like any of the other Germans, only the ship-mechanics.'

I smiled as I heard Rodel gossiping away. 'Well, we'll see...'

***

The captain wasn't wrong about the weather changing. Although it was still warm, the sky was cloudy and a strong wind had come up, creating a heavy swell and showers. The waves banged into the ship from the sides and it wasn't safe to go to the fo'c'sle for a stroll.

I didn't feel much like doing things for the guide-book. I was still very tired and the next two days slept a lot, trying finally to catch up and get rid of my ship lag.

On Saturday, we passed Taiwan. In the afternoon, the island suddenly appeared as a narrow strip of land on the horizon. Passing Taiwan, we sailed into the Pacific Ocean, but were not there for long.

Soon we went further north and into the East China Sea, thereby leaving tropical waters behind us.

Even though I had expected it, I still got a bit of a shock when I went outside the next morning on Sunday to check out the weather. The temperature had dropped from 26°C to 12°C almost overnight and the wind was bitterly cold.

Inside it wasn't much better. My cabin, being on the corner of the accommodation block, caught the ice-cold wind from two sides, making it a very draughty place. Although the air-conditioning wasn't blowing cold air any more, the heating didn't seem to be switched on instead.

I raided my cupboard and drawers for as many warm clothes I could find and put them on, all over the top of each other.

That evening the clocks needed to be put forward an hour to get to Busan time. We had now reached the most easterly point of the trip and from now on until we reached New York, we would go back westward and start turning the clock back instead of forward.

On the *FTK Kowloon*, ten months before, we *had* continued further east as our route had taken us from Asia, across the Pacific Ocean, to the west coast of the United States.

It took us nine days to cross this biggest of all oceans. Moving east continuously we had to change our clocks every night for eight nights in a row, resulting in the mother of all ship lags.

After four days sailing on the Pacific, we reached the 180° meridian. The day we crossed this line happened to be a Saturday (not one of my favourite days as eintopf was on the menu...). It was Saturday 8th June and in time, we were ten hours ahead of Central European Time. In other words, when it was 21.00h on the ship, it was only 11.00h in Europe.

The next day, lo and behold, it was Saturday 8th June again! We had crossed the 180° meridian, also known as the International Dateline, and had to get through yet another Saturday. Time had overnight changed from being 10 hours ahead into being 13 hours behind Central European Time, making 09.00h on the ship, 22.00h in Europe. By crossing the Dateline the whole world had caught up with us in time, and we were now the last to experience sunset, while the day before we had still been the first to see this happening.

Luckily, the cook had forgotten about the two Saturdays in a row and on the second Saturday had prepared his usual Sunday menu, so in the end I didn't have to suffer through two eintopf lunches.

Our crossing of the dateline caused an interesting problem for one of the ship-mechanics on board. His birthday happened to be on the 9th June and I wrote about it in my journal: "Yesterday his birthday was today, but today his birthday is tomorrow."

On our way back from the United States to Asia, we crossed the dateline again. It then resulted in us losing one day, making it go from Friday 21st June to Sunday 23rd June the next day.

Going back across the Pacific only about five days after we had arrived on the US west coast meant that I had only just recovered from one enormous ship lag as the other started. This time it was a westward ship lag, which differed from an eastward one in that it made me want go to bed at 20.00h in the evening and wake up and have breakfast at 04.00h in the morning.

***

It was Monday afternoon, 3rd February, on the *Serenity River*, when land appeared again on the horizon. We had reached Busan, our next port of call. Busan is the second largest city in South Korea and is situated on the south eastern tip of the Korean peninsula. It is surrounded by, and built in between, a number of high rocky hills that are covered in shrubs and trees.

The approach to the port was very picturesque. First visible were the hills, some almost as large as mountains. Then buildings appeared, situated on the flanks of the dark green hills. Some buildings were small, not more than one to two stories high; others were skyscrapers. The entrance to the port was guarded by a steep hill, covered in scrub, with a white tower on its top. We slowly glided past this semi-island, as other ships, smaller and larger, past us on their way to and from the port.

The wind was still biting cold and I was glad to go inside when we had berthed, and have my evening meal.

The captain had already told me that shore leave was expected to be until 18.00h the next day, which would give me plenty of time to explore the city.

***

I was still clutching the piece of paper on which the ship's agent had written the names of the underground stations in Korean, as I lowered myself on to a seat in the reasonably crowded underground train at Goejeong. It worked out that I hadn't needed the paper after all, as the signs at the station were in Korean as well as English.

It was 09.00h when I boarded my train and the rush hour seemed to come to its end, even though there were still a lot of people in the train. Most of them were wearing suits and carrying bags with laptops, clearly on their way to work. Even though

122

foreigners were by no means rare in Busan, I attracted some curious looks as I sat down, but the novelty soon wore off.

I had left the ship that morning at 08.30h. Rodel had told me that the people at the gate would call a taxi for me and they did. When it arrived, I showed the driver the piece of paper with the name of the station, which the agent had given me the evening before. Apparently, the cheapest way to get to Busan's city centre would be by underground. In my experience, it would probably also be the more interesting way. To me taking a taxi always felt a bit like cheating - the easy way out. I liked taking local transport. Taxis were for emergencies, or if there wasn't any other choice.

I was dropped off at Goejeong, the closest underground station to the port. The taxi ride had taken me north from the gate, along the port and into a suburb with apartment blocks. Close to the station was a street with shops and round the corner from it a market. As I got out of the taxi, I was curious to see the market, but decided I had better find the tourist information first and get the 'work' part of my shore leave out of the way.

The weather was still very cold. I wore my gloves, scarf and woolly hat and my summer coat over which I had put my fleece. It was sunny, but the biting wind went right through me. Very different from the warm tropical temperatures I had got used to almost since the *Serenity* had left the Suez Canal, more than three weeks before.

The agent had told me to get off at Busan Station if I wanted to go to the tourist information. It was only eight stops and after 10 minutes, we arrived. I stepped on to the platform and took a long escalator up, surfacing on to a large square in front of the station. Following the signs to the tourist information, I crossed the road and entered Busan's China Town. I found the tourist information in one of the side streets and after I had stocked up on leaflets, discovered they had free internet access and took the opportunity to check my email. I wasn't the only one, as the other four computers were also occupied, mostly by Westerners.

It took me 45 minutes to catch up with my emails. At least it was warm inside.

After the tourist information, I walked around China Town for a bit. It wasn't very busy, probably because it wasn't the tourist season. Most of the shops turned out to be restaurants and they were still closed. Then I moved south, back towards the city centre that I had bypassed on the underground earlier. It was now getting towards lunchtime and I wasn't surprised when I felt my stomach rumbling. I started to look out for a place to eat and soon I spotted a small restaurant in a side street. A large railway viaduct loomed over the houses in the street, giving it a gloomy atmosphere. The restaurant turned out to be Chinese and was already open. I went in and ordered some fried rice. It was still early and for a while, I was the only customer. Then another woman walked in and ordered some food. After a cup of green tea for dessert, I continued on my way to the city centre. It wasn't very far and along the way, I checked out some of the shops I passed. I was especially curious about the prices of dvds, but they turned out to be nearly the same as in Europe.

At 14.00h, I had had enough. I was thoroughly frozen and decided to take the underground back to the port.

Before hopping in a taxi, I had a look at the market I had spotted earlier. It was very colourful, with lots of little stands from which people were selling vegetables, meat, fish, clothes and other knick-knacks.

Arriving at the gate half an hour later, I noticed a little shop I hadn't seen in the morning. It was more like a shack, built of bits of wood and corrugated iron. Curious, I walked towards it and obeyed the sign saying Please Enter.

The shop was tiny with irregular shelves along the walls, filled with different types of Korean sweets, crisps and chocolate. Cigarettes and phone cards were also on offer. In one corner stood a cylindrical stove, radiating a gentle heat.

An old woman appeared from a small room in the back that was partitioned off by a piece of cloth. I bought some chocolate and peanuts with my last Korean wons.

Back on the ship, I went into the pantry. Rodel wasn't there and I figured he was probably taking a nap. I got myself a drink from the hot water machine and added a teabag. Sipping the hot liquid, I walked upstairs to my cabin.

We departed at 18.15h. I watched for a little while from deck 5, but soon found it too cold and went back inside.

That night the clock was turned back one hour. We were now on Singapore time again and would stay on it until we were back in the Bay of Bengal.

CHAPTER FIFTEEN

When I woke up the next morning and looked out of the window, I was surprised by the sight of the seawater that, overnight, had turned from a greenish/greyish into a light yellowish brown. It was the first sign that we were nearing the Yangtze River, although we weren't supposed to reach the river itself for at least another 12 hours.

With its 6385 kilometres, the Yangtze is the longest river in Asia and the third largest river on Earth after the Nile and the Amazon. As it journeys across China, the Yangtze River erodes tonnes of soil, which give the river its distinctive yellow colour. When the river reaches the East China Sea, it colours the seawater for many kilometres off shore

Our destination on the Yangtze was the Chinese port of Shanghai, situated on the south bank of the river and about 15 kilometres north of the actual city.

In the evening, we still hadn't reached the river mouth and after the meal, while the ship floated about waiting for the pilot, I went into the crew-lounge to look for Mr Garrido, the electrician, who had expressed a wish to see my laptop, but before dragging it down the stairs, I thought I'd better look for him. He wasn't in the crew-lounge however and I was directed to the ship's office on the main deck as it was rumoured he was there.

Walking into the ship's office I discovered the chief engineer, second engineer, the electrician, third engineer and second officer sitting around a table, drinking beer. As soon as the chief saw me he remarked, 'I am angry with you for not congratulating me on my birthday before now.'

I was rather taken aback. 'I'm sorry, but I wasn't aware that it was your birthday. Congratulations.' The chief scowled a bit, but accepted my wishes for many happy returns. 'You must stay here and have a drink with us,' he said.

'Okay,' I said somewhat reluctantly, but pulled up a chair from one of the desks. I accepted a glass of orange juice from the second officer.

'You know,' the chief said. 'None of the passengers ever come to visit the engine-room.' The remark came a bit out of the blue and I wondered where it was all going. 'No one is interested in the engine-room,' he continued.

'Well, I don't think that is entirely tr-' I started.

'The engine-room is the most important part of the ship, you know,' the chief interrupted me. He took a large swig of beer from the bottle he was holding. 'But passengers much rather go to the bridge and look at the charts and the radar screen. They find that far more interesting. It's not fair.' He stopped to draw breath.

I looked around at the others. They all looked a bit sheepish.

'You have not been to the engine-room,' the chief said accusingly, pointing a stubby finger at me.

'That's not true,' Mr Chavira, the second engineer came to my defence. 'She came and had a look at the new generator.'

I nodded vigorously. 'And I took pictures of the engine crew at work.'

'Exactly,' Mr Garrido said. 'She has been in the engine-room loads of times.' I smiled at him.

The chief waved his hand and mumbled something. Then he got up. 'Let's move this party to the crew-lounge.'

We all got up and followed the chief. The second officer and I were the last in line.

'Don't listen to him. He's very moody today,' the second officer whispered as we turned into the corridor.

'Just today...?'

'Well, more than usual it seems.'

'What's wrong with him?' I asked. 'I don't understand. He's always complaining and never smiles.'

'Low self esteem, I guess. And he hates the west Germans. He's from east Germany.'

'You're from west Germany.'

'Yes, but I'm half South African. That makes me less bad.'

'Ah...'

We had reached the crew-lounge. Some of the Filipinos were playing cards, while at the same time watching a video about bears in Alaska.

The chief sat down on a barstool and opened another bottle of beer.

'Have you ever been to Shanghai?' he asked as I sat down on a couch.

'No, you?'

He shook his head. 'I don't like big cities. Too many people and traffic.'

'Shanghai is quite nice, though,' the second officer said. 'It's got this old English part, very posh.'

'I would love to go to Shanghai,' Mr Chavira said. 'But there is never enough time to go on shore leave.'

'Hopefully we will have tomorrow morning, at least,' I said. 'I need to find a tourist information to get some info for the guide-book.'

'I wish I could come with you,' Mr Chavira said, looking wistful. 'See something of the town.'

'Well, why don't you go with her,' the chief said. 'We can do without you for three hours.'

'Really? Could I go?' Mr Chavira said perking up. He turned to me. 'Would you mind me tagging along?'

'No, of course not. You can join me, no problem.'

The phone rang and Mr Morayta answered it. He listened for a few seconds and hung up. 'The pilot is coming onboard. We're entering the river.'

The chief got off his stool. 'I better go to the engine-room,' he said and walked out. Mr Chavira and the third engineer followed him.

'When are we berthing?' I asked the second officer.

'Not until after midnight,' he answered. 'At least four hours from now.'

'I see.' I got up as well. 'I think I will retreat to my cabin, before the chief comes back...'

The second officer smiled. 'Yeah, good idea.'

I turned to walk away but the second officer's voice came from behind me, 'Oh, by the way...' I turned around again. 'Did you hear that my wife has had the baby?' I shook my head. 'It's a boy. He was born this morning.'

'Congratulations,' I said and shook his hand. 'I hope everything went okay. Any news on when you can return home?'

'Hopefully when we get back to Singapore. I can't wait to see him.'

'Yeah, I can imagine that.'

The *Serenity River* berthed at Shanghai port at 02.30h that night. I woke up as we were drawing near and watched from my window for a little while before going back to bed. When the agent came on board an hour later, the captain, at my request, asked him a few questions about how to get into Shanghai. To make it easier the agent wrote down the name of the port in Chinese on a piece of paper. I found it on the doormat when I woke up in the morning, shoved under the door by the captain.

∗∗∗

It was Thursday 6ᵗʰ February, and the day of the Shanghai shore leave. Mr Chavira was still enthusiastic about going into Shanghai with me. We had to be back at 13.00h and therefore left as early as possible. It was still cold, although not as cold as in Busan. The sun was shining and the air smelled crisp.

At 08.00h, we stood at the bottom of the gangway, waiting for the shuttle bus to take us to the gate. Just before breakfast, I had quickly read the info I had brought from home. Shanghai, it said, has a population of 20 million people and is the largest city in China. The city is bisected by the Huangpu River, which flows into the Yangtze about 15 kilometres to the north of the city centre. The west part of the city is the oldest. The east part, Pudong, is the modern economic hub, dominated by skyscrapers.

We boarded a taxi at the gate. That seemed to be the only way from the port to the city centre. The ride took 45 minutes. The area around the port was mainly industrial, with factories and several chemical plants. From their chimneys billowed a horrible smelly yellow smoke. In between the chemical plants were some residential areas. I hoped that they were deserted but then I saw a woman carrying some large shopping bags, going into the front door of a house.

The taxi ride took us through the centre of Pudong and along a three-lane highway into a tunnel under the river. Just before we entered the tunnel, we had a good view of the Oriental Pearl Tower,

131

which featured a larger and a smaller sphere, both covered in pink glass. Definitely one of the more impressive towers I have ever seen.

We emerged on the other side of the river to a big surprise. I would have thought I was in London, if I hadn't known I was in Shanghai. Old Victorian buildings lined the streets left and right, three or four storeys high, with large sash windows and columns that surrounded doorways or supported cupolas on the roofs. We were in The Bund, Shanghai's old English quarter along the river. The taxi stopped at the kerb and we got out. Across the river, the Oriental Pearl Tower dominated the skyline of Pudong.

'Do you know where the tourist information is?' Mr Chavira asked me.

'No, not a clue unfortunately,' I answered. 'Do you mind if we go looking for it first and then do some touristy things?'

'Of course not. You are working, right?' Mr Chavira asked.

I smiled. 'Yes, I am working.'

'Then we must do that first.'

I looked at the Victorian buildings. It was weird. So English, and yet I was in China. There were colonial buildings in Singapore as well, but these ones in Shanghai topped those. I spotted a large hotel and pointed to it. 'Let's go in there and ask at the reception where to find the tourist information.'

'Good idea.'

We walked up a few steps and through two large double doors, opened for us by a smiling doorman. We were in the foyer. At the reception a friendly man showed us on a map where the tourist information was.

'It is not too far, ma'am. Maybe a 15-minute walk along The Bund.' He waved his arm in the general direction we had to go.

'Thank you,' I smiled. 'Have you got any more of those maps?'

'No, I am sorry ma'am, I don't. Unfortunately I can't give you this one, as it belongs to the reception.'

'I understand,' I said. Then I noticed two stacks of what looked like English language newspapers on the counter. I picked one of them up. 'Are these for sale?'

'Yes, ma'am.'

'Can I buy one of each?'

'Of course. That is two yuan, please ma'am.'

I handed him the money and stuffed the two newspapers, a China Daily and a Shanghai Daily, into my bag. I loved reading foreign newspapers.

We walked out of the hotel.

'I bet we have a nice view over the river if we cross the road,' I said. 'It looks like there is some sort of path going along the river in the direction we have to go.'

'Let's cross the road at the traffic lights,' Mr Chavira said.

As we waited for the green man, a large group of tourists joined us. Most of them were wearing cameras around their necks. I listened to them talk and realised they were speaking Chinese.

The light turned green and we crossed. We had to walk up a bit of an embankment to see the river properly, and as we came to the top saw a large sightseeing boat that was moored at a jetty. Our fellow crossers-of-the-road had followed us up the embankment and were now making a beeline for the jetty. Clearly, they were going to take a tour.

'Are they Chinese tourists?' Mr Chavira asked.

'I think so,' I answered. 'It seems a bit strange though that there are so many of them.' As I said it, I remembered that the Saturday before had been the Chinese New Year. Hadn't Nick said something about an annual public holiday when we had walked past that Chinese temple in Singapore? I looked across the road and noticed more Chinese tourists, happily wandering about, snapping pictures. It had to be their national holiday week and clearly many of them had decided to visit Shanghai.

We walked along and looked at the river, the people, the skyscrapers on the other side and the buildings along The Bund. Then we arrived at the tourist information.

A woman was sitting behind a desk smiling, gesturing for us to sit down. Still smiling she said, 'I... help ... you...?' I smiled back.

'Yes, do you have a map, and some brochures of the city that I could take with me, please?' I looked at her expectantly, waiting for an answer, but instead had to content myself with her puzzled face. She hadn't understood a word I said. I changed tactics and pointed at the map of the city that was taped to her desk. 'Can I have one of those, please?'

She nodded, smiling and got one from the drawer in her desk.

'Any brochures or other information?' I tried again.

'I... no... English...' she said with an apologetic smile.

I returned her smile. 'No problem. Anyone else here who speaks English?'

'No... sorry...'

'Okay, no problem.' I got up. 'Thank you very much for the map.'

Back outside I heaved a big sigh. 'Unfortunately I don't speak hand-and-foot very well.'

'I don't think it would have helped much in this case,' Mr Chavira said. 'I didn't see any brochures inside any way.'

'That's true. Let's walk back and see if we can find some souvenir shops. I want to buy some postcards.'

It had become a little bit warmer and as we walked back along The Bund, I spotted an old man selling postcards on the street. I bought some.

Back near the hotel, we turned away from the river and walked west for a while. Soon, the old colonial buildings made way for a square lined by modern high-rises. Most of them seemed to contain electronics shops. In the middle of the square were a few stands that were selling souvenirs. The Chinese tourists were milling around, looking for something to take back home. I bought a wind chime with dragons and bells.

It was now 10.30h and we suddenly realised we were quite hungry. At the far end of the square, we found what looked like a McDonalds type Chinese restaurant. Although it was still early, the restaurant was packed, mostly with young people, chatting away to each other. We sat down and looked at the menu card. Each choice was given in the form of a picture and a short description in Chinese as well as in English. I went for the fried rice again, but this time Japanese style. I had no idea if it would be any different from the fried rice I had had in Singapore or Busan.

Our meals were soon brought out and I decided to eat with chopsticks. Some Japanese friends had taught me how to use them a year ago, when I was in Tokyo on the *FTK Kowloon*, but I was a little out of practice. Mr Chavira played it safe and used the knife and fork that had also come with the food.

After a cup of jasmine tea, we went back outside and wandered around. Then at 11.30h, we walked back to The Bund. We figured it would be easier to get a taxi from there.

We were back at the gate at 12.45h. No one wanted to check our passports as we walked back in. The shuttle bus soon came and dropped us off at the *Serenity*.

When we were halfway up the gangway a police car approached at considerable speed and with screeching tyres came to a halt at the bottom. Two men clambered out. One of them pointed at me angrily.

'You... crew... member?' he asked in broken English.

'Yes, of course,' I said somewhat indignantly. 'Do you want to see my passport and shore leave pass?'

'No, no... Okay, okay...' They climbed back in the car and drove off.

'If they had bothered to check the passports when we came in, they wouldn't have had to chase us like that,' I said. 'What did they think I was? A tourist curious about the ship? A prostitute?'

I sighed and continued walking, thinking that this surely would not have happened if I had been a man.

We left the port of Shanghai at 14.30h. As we slowly made our way down the river towards the sea, we passed many small fishing boats. I was still looking out over the river half an hour after our departure when Mr Morayta and some of the other deck crew walked past me.

'Do you want to have a cup of tea with us in the crew-mess? he asked. 'We always have a tea break at 15.00h. Come.'

I followed them and in the mess sat down at one of the three tables. Most of the Filipinos were present. We chatted for a bit, while sipping our tea. They were curious about my shore leave. At 15.20h, the crew went back to work and I returned to my cabin. I spent some time reading the two newspapers I had bought and then started working on the Shanghai chapter of the guide-book.

CHAPTER SIXTEEN

In the evening after our departure from Shanghai, I took my laptop to the crew-lounge to show it to Mr Garrido. He was curious to see what programmes I had on it. Soon Rodel joined us. He was also very interested and together the three of us checked out some of the work I had already done on the book.

'I have studied computer engineering, you know,' Rodel said after a while.

'Really? I had no idea,' I said. 'Then you probably know more about my laptop than I do.'

He smiled. 'Maybe.'

'So, if you don't mind me asking, why are you working on a ship?'

'Money,' he said. 'I can earn more money on a ship, even at the lowest rank of steward, than I could ever earn if I worked as a computer engineer in the Philippines.' He looked around at his fellow crew-members, some of whom had been playing cards or watching tv. They were now all listening to our conversation.

'It's probably the same for all of us,' Rodel continued. 'We don't like working on the ships and being away from our families for nine months at the time. But if we don't do it, we are not able to feed them.'

Mr Garrido nodded. 'It's true,' he said. 'We don't really have a choice.'

'That's horrible.'

'Yes, it's not very nice,' Mr Reyes remarked, 'but, *because* I am working on a ship, I earn enough money to look after my family in the best possible way. At least my wife and children live in a good house and have a good education. If I didn't work, we would be living in real poverty. So in a way I am lucky to have this job, even though I am away from home a lot of the time.'

'And that's the way you all feel?' I asked in general. They nodded their heads.

'Of course we feel low and horrible at times, missing our family and wishing we weren't here,' Mr Garrido said. 'But in general we try to make the most of it and think positively.'

'Now I understand why everyone is always smiling when I meet them,' I said. 'You're thinking positively and are making the most of it.'

'Or we are just happy to see you,' Mr Reyes said with a smile.

'That's also a possibility of course,' I nodded, returning his smile.

After Mr Garrido and Rodel had satisfied their curiosity about my laptop, I switched it off and sat down at a table where Mr Toribio, Mr Navaez and Mr Orozco were playing cards. I watched for a while and soon recognised the game as tong-its, a popular Filipino card game that I had learned to play on the other ships.

'You're playing tong-its, aren't you?' I asked. All three men looked up from their cards with surprise.

'Yes, we are,' Mr Navaez answered. 'Do you know how to play?'

'Yes, the Filipinos on the other ships taught me how to play it.'

'Then you must join us.'

'Thanks, I will.'

I joined in the next game and the guys soon realised that indeed I knew how to play tong-its. After about half-a-dozen games I had enough.

'It is getting a bit late,' I said looking at my watch. 'I'm going to bed.' I stood up and grabbed my laptop from the table. 'I will see you guys tomorrow. Thanks for letting me play.'

'You're welcome, and don't forget you can always join us for cards again.'

'I will remember. Goodnight.'

The next day we had left the yellow waters of the Yangtze far behind us and were well on our way back to the warmer climates. We were due to arrive in Hong Kong on Sunday, in two days time.

As I came down for lunch and walked past the panty, Rodel ask me to come in for a minute.

'What's up, Rodel?'

'As you might know we are getting some new crew in Hong Kong.'

I blinked at him for a second. 'Er... no, I didn't know that.'

'Well, we are. Six of the Filipinos are leaving and we are getting six new ones in return.'

'Ah.'

'There is going to be a farewell party for them tonight in the crew-lounge and the guys have asked me to invite you.'

'That is very kind. Tell them I will come.'

'Great. Now, do you want to have mashed potatoes and peas for lunch?'

'Yummy, yes, I do. I love mashed potatoes.'

The farewell party that evening was fun. Mr Garrido was one of the Filipinos leaving and he sang one karaoke song after another, sometimes on his own, and sometimes with Mr Orozco or Mr Jimenez, who was also leaving. The Germans had also been invited and most of them joined us for little while, except for the captain, who was in bed with a bad cold and didn't want to risk infecting everyone else on board.

After a couple of hours of karaoke, the Vengaboys cd was put in the player and most of us danced to their songs for a while. As the evening wound down Mr Reyes got out his guitar and started playing and singing. He had a wonderful voice.

At 23.30h, the party ended.

***

I woke up on Sunday 9th February, to find the *Serenity River* had gone for anchor at Hong Kong. We were not going to berth in the port as usual, but instead were going to be offloaded by floating cranes while at anchor. This was not too unusual a procedure, but it was the first time it happened on a ship I was on.

The view was brilliant. We were situated just to the west of Hong Kong Island, the sky was blue and it was a pleasant 22°C. The city's skyscrapers were gleaming in the sunlight and the green hills of Hong Kong Island seemed to beg me to visit them. Unfortunately, there was no chance of going on shore leave.

After breakfast at 08.00h, the first floating crane arrived, towed by a tug-boat. It was actually not more than a large barge, with room for containers in the middle, a sort of low bridge on one side and a steel tower, with a large swinging arm, on the other side.

The barge was positioned alongside us, and two workers climbed on board. They hauled with them one end of a steel cable, which was fastened around one of the bollards on our aft deck. The other end of the cable was attached to a winch on the deck of the crane. After that, the crane, dragged by the tug-boat, moved towards our fo'c'sle, while the steel cable slowly uncoiled itself. Then the cable was, via the winch, attached to a bollard on our fo'c'sle.

Arriving in Busan.

The author posing in front of the skyline of Pudong, Shanghai's modern 'suburb', where the Oriental Pearl Tower takes centre stage.

*Afternoon tea in the crew-mess with the guys. From the left: Rodel,
Mr Hernarez, Mr Reyes and Mr Morayta.*

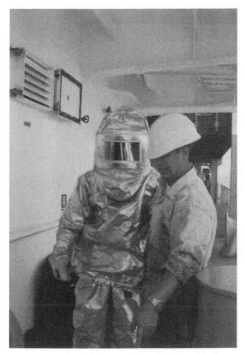

*The heat suit in action
during the fire drill.*

A floating crane is unloading the Serenity River *in Hong Kong.*

Supplies arrive by boat in Hong Kong.

*Port Kelang's Westports container terminal is decorated
with trees, shrubs and flowers.*

From great height the crew of
the Kowloon *watches as the
jerry cans on the Sri Lankan
boat are filled up with water.*

Suez anchorage – waiting for the north-bound convoy to start moving into the Suez Canal.

Traversing the Suez Canal near Ismailia, with the bayonet of the memorial of the 6 October 1973 sticking out of the desert sand on the right.

People are driving goats along the Suez Canal.

The bridge of the ship.

The outside stairs on the
FTK Kowloon.

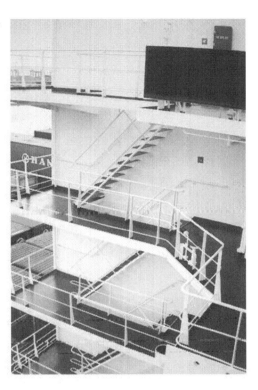

The author photographed from the mast, lying on the deck of the fo'c'sle
of the Colonial Star.

Back in La Spezia for the second time.

Hanging around on the fo'c'sle, while berthed in Valencia.

After this the tug-boat released the crane and moved away, slowly disappearing in the distance, leaving the floating crane able to winch itself along our hull by means of the steel cable. Large rubber tyres fastened around all sides of the crane prevented it from scratching our hull.

I had studied the whole procedure with Mr Reyes from the aft deck.

'This is very dangerous,' he said with a serious face. 'As the crane pulls itself along the cable there is an enormous strain on it with the real chance that it will snap. If that happens it will suddenly pull back like a whip and it could cut you in half if you were near it.'

I nodded and looked at the cable. It looked pretty thin and flimsy. 'But if this is so dangerous, why don't we just berth at the quay as normal?'

'I understand it is much cheaper to do it this way. Apparently half the price of being berthed.'

'I see,' I said, as we watched a second floating crane approach the other side of the ship. 'I think I will stay indoors today, or at least on the upper decks.'

'Yes, that would be best. Truly. Even the crew is scared most of the time when the floating cranes are around.'

I walked to my cabin and opened one of the windows. The first floating crane had started to offload containers near the fo'c'sle. The swing arm of the barge was manoeuvred over the top of the stacked containers on our deck and a cable with four shorter cables attached to it, was lowered over them. Then a worker fastened two of the shorter cables in two corners of one container and the two other cables in two corners of the container right next to it. The two containers were then winched up together, swinging precariously over the head of the workman. Sometimes it seemed as if the crane operator had little control as he winched up the containers. The result was that they started swinging wildly, bumping with a loud bang into other containers still stacked on deck and even once or twice into our hull.

Once lifted off, the containers were stacked in the middle part of the crane, waiting to be transported to a smaller barge, which would take them to the shore. The whole morning it was a coming and going of barges, taking containers to and from the *Serenity*. It all seemed a rather roundabout way of doing things.

Apart from the large and small floating cranes, other ships also visited us during the day. First, there was a wooden boat, manoeuvred alongside by an old woman, who came to bring us the supplies that had been ordered in advance. The deck of her little boat was full of cardboard boxes, mostly with food, which were one by one winched up by our deck crew.

At 11.15h, a water taxi arrived with the new crew. As they climbed onboard, their luggage was hoisted up via ropes. With the new crew also came the ship's agent.

As I went down for lunch 15 minutes later, Rodel introduced me to the new cook, Ramon. He was a big chubby man with a ready smile. He was already familiarising himself with the galley, while Mr Espinosa, the old cook, put the finishing touches to the last lunch he would cook on board.

'I like to cook Chinese food,' Ramon said to me. 'Do you like Chinese food?'

'I do, very much,' I said. I liked the sound of Ramon's meals, for although tasty, Mr Espinosa's meals had not been very varied.

A water taxi came to pick up the old crew at 14.30h. I watched as they climbed onboard the little boat and waved as it slowly disappeared out of sight.

The floating cranes kept loading and offloading containers into the night. As it got dark strong lights shone down from the towers of the cranes and illuminated the scene. On Hong Kong Island, the skyscrapers lit up like Christmas trees.

At midnight the work was done. The cranes moved off and after we had hauled in the anchor, we set sail for Singapore.

CHAPTER SEVENTEEN

Two days after our departure from Hong Kong, a Tuesday, I was typing away on my laptop, while I kept half an eye on the clock. Although I knew what was going to happen in five minutes time - there had been a notice on the board on deck 1 - I still liked to be prepared. Five minutes later, when the clock ticked over to 10.20h, the general alarm went off around the ship. It was a loud blering noise that came out of a speaker in the ceiling - seven short blasts and one long one. The safety drill had started.

I did as I had been taught to do during numerous other safety drills. I put on my boots (rule 1: wear sturdy footwear), and then got my coat out of the closet (rule 2: dress warmly), and grabbed the life-jacket and hard hat from the top shelf (rule 3: take your life-jacket). I pulled on my coat and walked down the outside stairs to reach the muster station on the starboard side of deck 3.

As I arrived most crew-members were already assembled, all of them wearing their hard hats and bright orange life-jackets. The 2nd officer hadn't arrived yet and while we waited, I put on my hard hat and life-jacket. I was still fastening the straps when the second officer stepped outside holding a clipboard.

'Is everyone assembled?' he asked. It was a rhetorical question. 'I will now call out your names.'

He started calling off our names and one by one, we raised our hands, just as we used to do in school. We all looked a bit bored, but safety drills were important, especially with a partially new crew and captain.

When the second officer had ascertained we were indeed all present, he started explaining about the rest of the drill.

'We are doing a fire drill today. There is a fire in the galley, which needs to be put out. Everyone knows their tasks, so do what you have to do.'

'Are we using the heat suit? 'Mr Navaez asked.

'Yes, we are. Get it ready.'

'Aye, sir.'

The crew moved off to their different predetermined stations. Some started rolling out the fire hoses, a few others went to get the heat suit.

'Captain, the crew is getting ready to fight the fire,' the second officer said into the portable two-way radio he was holding in his hand.

I looked up from deck 3 to the wing of the bridge, where I could see the captain looking down on us.

'Understood,' the captain's voice came back. 'Co-ordinate the drill and report back to me.'

'Aye, sir.'

Then the second officer looked at me. He and I were the only ones left at the muster station. As I was on the crew-list as a passenger, I didn't have a task in an emergency. Safety drills for passengers usually only involved showing up at the muster station with life-jacket, after which they could go back to their cabins.

'After the fire drill we will go into the lifeboat,' the second officer said. 'So I am afraid you will have to stick around for a bit.'

'That's okay,' I said. 'Can I watch?'

'Yes, as long as you keep out of the way.'

I followed him inside and we walked down the stairs to deck 1. The door of the galley was closed and the corridor was filled the crew, some holding fire hoses. Most life-jackets had been taken off and dropped near the crew-lounge. I took off my life-jacket and put it against the wall in the stairwell.

I kept back and watched as Mr Figueira, one of the new deck crew, struggled into a wide pair of trousers made of a silvery material. He then pulled on some large silvery boots. On his back was strapped a large canister of oxygen, which was connected to the breathing apparatus covering his face. Over all this went a big coat, made of the same material as the trousers. Mr Navaez helped him pull on some long silvery gloves over the sleeves of the coat and then pulled the attached large hooded headpiece over his head. The silver hood had a shiny gold faceplate. Thus swaddled it looked like Mr Figueira had been transformed into an astronaut, ready to be launched into space.

I didn't think he was able to see very much, as Mr Navaez had to lead him by the hand to the door of the galley, where someone pushed a fire hose into his hands. Everyone moved back as Mr Figueira opened the door to the galley with some difficulty. Then he stepped inside, pulling the hose with him and pretended to put out the imaginary fire.

The second officer had watched it all and timed the whole procedure. He looked happy.

As Mr Figueira, with the help of Mr Navaez, peeled himself out of the heat suit, the second officer said that we were now all going back to the muster station to board the lifeboat. I was quite excited about the prospect, as I had never been inside a freefall lifeboat before.

Back at the muster station, we trooped around the entrance to the lifeboat, which was hanging in its launching contraption at a downward angle of about 45°. One by one, we were led inside and sat down. Unlike the lifeboats I had been in before, this freefall lifeboat had two rows of seats on either side, with a passage through the middle, not unlike a bus. The seats were at an angle and all facing backwards. This was obviously done to cushion the body from the blow when the boat was dropped into the water from up high.

When we were all seated, the second officer told us to fasten our seatbelts. He then explained a few things about the lifeboat, after which we all climbed out again.

Then the drill was completed and everyone went back to work.

As I walked upstairs to my cabin, I remembered I had left my life-jacket at the bottom of the stairs on deck 1. Not wanting the captain to trip over it on his way to lunch, I thought it better to retrieve it at once. As I walked down, I thought back to a previous safety drill, which had not worked so perfectly, at least, not from my point of view.

I was working on the *FTK Kowloon* at the time, and we were in the Red Sea on our way to Singapore. I was in my cabin, also typing away, when totally unexpected the general alarm went off.

I froze, my fingers hovering over the keyboard. My stomach tightened. Thoughts flashed through my brain. Was this for real? Was this a real emergency or had there been a notice on the board about a drill? No, I would have seen that. I looked on the board every time I went down for a meal, three times a day. I quickly looked at my watch. It was 10.20h, a time that was often picked for a drill. So was it a drill? I decided to check the corridor. As I got up, I noticed that my knees were trembling. I opened the door of my cabin, and stepped into the corridor. Apart from the dying echoes of the alarm, everything was quiet. How strange. Somehow, I would have expected a lot of noise, shouting voices etc., when the alarm went off for real. For sure, this was a drill and I had missed the notice.

Having already lost nearly a minute of valuable time I had no choice but to obey the alarm. I had to get down to the muster station.

I quickly dressed warmly, put on my shoes and went down the stairs with my life-jacket under my arm.

As I emerged at the muster station, my legs were still shaking. Everyone was there, waiting with bored faces, as the second officer called their names. Then I was sure it was a drill. There was no way that everyone could be so calm and relaxed if it had been a real emergency.

Pretending I had known all about it, I put up my hand as my name was called. After that, the drill was over for me and I could go back to my cabin.

Back upstairs, I saw that I had left my cabin door standing wide open. As I closed it behind me, I reflected that this had truly been a proper drill for me. I was glad to discover that I hadn't panicked and had stayed reasonably calm and done all the right things, even though I had lost time by trying to figure out if it was a drill or not. I was sure that had the alarm gone off at a less 'normal' time, like in the evening, I would have known it was real and would probably have reacted faster. I hoped so anyway.

At lunchtime two hours later, I told the captain I must have missed the notice on the board. No, I hadn't, he said. The second officer should have told everyone about the drill, but had clearly forgotten to mention it to me.

At least there had been no harm done, I thought as I picked up my life-jacket from the bottom of the *Serenity's* stairs and trudged back up. It was good to be tested every now and then.

***

During our trip from Hong Kong to Singapore, I got into the habit of going down to the crew-mess in the afternoon for a cup of tea. It was during one of these tea breaks that I noticed an English language newspaper lying on one of the tables. The newspaper looked well thumbed; in fact, Mr Morayta was still leafing through the sports section.

'Where did this paper come from?' I asked him.

'Mr Sanroma, the new cook, brought it with him from the Philippines when he came on board.' Ramon chose that moment to walk into the mess and hearing his name sat down at the end of our table.

'I didn't realise there are English language newspapers in the Philippines.' I said.

'Yes, there are,' Ramon nodded. 'Of course there are also newspapers in Tagalog, and the other languages that are spoken on the different islands, but newspapers in English are very common.'

'Interesting,' I said, taking a sip of my tea. It was still a bit hot. 'Is it possible for me to borrow this newspaper, whenever you guys are finished with it? I would love to see what it is like.'

'Of course you can. I think most guys are finished with it anyway, so you can take it back to your cabin later.'

'Thanks. I will bring it back down when I am finished with it.'

The evenings on the ship had gradually changed since the old captain and first officer had left in Singapore. The beer-drinking, cigarette-smoking, hanging-around-the-bar-in-the-lounge culture had disappeared.

The new captain didn't smoke and seemed to prefer to spend his time in the evenings gently jogging from the accommodation block to the fo'c'sle and back. The new first officer loved movies. In every port we berthed, he had a man who would bring him a pile of the latest, illegally copied dvds, from which he would choose five or six to buy for a fraction of the price they would have cost if they had been legal. He would watch these dvds on his laptop in his cabin, where he, according to his own words, had set up a mini home theatre.

The other officers, who, when the old captain was still on board, had often hung around in the lounge in the evenings, had almost stopped doing that. Maybe a couple of nights a week they would still come and watch a movie, but in general, they would retire to their cabins in the evenings.

I was now the only 'passenger' on board and I had stopped hanging around in the officers' lounge as well. Instead I now often spent part of the evening with the Filipinos, or the guys as I had started to call them, in the crew-lounge, playing tong-its or listening to Mr Reyes play his guitar.

Sometimes we would have interesting discussions about world news, current affairs or politics. Especially Ramon, Mr Reyes, Rodel and Mr Morayta were interested in those subjects and loved to talk about them.

The evening of the fire drill, I went into the crew-lounge after the meal. It was quieter in the lounge than usual. Mr Toribio, Mr Orozco and Mr Ibanez, the new electrician were playing cards in the corner. I joined them.

After a while, I noticed Mr Reyes wasn't in the lounge. This was a bit odd, as he would normally spend time in the lounge every evening.

'Where's Mr Reyes?' I asked.

'Oh, haven't you heard yet?' Mr Orozco said. 'He got a message from home today. His father has died.'

I looked up from my cards. 'That is terrible. He must feel very sad and lonely right now. Can he make it back to the Philippines in time for the funeral?'

'Maybe. But it depends if the company can find a replacement for him at such short notice. If they do, he will leave in Singapore.'

'Poor Mr Reyes. I am sure he wishes he was with his family right now.'

We continued to play for a while in silence, but we were all a bit distracted. Soon I excused myself and retired to my cabin.

CHAPTER EIGHTEEN

On Thursday 13th February, we went for anchor near Singapore at 08.00h. We had all been looking forward to a day of shore leave, but during the night the disappointing news had come that we wouldn't be able to berth until at least 20.00h and would likely leave the next day as early as 06.00h.

I was on the fo'c'sle with Mr Adega and two other deck crew, waiting for the captain's order to drop the anchor, as the *Serenity* slowly drifted towards the designated anchorage spot. While we waited, we stared at Singapore's skyline in the distance.

'I wanted to go to People's Park Complex, to do some shopping,' Mr Adega sighed. 'But it looks like we will be arriving too late.'

Mr Figueira and Mr Morayta nodded with sombre faces. They too had been hoping to visit People's Park, a large shopping complex in Singapore's China Town, not too far away from the port.

'I went to People's Park a few times in the past,' I said. 'It's amazing the amount of stuff they sell there.'

'And very cheap too,' Mr Morayta said. 'It is the perfect place to shop.'

We kept staring at Singapore's skyscrapers. To the left of them we could see the large cranes of the container terminal.

'Do we already know if Mr Reyes is going home in Singapore?' I asked, breaking the silence.

'He is not going home,' Mr Adega said. 'He is staying on board.'

'Really? Why?'

'The company couldn't find a replacement for him, so he has to stay.'

'But that means he will miss his father's funeral. How terribly sad for him.'

'Indeed.'

At that moment Mr Adega's two-way radio crackled with the captain's voice, telling him we had almost reached our anchorage and to get ready to drop the anchor. As the men jumped into action, I stayed at the side.

'Don't forget to look down to see the anchor drop in the water,' Mr Adega said over his shoulder to me, as he walked towards the anchor chain release-mechanism.

I watched as Mr Figueira and Mr Morayta released the safety catches from the chain.

Then the order came to drop the anchor and Mr Adega flicked a lever. As he did so, the anchor chain started to unwind with a loud rattling noise. I quickly looked over the side at the anchor hanging halfway down our hull. As more and more of the chain unwound, the weight of the anchor dragged it down the hole in the deck, gaining more and more speed. Then, with a loud splash, the anchor dropped into the water. It disappeared out of view immediately. The chain however, kept unwinding, throwing in the air a large cloud of fine rust coloured dust.

When the anchor hit the bottom of the sea, the chain ceased unwinding and the loud rattling stopped. Mr Adega flicked the lever back and applied the safety catches. As the red dust settled on the deck, Mr Adega let the captain know the anchor had been dropped successfully.

We now had to wait for our berth.

After I had walked back from the fo'c'sle, I dropped in at the galley to get a cup of tea before going back to my cabin. Ramon and Rodel were both in there, clearing up after breakfast and getting ready for lunchtime. They were talking about the lack of shore leave in Singapore.

'We haven't had a proper shore leave since Busan,' Rodel complained in an uncharacteristic way. 'And now it is likely we won't get off the ship until we are back in La Spezia.'

'You are disappointed because you won't have a chance to go to People's Park,' Ramon said. 'But maybe we will be lucky and get a berth earlier than expected.'

'Yeah,' I said. 'It's possible you know.'

'I am not going to count on it,' Rodel said as he slouched into the pantry to check on the dishwasher.

'Well, I think we should stay positive,' Ramon said.

'Yes,' I said. 'And keep smiling.'

'Absolutely, otherwise our lives will be miserable.' Ramon held out his hand and we shook hands, as if to seal our happiness pact.

In the evening, it became clear that Ramon's hopes for an early berth wouldn't come true. I was in the crew-lounge with many of the guys. Rodel had perked up a bit and he tried to teach me some words in Tagalog, one of the main languages of the Philippines. We had got there via a more serious subject that had started to come more and more to the foreground in the last couple of days, namely America's intentions towards Iraq. Rodel had explained that most Filipinos were pro-America, but that he could understand that I, as a European, didn't like the idea of an invasion.

Then he changed the subject and asked, 'are you interested to see where everyone comes from?' He opened a drawer and pulled out a map of the Philippines. As he pointed at the different islands the crew came from, he explained that Tagalog was the language that was spoken on Luzon, the largest island in the Philippines that also held the capital Manila.

'Tagalog has almost become the main language of the Philippines, but on many of the other islands they speak separate languages.'

'I didn't know that,' I said. 'So what is Hello in Tagalog?'

'Ayos. But ayos also means okay or fine. Using it as hello is like slang.'

'What about Thank you?'

'Thank you is Salamat.'

'Ah... like in Malay and Indonesian.'

Ramon walked into the lounge and sat down near Rodel and me.

'Any word yet about berthing?' he asked in general.

'No,' Mr Morayta said. 'But it is likely going to be after nine o'clock.'

Ramon nodded and then turned to me. 'I hear your brother is embarking in La Spezia. Is he older than you?'

'No, two year younger.'

'Do you have any other siblings?'

'No, it's just the two of us.'

'What does he look like?' Rodel asked. 'Does he look like you?' Everyone was now listening.

'I don't know if he looks like me. I don't think so. He's taller than I am and has short blonde hair. He does have blue eyes, though.'

'Is he married?' Mr Morayta asked.

'Yes, he is.'

'Has your brother been on a container ship before?' Mr Orozco asked.

'Well, when I was a passenger before on the *Colonial Star*, he came to drop me off. But he has never been on a container ship that was at sea.'

'It will be interesting to meet him,' Ramon said, and everyone nodded in agreement.

***

We berthed at 21.45h and by pure coincidence ended up right next to one of the *Serenity River's* sister ships, the *Serenity Valley*, one of the other three ships I was writing the guidebook for. I looked at the *Serenity Valley* with interest and noticed it was exactly like us.

After we had berthed, the agent came on board. At the captain's request he had brought me a Straits Times newspaper. The captain knew I liked to get newspapers wherever we berthed and as it was unlikely I would be able to go ashore, he had phoned the agent during the day and asked him to bring me one.

At 23.30h, I walked down the gangway with Mr Navaez, Mr Pachero and one of the ship-mechanics. I wanted to call my parents from the port canteen, which was only a 5-minute walk from the ship.

It was busy in the canteen and I was lucky to find an empty phone. As I talked to my parents, my eyes scanned the canteen and spotted nearly all of the *Serenity River's* crew. They were either making phone calls themselves, hanging around the little shop in the corner, or sitting around tables, chatting.

When my call was finished, I saw that Rodel was gesturing me over to his table, where he was talking to a man I didn't know.

'This is my friend Antonio,' Rodel said, as I sat down. 'He is the steward on the *Serenity Valley*.'

'Nice to meet you,' I said. 'It's a coincidence our ships are berthed so close together.'

'Yes,' Antonio said. 'But lucky because now I can catch up with my friend Rodel.'

'Where did you meet?'

'At stewards training a couple of years ago,' Rodel said.

'Rodel tells me that you are writing a book?' Antonio asked me.

'Yes. It is a guide-book for the passengers on our ships,' I answered. 'Do you have any passengers at the moment?'

'Three,' Antonio nodded. 'And one more will be arriving tomorrow.'

'You must be busy then.'

'Not too busy. It all belongs to a steward's job.'

'True. So you are on your way to Busan?' I was curious about the order in which the four ships journeyed across the seas.

'Yes, our last port was Port Kelang and before that Khor Fakkan.'

'Ahhh... Khor Fakkan. Seems like ages ago we were there.' I looked at Rodel. 'Have you told Antonio the story about the crazy crew-member?'

'No, not yet...' and he started to relate the story.

The three of us continued to chat for a while longer and at 01.00h walked back together to our respective vessels.

Back on board I heard the news that shore leave would be until 09.00h. I decided that if I could go early I might just have enough time to walk to the shops at Tanjong Pagar Road and buy a newspaper.

I didn't sleep until 03.00h and felt very groggy when my alarm clock woke me up only four hours later.

I stumbled out of bed at 07.00h and was walking down the gangway at 08.00h. Our departure time was still 10.30h, so I had to be back on the ship at 09.00h. I was hoping I would be lucky enough to find a photographers shop, as I would like to develop some films, but only if there was enough time. At least I would be able to do a little shopping.

I had noticed the evening before that the canteen was almost next door to the gate, so I decided to walk to the gate via the canteen, instead of losing valuable time waiting for the shuttle bus.

As I reached the gate, I saw an immigration officer coming out of the little booth. I recognised him immediately as my friend from two weeks before. As soon as he spotted me, a broad grin appeared on his face. He had recognised me as well.

'So you have come back to Singapore,' the officer said as I neared the booth. 'Welcome back!'

'Thank you,' I said and pulled out my passport. 'I want to show you something.'

I flipped my passport open and held out a stamp for him to see.

'I think I have the right stamp this time,' I said with a smile.

'Indeed, you have,' the officer nodded, smiling back. 'Very good.'

'And I have brought the crew-list...' I pulled it from the back pocket of my jeans, '...on which I have written the agent's phone number.'

The officer's smile became even broader. 'That's excellent,' he said. 'Now you can come back here and go to your ship, no problem.'

'I was hoping you would say that. Thank you.'

'So how long is your shore leave today?'

'Only one hour. I am just walking to Tanjong Pagar Road to get a newspaper and maybe develop some pictures.'

'Well, good luck with that,' the officer said, still smiling. 'Goodbye.'

'Bye.' I said and walked past the barrier out of the gate.

I arrived at Tanjong Pagar Road about 15 minutes later. It was by then 08.30h. Luckily, the first shop I saw was a photographers and I found on enquiry that they did a one-hour developing service. This meant that I had to wait for the pictures until 09.30h. I decided to take the risk, as I really needed them, and didn't want to wait with developing until we got to La Spezia.

Even though I had decided to take the risk myself, I had a nervous hour waiting. I walked around the shops, keeping all my fingers crossed that the *Serenity* wouldn't leave early, as they wouldn't wait for me.

While waiting I bought a souvenir t-shirt and two Straits Times newspapers, one for me and one as a present for Ramon. I also bought some fresh fruit at a greengrocer that I would be able to keep in the small fridge in my cabin.

At 09.30h I picked up my pictures and walked quickly back to the port. The immigration officer smiled at me and let me through without having to see my passport.

As I neared the ship, I was glad to see that they were still loading. In the ship's office the first officer told me the loading had been delayed by an hour, so I could have stayed out a bit longer.

Ramon was pleasantly surprised when I handed him his newspaper and Rodel, curious, checked out the developed pictures.

We departed Singapore at 12.00h and were on our way to Port Kelang.

That afternoon I was on my way to the fo'c'sle when I bumped into Mr Reyes halfway down the ship. He was chipping some rust off the railing in preparation to have it re-painted. He looked up at me and smiled.

'How are you feeling?' I asked.

'I am okay, actually,' he answered. 'Of course I am very sad my father died and that I can't be there for the funeral, but I know my father had a happy life and I am trying to focus on that. And I spoke to my wife on the phone for a long time last night. That helped a lot.'

'I am glad to hear it.'

'I will play you some songs in the crew-lounge tonight.'

'That would be lovely.'

CHAPTER NINETEEN

'It's *how* late where you are now?' my brother's surprised voice came over the phone.

'Two o'clock in the morning,' I answered. 'I woke up especially to phone you.'

'Wow, I had no idea. It's only seven in the evening here.'

I was talking to my brother Arjen over the phone. He was still in the Netherlands and as it was just over a fortnight before he was coming onboard the *Serenity River*, I was curious to hear if he was still looking forward to his trip.

'So where are you now?' Arjen asked.

'In Port Kelang, Malaysia. We arrived here half an hour ago. This morning we were still in Singapore.'

'I see... What's the weather like over there?'

'Warm. It's the middle of the night, but it is still about 25°C.'

I watched as some stevedores came into the canteen from where I was making my call. They walked to the little shop where I had bought the phone card and ordered some take away coffees. The canteen was situated in a large modern building opposite the Hindu temple and only a 5-minute walk from the ship. Although the canteen was open 24-hours a day, it was almost deserted at this time of night.

'How are you travelling to La Spezia?' I asked into the phone.

'I will fly from Amsterdam to Nice in France and then take a train, along the Mediterranean coast to La Spezia.'

'I did part of that train ride. It's very picturesque.'

'When do you arrive in La Spezia?' Arjen asked.

I had to think for a second. 'Possibly on the same day you arrive in La Spezia. Otherwise we will be there the next day.'

'Great.'

'I hope you are looking forward to the trip?'

'Yes, very much. Not just to the voyage on the ship, but of course also to spending a few days in New York, before flying back.'

The phone beeped in my ear, indicating the time left on the card was running out.

'We've got less than a minute left. I will send you a fax from the ship with some information about La Spezia.'

'Yeah, thanks, that would be handy,' Arjen said. 'I hope you have a good trip back to Europe.'

'Thanks. I will see you in two weeks.'

'Yes, absolutely. Bye.'

'Bye.'

I hung up the phone and walked back to the ship, which was illuminated by strong lights that were placed, four together, on the top of high posts standing at regular intervals along the quay. I looked at the ship with some tenderness, as after all, it was my home.

The loading had not yet started and the port seemed unusually quiet. As I arrived on the main deck, I met Mr Morayta, Mr Navaez and Mr Toribio, who were standing at the top of the gangway. They had the night shift of keeping an eye on the loading, but had nothing to do as yet. They didn't seem at all surprised to see me up and about at 02.30h in the morning.

We didn't have much loading to do, so as expected shore leave the next day was only until 10.00h. It meant that again I wouldn't have a chance to go into the town of Port Kelang.

I had woken up at 07.15h, after another short night. It was Saturday 15th February. After breakfast, I made my way to the port authority building, to buy a newspaper. I got three - two New Straits Times and the Star. The latter was the newspaper about which a passenger on the *FTK Kowloon* had said that I shouldn't buy it, as it looked too communist. I however, had only ever found it to be slightly left-ish.

Walking back, I tried to find the small canteen where Nick and I had drunk teh tarik on our previous visit. I would happily walk in there on my own this time, but unfortunately, the little wooden building seemed to have vanished. Pity, as I really felt like a cuppa.

Back on the *Serenity* I realised I was actually very tired. I gave Ramon one of the New Straits Times and walked upstairs to my cabin. I tried not to fall asleep as I listened to the World Service on my little radio.

It being Saturday, there was eintopf for lunch, so I didn't hurry to get down. But as I walked into the galley, I was pleasantly surprised to find that instead of the traditional German potato and cabbage eintopf, Ramon had made a wonderful delicious pea soup. When the smell of the soup reached my nose I suddenly realised I was more hungry than I thought, probably from the lack of sleep for the last few nights. I sat down in the mess and wolfed down two large platesful of the soup and several slices of bread.

I was the only person for lunch as everyone else was busy, getting ready for departure. Ramon came in from the galley and sat down with me for five minutes and we talked about the different traditional foods in our countries. I explained to him that in the Netherlands pea soup was a typical winter dish, but that for some reason I really enjoyed eating it even though it was 28°C outside.

***

We departed Port Kelang at 12.00h. Our next port of call was Gioia Tauro and it would take us 14 days to reach it.

I watched from the sun-deck as the *Serenity* slowly made its way out of the mouth of the Kelang River. Back in the open water of the Malacca Strait, I could see where we had anchored on our previous visit to Port Kelang. Watching as the container ships patiently waited at anchorage in the hot tropical sun, I thought back to an incident that had happened at this very spot, on the *FTK Kowloon* ten months earlier.

We had arrived from Singapore on a Sunday afternoon and as no berth was available yet at Port Kelang, we were ordered to go for anchor and wait.

We approached the anchorage from the south in what was a reasonably busy part and several ships were near us, either coming or going from the anchorage.

One of those ships was a tanker called *Rosalie* that, with its 150 metres in length was about half the size of the *FTK Kowloon*.

The *Rosalie* was sailing away from the anchorage and coming from starboard, or right, was about to cross in front of us. According to the international rules at sea, the *Rosalie* had the right of way and should have just continued on its course, without being too worried about us, even though we were so much larger.

The first officer of the *Kowloon*, who as it happened had just started his watch, saw the *Rosalie* coming from starboard and realised it had the right of way. He decided to give the *Rosalie* a bit more space and steered the *Kowloon* slightly to starboard, so that we would pass behind the tanker. Large ships are always a bit slow to react, so it took a few seconds before the *Kowloon* started to move to starboard.

As the first officer steered to starboard, the person on watch on the bridge of the *Rosalie* became very nervous about the big container ship coming from their port, or left, side and contrary to all international rules decided to steer the *Rosalie* to port, in an attempt to pass behind the *Kowloon*. Obviously the *Rosalie's* watchman didn't realise the *Kowloon* was already making way for them, otherwise they would have just kept on course and everything would have been okay.

By the time the *Rosalie* started moving to port, the *Kowloon* had started moving to starboard and suddenly both ships were on a head-on collision course.

The first thing the first officer on the *Kowloon* did was sounding the horn a number of times to warn the *Rosalie* and to try to make them see sense and get back on their original course. This they didn't do. Instead, panicking, they steered harder to port in an attempt to avoid crashing into our hull.

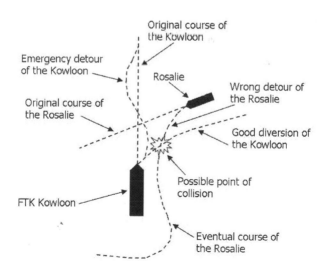

I was at the time of the incident in my cabin and as I heard the horn, I realised something extraordinary was happening. I had never heard the horn sound in such an urgent way before.

I jumped up from my chair and looked out of my window to see the *Kowloon* still moving slowly to starboard, while at that same time a tanker was heading straight towards us. Instantly realising the seriousness of the situation the thought flashed through by mind to go and start looking for my life-jacket. However, the scene outside had me spellbound, and as I kept watching I saw that the *Kowloon* slowly changed its course and at a snail's pace, started moving to the portside. The first officer was clearly trying to turn the ship back as soon as possible, hoping to create some much needed space between the two ships.

The *Rosalie* meanwhile, kept turning to portside, but was still getting dangerously close to our hull. At one point, the tanker actually disappeared from my view as it moved so close that it became hidden behind the stacked containers on our deck. As I couldn't see how close the *Rosalie* actually was to our hull, I braced myself for the impact of the collision, but luckily, nothing happened.

I waited for a bit longer to be sure the danger of a collision was over, then, immensely curious; I walked outside to have a good look at the *Rosalie*. As I arrived on our starboard sun-deck, the tanker was just passing below and was now actually moving away. I kept watching as it moved in a large circle behind us and then returned to its original course. After a bit of a zigzag, we also returned to our original course.

That evening in the officers' mess, I asked the first officer if it really had been as close as it had looked.

'Yes, it was,' he said. 'There was about five metres between them and us at one point. It could have been very nasty.'

'But if he had the right of way, why did he suddenly change his course?'

'Because he thought we hadn't seen him. He panicked, thinking we were not going to give him the space.'

'But we did.'

'Yes, we did. But by then it was too late for him to return to his original course.'

The first officer sighed. 'As long as I meet this sort of idiot not more than once a year, it is okay.'

I watched the *Serenity River* glide past the ships at anchorage and I hoped that the first officer of the *FTK Kowloon* had not bumped into any more people like the person on the *Rosalie*.

In the evening, I hung out with the guys in the crew-lounge for a while and played a few games of cards.

That night we turned the clocks back again, the first of seven occasions before reaching the Gioia Tauro time zone.

CHAPTER TWENTY

'Yeehaa,' I yelled as a large grey dolphin jumped out of the water right in front of my eyes.

I had been sitting quietly by myself on the fo'c'sle, when sudden splish-splash noises attracted my attention. I got up and ran over to the other side of the fo'c'sle in time to see a large pod of dolphins playing and chasing each other below me, quite near the nose of the *Serenity*.

Holding on for dear life, I leant over the bulkhead to get a better view of the playing creatures, the largest of which occasionally jumped high out of the water and with a joyful back flip crashed back in with a loud splash. For ten minutes I watched, ecstatic, as the pod kept up with the fast moving ship, having a great time chasing each other and playing in the waves created by our bow.

Never before had I seen dolphins, up close, from the fo'c'sle, but now my dream had come true. Sometimes you just had to be lucky and be at the right place at the right time, I thought to myself as the pod, now tired of playing, moved away from our bow and slowly disappeared out of sight.

Still totally excited about what I had just seen I made my way back to the accommodation block, eager to tell someone about my luck. Halfway down the path I saw Mr Navaez and Mr Figueira, who were painting the railing.

'You can't believe what I just saw,' I said with the biggest grin on my face, as I walked up to them.

'What?' Mr Figueira asked, imitating my grin.

'A whole pod of dolphins, playing in the water, near the fo'c'sle,' I answered enthusiastically. 'I have never seen dolphins from the fo'c'sle before, I am so excited!'

'That's great, congratulations. You were lucky.'

'Yeah, I was,' I said and leaving the two men behind I happily continued on my way to the accommodation block.

The day had been boring up to that point; everyone was resigned to the fact that it would take us ten days to reach the Suez Canal.

I had, with the best intentions, made a list of all the things I wanted to do for the guide-book before we reached La Spezia and my brother came on board. But so far, I had not wanted to do anything. Bored, I had made my way to the fo'c'sle, not knowing that my reward for doing nothing would be seeing dolphins.

Everyone was lethargic in the days after we left Port Kelang. The piracy watch had been suspended as soon as we left the Malacca Strait behind and turned into the Bay of Bengal. The evenings were long as on Sunday, Monday and Wednesday night the clocks were turned back, one hour at the time.

I spent my days reading, playing cards with the guys in the lounge, walking to the fo'c'sle, taking naps, watching movies on my laptop and taking close-up pictures of the new crew. Every now and then, my list would float to the surface of my thoughts, but I managed, guiltily, to push it as far back again as I could. I didn't feel like working at all.

On Tuesday morning 18th February, we passed Sri Lanka and were back in the Arabian Sea. The weather was warm and sticky, 30°C, with rain in the mornings and clouds all day. The sea was calm and the wind light, but the *Serenity* had started to roll gently from side to side. Every time we rolled a loose runner in one of the curtain rails in my cabin moved with a soft 'rrrrrrrrrrrrrrrr' back and forth. At times, the sound really annoyed me, but not as much as some of the other little regular creaks that had started to become audible around my cabin with the constant monotonous drone of the engines.

One of the creaks came from a vent in the ceiling. I managed to stop it by wedging a piece of folded paper in between it and the metal ceiling plate.

Obviously the empty hangers in my wardrobe, wire and plastic, had long been exiled to a drawer, to stop them from making soft clicking noises as they swayed with the movement of the ship, day and night.

I once, when I first moved into a cabin, removed a piece of paper that was clumsily stuffed in between a cupboard and the small fridge by the previous inhabitant. As soon as we left the port, I realised why the paper was there and hastily stuffed it back to get rid of the irritating creaking sound.

Hunting all the creaks, ticks, clicks and swishes in my cabin, became nearly a daily task, for as soon as one tick had stopped another creak appeared.

Wednesday was Ramon's birthday, but he didn't celebrate it. Instead, I drank a cup of tea with him in the morning, during his break. He showed me pictures of his house and garden where he hoped to be able to retire in the foreseeable future. His garden was large with different types of tropical plants and plenty of space for the vegetable patch he wanted to have and a corner for the pigsty, where he was planning to breed pigs to sell.

The next day at lunchtime the captain told us that we were going to slow down, as we were ahead of schedule and couldn't arrive in Suez too early.

'Our transit for the Suez Canal is scheduled for next week Thursday,' the captain explained. 'If we arrive too soon, we will have to pay extra money to be able to go for anchor at Suez.'

'Can't we take an earlier convoy if we arrive too soon?' I asked.

'No,' the captain said, shaking his head. 'We have been scheduled for the next Thursday transit for about three weeks now. If we change the date, it will cost the company a lot of money. Better to slow down and kill some time at sea where we don't have to pay for it.'

'Ah, I see.' I got up as I had finished my lunch and was ready for a nap. Ship lag was catching up with me again and I was hoping for a lazy afternoon, lying in bed alternately sleeping and reading.

I nodded a good afternoon to the captain and walked to the door.

'Oh, I forgot...' the captain's voice came. I turned around.

'This coming Saturday we will have a barbecue,' he continued. 'I thought you would be interested to know.'

'Yeah, thanks. I am looking forward to it.' I continued on my way.

As I walked past the pantry Rodel stuck his head out the door and whispered, 'the chief engineer has been badgering the captain about that barbecue since we left Singapore.'

'Really?'

'Yes. We all know the real reason why he wants a barbecue so badly.'

'We do?'

'Yeah,' his whisper became even more inaudible. 'The chief is only interested in free beer...'

On Friday, I was sick of doing nothing and worked on the guide-book the whole day. It felt good to do some proper work again.

In the evening I was hanging around the outside on deck 1 for a while, my hands on the railing, as I watched the almost waveless sea. The sun was about to set and as there were no clouds I was sure I would be able to see the sun sink into the water all the way until the end.

Mr Morayta walked by.

'Are you watching the sunset?' he asked, joining me at the railing.

'Yes, I am. It's so peaceful this evening.'

'Looks like you will be able to see the green flash. It's the perfect evening for it.'

'The green flash?'

'Yes. As the sun sets, at the end, just before it disappears, there is a bright green flash of light on the horizon,' he explained.

'Really?' I said, intrigued.

'Yeah, but you mustn't blink. If you blink you'll miss it.'

'You're pulling my leg, surely.'

'No, really,' said Mr Morayta and he walked towards the door. 'As the sun goes down, watch, and don't blink.' He went inside.

Still not sure if he had been joking, I watched as the sun set. The yellow circle slowly became smaller and smaller as it disappeared into the sea. When there was only the tiniest sliver of light left, I felt it safe enough to watch continuously and tried not to blink.

To my surprise at the moment the last part of the sun disappeared, there was a sudden, very brief, flash of bright green, where the sun had been. Mr Morayta had been right.

Still a little overawed by this unexpected, natural phenomenon I had witnessed, I also went inside.

I stopped at the open door of the crew-lounge and looked inside. Catching Mr Morayta's eye, I grinned and gave him a thumbs up. He grinned back and then continued playing cards as I made my way upstairs to my cabin.

*****

'So we are on piracy watch again tonight,' I said to Mr Adega. We were on the bridge, where it was Mr Adega's morning watch. I had come to the bridge, as I did every day, to write down our position and to have a peek at the current chart, to find out if there would be anything interesting to see that day.

It was Saturday 22nd February, and we were back in the Gulf of Aden, having recently sailed passed Socotra Island, an island to the south of the Gulf of Aden, close to Somalia, but actually belonging to Yemen.

'Yes,' Mr Adega said. 'We are on piracy watch again. Probably until we are halfway up the Red Sea, as Bab el Mendeb and the southern part of the Red Sea are also considered high risk areas for pirate attacks.'

'Yeah, I remember that from previous ships,' I nodded.

Suddenly we became aware of a strange sound that was getting louder and louder.

'What's that noise?' Mr Adega asked, looking through the windows to locate its source.

'Sounds like a jet plane.'

'You're right.' He stepped out to the wing of the bridge and pointed at the sky. 'Look there.'

I stepped outside, just as two fighter jets roared low over our heads. We watched as they made a sharp turn and came over again, this time even lower.

'What are they doing?' I shouted as the jets flew over our heads and then moved off.

'Looks like they were doing a fake attack.' He stepped back inside and looked at the radar screen. 'No large vessels in the vicinity, but that doesn't mean they're not there.'

'What are you talking about?' I asked, also peering at the screen.

'I have the feeling those jets belonged to an American aircraft carrier. They're on the way to the Persian Gulf, you know, to invade Iraq. Normally they want us to stay at least 40 nautical miles out of their way, but I don't think we are anywhere near them at the moment.'

'Wouldn't it be cool to see one close up?'

'Yes, that would be interesting, but it is not going to happen.'

'Pity,' I sighed.

'I thought you were against America invading Iraq?'

'I am, but I have always had a soft spot for fighter jets, so in that light it would be interesting to see a real aircraft carrier.'

'Yeah, I guess.'

That evening we had the promised barbecue. Again, a pig had been roasted on the aft deck and carried upstairs to deck 1. During the meal, the captain told me that although he was German, he lived in Brazil, as he was married to a Brazilian lady.

'Where exactly do you live in Brazil?'

'I live in Manaus. That is a large city up the Amazon River. I have lived there for 30 years.'

'In that light, isn't it strange to be working for a company that is based in Germany?'

'Not really,' the captain shrugged. 'I have always worked for German based companies, so to me it is normal.'

As it got dark, some of the crew left the party, as they were on piracy watch. From deck 1, we could see the strong light beams shine into the water from the bridge and the aft deck.

Soon Mr Orozco put on the Vengaboys cd.

'Maybe it will keep the pirates away,' he said to me with a grin.

'Yeah, it might very well,' I nodded.

I watched for a while as some of the Filipinos danced. To their big surprise, the captain joined them, under loud applause from everyone. The rest of the Germans looked on a bit embarrassed. It was clear they didn't want to dance, but felt they had to because their captain was. Soon the first officer mumbled an excuse and escaped inside.

As another song started up I joined the dancers and soon the second officer and third engineer were dancing as well. The captain looked happy.

Later on, I was drinking an orange juice, when Mr Lozada, the new second engineer, sat down next to me on a chair. He was tall and broad with very large muscles and a thin moustache, but he had turned out to be painfully shy.

Now he gave me a quick smile and said, 'the Vengaboys are nice, aren't they?'

'Yeah, very cool,' I nodded. It was the first time he had ever spoken to me.

'Your brother is coming on board in Europe?' he continued.

'Yes, in La Spezia.'

'That is nice.'

'Yes, indeed.' I smiled.

'Er... I am going to get some more rice.' He got up from his chair and walked off.

As I watched him go, Rodel sat down on the chair Mr Lozada had just vacated.

'Did he speak to you?' he asked curiously.

I nodded.

'First time, wasn't it? He's very shy.'

'Yes, I have noticed. '

'Maybe he will speak to you again tomorrow.'

'Yeah, who knows...'

The barbecue finished at 00.30h, but as we had to turn the clock back one hour that night, it was only 23.30h as I got into bed.

CHAPTER TWENTY-ONE

A serene rest came over the *Serenity* when the ship came to a halt and started floating around in a quiet part of the Red Sea. For nine days, since Port Kelang, the drone of the engines had been our constant companion, never ceasing, day or night. Now, on Monday 24th February, two days after the barbecue, we came to a halt as we were still too early for the Suez Canal, and the vibrations caused by the engine stopped. Having finished nearly all the work on the guide-book, I was getting ready for a quiet day.

In the early morning of the day before we had gone through Bab el Mendeb, following one of the two narrow shipping lanes, which separated north-bound and south-bound traffic. Obviously, those lanes were not visible in the water, but were instead marked on the chart and pre-programmed into the radar screen.

Later that day I was lucky to see another pod of dolphins from the fo'c'sle. This time they weren't playing, but on their way to something and swimming with quiet determination, breaking the surface of the water only to breath.

When the clocks had turned back that night, we were on Suez Canal time and wouldn't have to change again until we were back in the Mediterranean. This would give everybody another chance to let their body clocks catch up with real time.

It was Monday morning when we came to a halt on the spot the captain had chosen for our floating session. We had diverted from the major shipping route through the Red Sea to a quieter part. Although there are no designated shipping lanes in the Red Sea, most ships will keep to a certain route, as it is the shortest way from Bab el Mendeb to the Gulf of Suez, at the northern end of the Red Sea.

On the *FTK Kowloon,* we also had the problem of being too early for the Suez Canal transit. Then, as now, the captain had decided to float around for a day in the Red Sea and we took the opportunity to do a lifeboat drill. The *Kowloon* had two lifeboats, which, unlike the *Serenity's* freefall lifeboat, were hanging from davits on either side of the accommodation block. During the drill one of those lifeboats was let down with a few crew-members on board. After being released into the sea, it made a little circle around the ship, and was then winched back on board.

But as I quietly sat on the sun-deck of the *Serenity* that Monday afternoon, I wasn't thinking back to the lifeboat drill on the *Kowloon,* but to something more remarkable that had happened afterwards, in the early evening.

It was time for the evening meal and the second engineer and I were the only ones so far who had showed up. The steward, Gene, had just put a plateful of food in front of me, when I heard some shouting from the direction of the crew-lounge. The second engineer and I looked at each other with questioning faces, but as the noise stopped, we shrugged our shoulders and continued to eat.

Then the first and second officers walked in and sat down in their places.

Soon there was some more shouting and Gene walked out to check on what was happening. The first officer went with him.

In the meantime, the atmosphere in the mess had become slightly tense, but the second engineer and second officer kept eating, so I munched away as well.

Gene returned and I looked a question at him.

'A little boat has come alongside with 20 people in it,' he said.

'A little boat?' I asked, thinking that was a bit strange, as we were in a rather deserted part of the Red Sea, with no land in sight.

Before Gene could answer, the third officer came running into the mess and shouted to the second officer, 'Second, come! Plenty pirates!'

At this, both the second officer and second engineer jumped up from their seats and together with Gene and the third officer ran out of the mess, leaving me by myself. My heart was thumping wildly and my knees were shaking. Pirates? Great Scott! I wasn't sure what to do, but concluded it was probably best to stay out of everyone's way. After a while, I had a peek into the corridor and saw Gene, the first and second officers walking back towards the mess.

'Can we continue eating?' I asked the first officer as he sat down.

'Yeah, why not?' he answered, picking up his knife and fork.

'What is happening?' I asked.

'A boat has come along side and the people in it are asking for drinking water. The crew is letting water down with hoses. A lot of fuss about nothing.'

'But what about the pirates?' I asked a bit surprised by the first officer's calm demeanour.

'Pirates? What pirates?' he asked with a puzzled look on his face, his fork halfway to his mouth.

'The third officer came in and said there were pirates,' the second officer explained.

'Ah...' the first officer said. 'No... no pirates. Just some people in a boat.'

I continued eating, but I was now very curious about this boat and ate as fast as I could.

My plate empty I went upstairs to my cabin first, to get my camera, before I walked down the outside stairs to B-deck, where a small group of Filipinos were looking over the railing. I joined them.

Below us, a small boat had come along side, probably about 20 meters long. It was crammed full with men, Sri Lankans as it turned out, 59 in total. Most of them were sitting or lying listlessly on the open deck. Placed in between them were about a dozen large blue plastic jerry cans that were now one by one, being filled with fresh water, via one of our hoses. Half of the boat was covered with a low roof, but I couldn't make out if there were any more men under it or not.

The men on the deck were nearly all dressed in baggy shorts, their upper bodies, legs and feet bare. I figured it would be terribly hot for them on the open deck when the sun was shining. Some of the men were looking up at us.

I walked further down to the main deck from where the hose was hanging down over the railing. The bosun was keeping an eye on it. The men on the boat had told him, they were on their way to Cairo and had been running out of water. They were refugees, fleeing from the hostilities between the Tamils and the Sri Lankan government. They had been at sea for a month and hoped to find work in Egypt.

After taking a few pictures, I walked back upstairs. As I walked past A-deck, I saw the third engineer standing near the railing with a fire hose in his hand, pointing it at the men in the little boat.

Back on B-deck, I joined the still growing group of crew-members. There was less and less space along the railing to hang over to gawk at the boat.

'So what was all the shouting about?' I asked the third officer, who was standing next to me.

'The first officer had been on watch on the bridge and had seen the little boat coming,' the third officer said, starting his story. 'When it was time for the first officer to eat, the boat had come so close that on his way to the mess the first officer came into the crew-lounge and told us to roll out some fire hoses, just in case they were pirates.'

I watched as another of the blue jerry cans was filled and the hose transferred to the one next to it.

'You must know,' the third officer continued, 'that this part of the Red Sea is still dangerous for pirates, although mostly at night, but you can't be too careful.

'As it happened our third engineer has been in a few pirate attacks and when he heard what the first officer said he jumped up to get the fire hoses out. The electrician and I followed and when we reached A-deck, I saw that four men in the boat were swinging ropes and it looked as if they were trying to grapple on to our railing with the intention of climbing on board. Obviously, we didn't want that to happen, as they numbered more than us they might try to take over the ship.

'When the men on the boat saw that we had some fire hoses pointing at them, they stopped swinging the ropes and said they just wanted some water, as they were almost out. We said we would give them water as long as they stayed on their own boat, and they agreed to that.'

'Do you think they had any hostile intentions?'

'Probably not. But you just never know, that's the problem.'

'I saw that the third engineer was still holding on to the fire hose,' I said.

'Yes,' the third officer nodded. 'He panicked a bit, which is not so strange really, keeping in mind what he has already gone through.'

When all the jerry cans were filled, our hose was pulled back on board. The men in the boat shouted their thanks and said they would be on their way. The little engine was started and as they drifted away from us, they waved. We all waved back. With a slow circle, the little boat made its way around the back of the *Kowloon* and then set course for Egypt. As they sailed into the setting sun, I walked back upstairs and watched from the sun-deck, as the boat got smaller.

It had been a really strange experience seeing all those men in that little boat. What happened to them? Had they ever made it to Egypt? Had they been able to find work there, or would they have disappeared into illegality and tried to reach Europe?

Whatever had happened, I hoped they were okay.

***

A cold strong wind was tugging at my clothes as I walked back up the outside stairs after breakfast on Wednesday morning, 26th February. Two days before the *Serenity River* had been floating around in the Red Sea, the temperature a nice warm 28°C. Now it was only 12°C and I was sure that we had now left the warm weather behind us for the rest of the trip.

It was only 08.00h and we were slowly nearing the Suez anchorage. The north-bound convoy had only left two hours before and we were one of the first ships to arrive to wait for next day's convoy.

At 14.00h, the ships from the south-bound convoy came out of the Suez Canal one by one. I went down to the main deck to see them glide by - most of them were container ships.

One of the ships coming out of the Canal however, was a large US navy ship. It looked like a vehicle carrier. It was painted grey and on its deck tanks were stored under dark green tarpaulins. A helicopter was escorting the ship, circling around it like a fly. The ship was also escorted by a small grey boat that stayed in front of the large ship. Through my binoculars, I could see the little boat had guns on its fore and aft decks and was manned by six soldiers.

After the navy ship and its escorts had gone by, I noticed Mr Toribio, who was talking over the railing with two guys in a small wooden boat. They wanted him to buy some bags of unshelled peanuts, but he didn't have any money.

'I can trade you some old working clothes and shoes for it?' Mr Toribio shouted down. I joined him and together we waited and watched as the two men discussed the offer.

'Okay,' one of them nodded after a little while. 'Six bags of peanuts for the clothes.'

'Done,' Mr Toribio said and walked off to get the clothes and shoes.

Soon he returned with a rope and a bag full of clothes. He tied the rope to the bag and let the bundle down to the boat. After the two men had untied the bag, they tied the rope on to a string of six large plastic bags. Mr Toribio hauled it up. With a wave of their hands the two men steered their boat away from the *Serenity* and made their way to another one of the anchored ships, in the hope of selling some more.

Mr Toribio meanwhile untangled one of the bags and handed it to me. 'Here,' he said, 'a present. I hope you like peanuts.'

'I do. Thank you.'

'You're welcome.'

In the evening, I tried to teach Rodel, Mr Reyes and Mr Figueira some Dutch, but it wasn't a great success. We had a lot of fun though.

I went to bed early, as I wanted to wake up in time to see us going into the Suez Canal at 06.00h.

195

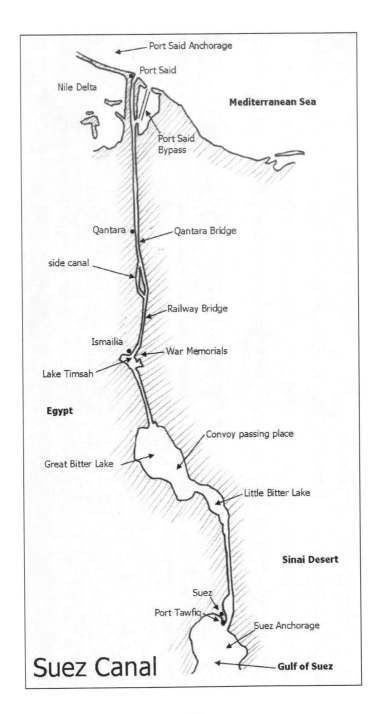

CHAPTER TWENTY-TWO

When the Egyptian ruler Necho II, around 600BC, came up with the plan to connect the Mediterranean Sea with the Red Sea via a man-made canal, he, although he didn't know it, was way ahead of his time.

Necho decided that his canal would run from the River Nile to the Bitter Lakes and from there to the Red Sea, which in those days was much closer to the Bitter Lakes than it is today. The project however, was abandoned before it was finished, but a hundred years later Darius, a Persian ruler who had conquered Egypt, finished the job. Unfortunately, silt from the Nile soon clogged this canal, making it unusable.

Several rulers in different times, consequently dredged the canal in order to reopen it, but it was never a big success and after 800 AD, people gave up idea of having a connection between the Mediterranean and the Red Sea.

Until 1798, when Napoleon Bonaparte started thinking it would be handy to have a quick route between the Mediterranean Sea and Asia, he had his engineers look into the possibilities of a canal going from the Red Sea, via the Bitter Lakes and Lake Timsah, north to, what is now, Port Said. He hoped that bypassing the River Nile altogether would make the canal less liable to silting up, which had been the major problem with the old canal.

During this project, Napoleon's surveyors calculated that there was a 10-metre difference in sea levels, and the project was abandoned, as no one really felt like building a succession of locks.

Years later British surveyors recalculated the difference and concluded that Napoleon's team had been wrong. There was no difference in sea level to speak of, and it would be possible to build a canal along that stretch without locks.

It was the French consul to Egypt in 1856 who started the ball rolling and in 1858, the Suez Canal Company was established to oversee the building of the canal and, when it was finished, run it and collect revenue for the shareholders. Digging started in April 1859, from the northern end, near present-day Port Said. Ten years later the work was finished.

The Suez Canal was opened for ships on 17 November 1869.

From its opening, the Canal became very important to world trade and in 1888, it became a neutral zone under protection of the British, allowing ships from all nations to pass through it. The British protection lasted until 1956, even after 1936, when Egypt had become almost independent.

After the Second World War, the Egyptians became very resentful of the British presence in their country, but it took until 1956 for all the British troops to withdraw.

That same year the president of Egypt decided to nationalise the Suez Canal and use the money from its revenue to build the Aswan Dam in the River Nile. This decision rather angered the British, French and Israeli governments, who as a result, planned to invade Egypt. Intervention by the United Nations prevented the situation from escalating and consequently a United Nations peace-keeping force, the first ever, was sent to Egypt to keep the peace.

In June 1967, a war erupted between Egypt and Israel. It lasted for several years and became known as the Arab-Israeli Wars. Part of the Arab-Israeli Wars was the Six-day War, in which Israel invaded Egypt. It resulted in the occupation of the Sinai Desert by Israel and the closure of the Suez Canal. For six years, the Suez Canal became the border between Israeli occupied Sinai and Egypt.

On the 6 October 1973, the Egyptian army crossed the Suez Canal in an attempt to drive Israel out of the Sinai Desert, after which in turn, Israel crossed the Canal into Egypt. In early 1974, a treaty was signed between Israel and Egypt. In stages, Israel withdrew from the Sinai Desert. They had all left by 1981.

After the treaty was signed, the Suez Canal was swept for mines and tidied up and reopened in June 1975.

The Suez Canal is about 170 kilometres long, and since it was built it has been widened and dredged several times to make it compatible for the ever-growing ships that pass through it. Three cities are situated along its banks; Port Said on the Mediterranean coast, Ismailia in the middle near Lake Timsah and Suez on the south side.

***

On Thursday morning 27ᵗʰ February, it was finally our turn to transit the Suez Canal. I woke up at 05.45h to see the start of the north-bound convoy. Still yawning I emerged on the sun-deck at 06.00h. The first ship in the convoy was already on the move, with another in close pursuit. The *Serenity River* was fourth in line and entered the Canal at 06.30h. We were preceded by another large container ship and in turn, were followed by a small tanker. The distance between the ships was about two kilometres - our speed a slow 8 knots (15 km/h).

The weather was cold and cloudy with a strong wind. It blew my hair in my face as I looked out over Port Tawfiq, Suez's twin city that hugged the entrance of the Canal on the west side. The town seemed quiet. Not many people were about yet on the boulevard that faced the Canal. At the end of the boulevard, I could see a large mosque with two slender minarets and a dome. It was built out of yellowish sandstone and surrounded by evergreen trees.

The boulevard and mosque were by far the most picturesque parts of the city that I could see. Most of the other buildings were modern 10-story apartment blocks, made of concrete or brick in the same colour as the mosque. Port Tawfiq and Suez were both very heavily damaged in the 1973 Arab-Israeli war.

As we passed the mosque, the Canal made a long curve to the left and I could see the three ships in front of us going around the bend in the distance.

I walked to the other side of the ship to have a look at the east side of the Canal. No buildings greeted me, just a very flat landscape with sand as far as the eye could see. This was the northern part of the Sinai Desert.

The bend straightened out and leaving Port Tawfiq behind us all signs of human habitation disappeared, except for the guard posts of the soldiers that lined the Canal on both sides. Huddled around their little guard huts, the soldiers, carrying guns, watched as we went by.

After a while, trees and shrubs appeared on the west side of the Canal, dotted here and there with small white houses, grouped together under the palm trees. The Canal's east side was still nothing but desert.

It was now 07.30h and it would be another two hours before we reached the Bitter Lakes, where we were to pass the south-bound convoy that had gone for anchor to wait for us.

I went downstairs for breakfast, glad to be out of the cold wind for a bit.

After breakfast I looked out of my cabin window at the banks of the Suez Canal that slowly passed by. The west side of the Canal remained relatively green. Occasionally I could see people on foot driving goats in front of them, going along the road that ran parallel with the Canal. The only other users of the road seemed to be the soldiers in their army vehicles.

Around 10.00h the Canal widened and we slowly sailed into the Little Bitter Lake. Concrete markers in the water indicated where the Canal was continuing. After about an hour, the Little Bitter Lake seamlessly turned into the Great Bitter Lake. Ahead of us, I saw the ships of the south-bound convoy that were waiting at anchor and soon we were passing them.

One of the ships at anchor was the *US Navy Ship Charlton*, which was very similar to the one I had seen gliding past us at the Suez anchorage the day before. The difference was that no helicopter was hovering around the *Charlton*, but through my binoculars, I spotted many soldiers, standing on the deck with guns in their hands, keeping watch as we went by.

The Great Bitter Lake isn't very large and I could see its shores, even though it was a bit hazy. A few small towns were visible on the western side of the lake, surrounded by narrow stretches of green.

When we had crossed the Great Bitter Lake, we once again entered the Suez Canal for the short stretch to Lake Timsah.

This smallest of the Bitter Lakes is popular with tourists, who come to swim in the brackish water and lounge on the sandy beaches. The west side of the lake especially, is dotted with resort towns. The Suez Canal passes through the east side of Lake Timsah. On its north-western shore is the city of Ismailia. This city was founded around 1860, during the digging of the Canal and is situated roughly halfway along it.

It was just after lunch and it had become a bit warmer as I went back out on to the sun-deck to see us glide through Lake Timsah.

The landscape along its eastern shore was still featureless desert sand, like it had been since the start of the transit, but as we neared the section where the lake ended and the Canal continued, I noticed two huge memorials protruding from the desert sand. They were impossible to miss.

The first one was made of stone in the shape of two slender, slightly triangular columns, standing close together, leaving a long vertical gap in the middle. This was the Anzac memorial, commemorating the Australian and New Zealand troops who had fought in this area in the First World War.

Close behind this huge memorial was another one, equally large, but totally different. It looked like a large knife sticking, blade up, out of the desert sand. Studying it through my binoculars, I saw it wasn't a knife, but a giant replica of the nozzle of a gun, with bayonet. I later discovered that this was the memorial of the 6 October 1973 and it commemorated the Egyptians who had been killed, as part of the Arab-Israeli Wars.

Opposite these memorials, on the west side of the Canal, was the city of Ismailia. Quite a few colonial buildings of the time of the construction of the Canal had survived. They were situated close to the Canal and sat in nice parks, surrounded by green trees. I saw people taking a stroll in the parks or relaxing around on the grass or benches, watching as the huge ships glided past. A few of them waved as they saw me and I waved back.

In between the large ships of our convoy, ferries darted back and forth across the Canal, transporting cars, people with bicycles and foot passengers. I reckoned they weren't running to a specific timetable, but just waited until a ship had passed, and then hurried across before the next ship arrived.

We left Ismailia behind us and were on the last stretch to the Mediterranean. The Canal banks on the left as well as the right were now covered in sand - no more green stretches with houses.

What *had* appeared on the west side was a train track, over which every now and then a long train rumbled, overtaking us, as they were much faster.

Things now became boring and I nodded off sitting in a deck chair on the sun-deck. When I woke up, I saw I had just opened my eyes in time to see the railway bridge across the Canal. It had swung open to let us through. Soon after the bridge we neared the side canal where we had spent seven hours on our way over, waiting for the north-bound convoy to pass.

I watched the ships moored in the side canal and was thinking that for them, it must look like we were floating through the desert, like the other ships had done when I had watched them, seven weeks before.

Then we reached the Qantara suspension bridge. The first time I had been in the Suez Canal on the *Galactic Star*, they had been putting the finishing touches to this enormous bridge, with one of the two huge pylons still covered in scaffolding. The bridge had been opened to traffic six months later. I never really understood the need to have such a large bridge in that particular spot, as the road east seemed to disappear into the nothingness of the desert. But apparently, the Egyptian government has big plans for that area, for housing as well as industry, so in that light, perhaps, it is not too crazy.

After the bridge, we reached the town of Qantara. It played a big role in the 1973 war and the scars are still visible. Many houses on both sides of the Canal lie abandoned and in ruins, riddled with bullet holes. The only new buildings near the ruins were the cone-shaped dovecots built out of red brick. Little square holes punctured them all the way around, giving the doves and pigeons access to the interior.

After Qantara the landscape became even drearier. Instead of the yellow sand that we had gone past so far during the transit, the soil became a boring grey, indicating we were now crossing into parts of the Nile delta. Small tufts of grass that could only grow in brackish muddy soil covered the landscape.

It was getting near time for the evening meal, but before I went down to eat, I watched as the ship entered the Port Said bypass. Through my binoculars, I could see the city of Port Said that was founded in 1859, at the start of the construction of the Canal. High rise buildings, domes and minarets punctured the skyline. A large salty floodplain separated the bypass from the actual city. These days only the ships that need to berth at the Port Said container terminal go through the city. The rest takes the bypass.

As I walked down the outside stairs to the mess, I caught a glimpse of the Mediterranean Sea and the exit of the Suez Canal. I realised that I had totally forgotten to take a look at the shop the mooring men had set up on our main deck. So before going in to eat I looked over the railing of deck 1 and saw that the mooring men had packed all their boxes back into their boat. Mr Morayta winched them back down into the water of the Suez Canal, and they moved off.

Eating my mashed potatoes, broccoli and carrots, I noticed that the drone of the engines soon grew more distinct. We were back in the Mediterranean and speeding up; free to go wherever we wanted, which in our case was Gioia Tauro.

CHAPTER TWENTY-THREE

The next day I entered the officers' mess for lunch at 11.30h. In the morning I had edited that part of the guide-book that was finished. Satisfied it was fit for printing, I could now relax until after La Spezia, when there would still be another five ports to write about. On my way down to lunch, I had taken a quick look outside. The weather had become a bit warmer again, with a sky that alternated between cloudy and sunny, and a calm sea.

As I entered the officers' mess, Rodel came out of the pantry.

'I suppose you don't want to have the pork,' Rodel asked, as I walked to my seat and sat down.

'Indeed, I don't,' I said with a half smile. He still seemed to find it a bit strange I didn't eat meat. 'What else goes with it?'

'Fried potatoes with mushroom, onions and vegetables.'

'That sounds great, thank you,' I smiled, and Rodel walked off to the galley to get me a plateful.

As I waited, the captain came in. Before sitting down he handed me a piece of paper. 'The first officer asked me to give you this,' he said apologetically. I looked at it.

It was an A4 colour print-out that had in large red letters 'Suez Canal Passport' across the top. Below that was a picture of a stylised container ship, under which it stated that I, Mrs Maria Staal, had successfully transited the Suez Canal on the *MV Serenity River* on the 27th February 2003, and that I was hereby initiated into the Brotherhood of the Sea by no one less than Neptune himself. At the bottom, there were the signatures of the captain, the first officer and, lo and behold, the chief engineer. I didn't really think he was into this sort of thing.

'I think it is a bit silly,' the captain said, sitting down, 'but the first officer loved it. He found it on the computer and printed it out for you.'

'I actually quite like it,' I said. 'I have never had a Suez Canal Passport before, so it will go into the scrapbook when I get home. Thank you for signing it.'

'You're welcome,' the captain smiled. Rodel brought me my plate and then turned to the captain to ask him what he wanted. When Rodel had disappeared back into the pantry, the captain asked, 'how are you doing with your guide-book?'

'It's going really well. I have almost finished the first part of the trip, so I don't have to work as much when my brother is on board.'

'Good. When is your brother arriving in La Spezia?'

'On Monday evening.'

The captain nodded. 'As it looks now we will be arriving on Monday as well,' he said.

'Great,' I smiled. 'Perfect timing.'

In the afternoon, I paid a visit to the bridge. The second officer was on watch. He was still on board as the company had not been able to find a replacement for him before we left Singapore, so he hadn't been able to fly home to see his wife and newborn son. But he now had the news that he was leaving the ship in La Spezia.

'You must be excited to be back in the Mediterranean,' I said, as I accepted a cup of rooibos tea from him. 'We will be in La Spezia soon.'

'Yes, I am really happy,' he said, gesturing to me to sit down in one of the two chairs that were positioned on either side of the radar screen. 'These last two weeks have been very long. I really want to go home and see my kid.'

We sipped tea and watched as the minor swell pitched the ship slowly up and down.

'Can I ask you a question?' the second officer broke the silence.

'Of course.'

'I want to buy my wife a present and I have no idea what to get her.' He looked at me in an expectant way.

'And you think I have any ideas?'

'Yeah... well... you're a woman, so...'

'I see... What about... er... some jewellery, or... er... a nice scarf or perfume?'

'She likes rings.'

'Well, there you are then. Buy her a nice ring.'

The second officer nodded, but a frown appeared on his face. 'The problem is when to buy it, though,' he said. 'I might not have time in Gioia Tauro and in La Spezia I will fly home soon after we arrive.'

'I am sure you will be able to find some time to go ashore and buy something,' I said, trying to be encouraging.

'Yeah, probably,' he sighed. 'I hope so, because I really can't go home without a present.'

We watched as a large passenger ferry came from our portside and passed behind us.

'Greek,' the second officer said, peering through his binoculars. 'Probably on its way to Crete.'

'We're not going to see Crete, are we?'

'No, we are too far south.'

I had finished my tea and got up to take the cup to the small sink to wash it.

'Anyway, I will see you later,' I said. I put the washed cup on a tea towel and walked towards the door to the inner stairs.

'Yeah, see you later,' the second officer waved. 'And thanks for your help about the present for my wife.'

'No worries.'

In the evening, I played cards with the guys in the crew-lounge. Mr Reyes tried to teach Rodel to play the guitar, but they didn't get very far. After Rodel had given up, he asked me if I knew any nice recipes for salads. The salads we had with our meal every evening were the responsibility of the steward and Rodel told me that not only did he want to bring more variety into his repertoire, but that he planned to become a cook one day, which was actually the only upward career move he could make as a steward.

After raking my brain for a while, I gave him some ideas, which he scribbled down on a piece of paper.

Before going to bed, I turned my clock back one hour. We had now arrived back on Central European Time.

***

It always surprised me how long it actually took to get from Port Said to Italy. The Mediterranean Sea was much larger than it looked on the map. It wasn't until the evening of the next day, Saturday 1st March, that Italy's coast came into view. It had taken us over two days to get that far.

After watching Italian coast glide past for a while, I went down to the crew-lounge and hung around with the guys for a bit. I didn't feel much like playing cards, and instead found a 6-month old Straits Times from Singapore in a cupboard and read in from cover to cover.

Again, it was dark as we went through the Messina Strait. At 22.00h, we arrived at Gioia Tauro. To everyone's surprise, we were able to berth at once. I went down to the main deck and sat down on a bollard to see us glide into the port, past the ships already berthed.

The second officer walked past on his way to the aft deck with some of the deck crew, to prepare the lines for berthing. He stopped as he saw me and asked, 'do you know the best way to get into Gioia Tauro?'

'Well, there is this guy who runs a shuttle bus...' I answered.

'Good. I want to try and get a present for my wife. Are you going into the town tomorrow?'

'That's the plan, but it depends on when we leave. You do realise it is Sunday tomorrow and the shops might be closed.'

'I know, but I just have to go. Maybe I will be lucky.' He started to walk away, but turned around again. 'Shall we catch the shuttle bus together?'

'Yeah, okay.'

'Great.'

At breakfast the next morning, the captain told me shore leave would be until 14.00h. That would give the second officer and me enough time to go into Gioia Tauro. I was planning to do some more sightseeing, as I still needed to see that picturesque cathedral Nick had told Lukas and me about, two months before.

At 08.30h, we walked down the gangway to the gate, from where we hoped to catch Guiseppe's shuttle bus. The agent had told the second officer that the shops would be open in the morning, so he was in high spirits, looking forward to finding something nice for his wife.

But we were out of luck. The two men at the gate soon told us that, because it was Sunday, the shuttle bus wouldn't come until 13.00h, and no taxis were available either. Realising that catching the bus at 13.00h wouldn't leave us enough time, we returned to the ship, a little disappointed.

Having nothing else to do I hung around on the sun-deck, reading, until at 14.30h, just before our departure, I became aware that Mr Morayta and his deck crew seemed to be searching the ship from top to bottom.

'What's happening?' I asked as he walked by on the sun-deck.

'We are looking for stowaways.'

'Seriously?'

'Yes. Italian ports are notorious for stowaways, so we always search the ship, before we leave one of those ports.'

'I see. I didn't realise that. Found anyone yet?'

'No, not yet. I will tell you if we do.'

'Cool.'

***

It was 19.30h when I went outside for a quick look at the hills surrounding La Spezia. It was Monday evening 3rd March, and we had arrived 30 minutes earlier, but as there wasn't a place for us to berth, we had gone for anchor instead.

It was pretty cold outside, with a strong wind. I looked down from deck 5 on to the aft deck and noticed Mr Navaez, standing by the railing, staring down into the water. Curious, I walked down the outside stairs to the aft deck to check it out.

'Hi,' I said as I arrived at the railing. Mr Navaez was still peering into the water, but I now noticed he had something in his hands. 'What are you doing?'

'I am fishing.'

'Fishing?' I said surprised. I had not expected that. 'And do they bite?'

Mr Navaez tugged the fishing line that was hanging down into the water, from a plastic coil.

'Not yet, but I have only just started.'

I watched as he slowly pulled the line up and down, trying to attract the fish.

'You've got hooks on there?'

'Yeah, with bait.' He tugged the wire a bit more. 'Normally La Spezia is a good place for fishing.'

'Is it?'

He nodded, concentrating on his line. 'I have caught loads of fish here before.'

He kept pulling the line, but the fish didn't seem very interested. The wind became stronger and colder, and tugged at my clothes. I shivered.

'Well, it's getting too cold for me,' I said. 'Good luck, I hope you catch something.'

'Thanks.' He flashed me a quick smile.

I walked back upstairs to the warmth of my cabin. I hoped Arjen's train had arrived in La Spezia and that he was coming on board the next day. I had no way of contacting him, as in 2003, neither of us had a mobile phone yet.

As I woke up the next day, Tuesday 4th March, we were still at anchor just outside La Spezia's breakwater and before I went down to breakfast, I looked through my binoculars at the city that bathed in sunlight. I followed the bay around from the west. The first thing I spotted was the naval base that had come to the city around the 1860s. Up to that point La Spezia, although inhabited since Roman times, hadn't been much more than a town.

North of the naval base was the city centre with an esplanade and marina, where the citizens of La Spezia went for their evening strolls. Behind the esplanade, the main street followed a narrow valley up into the hills. Here large neo-renaissance buildings had sprung up to cope with the expanding population of the city after the arrival of the naval base.

With my binoculars, I followed the bay around further to the east. The area between the marina and the container port was a somewhat eclectic mix of cargo docks and industry, above which towered the large apartment blocks of La Spezia's slightly run down suburb.

The container port was still further to the east, recognisable by the gantry cranes, all busy unloading the berthed container ships. It was clear there wasn't any room for us yet, as all the berths were full.

Past the container port were more cargo docks, until along the east side of the bay on the steep hillsides, appeared the village of Lerici – its castle visible on the craggy slopes.

The latest news was that we were going to berth at 13.00h, which would be a perfect time for my brother to come on board.

After breakfast, I hung around the ship, waiting for us to berth, but at 11.00h the disappointing news came that we wouldn't be able to do so until 17.00h.

In the afternoon, I walked to the fo'c'sle and sat there, looking at the beautiful view. It was now two months since the *Serenity River* had left La Spezia and Lukas and I had been watching the same view from the monkey-deck. I was happy that so far I had only been seasick that one time.

I walked back to the accommodation block and hung around on the aft deck for a while. I was thoroughly bored. There were no Filipinos fishing this time and I got my binoculars out of my coat pocket and looked at the city. Spotting the marina, I imagined Arjen hanging around there, while he would every now and then drop in at the agent's office to get an update about our berthing time. He was probably as frustrated as I was, possibly even able to see the ship, but not being able to get on board.

At 15.00h, I went inside and had a cup of tea with the crew. They were all a bit restless as they had been on standby since the early afternoon.

Nothing happened all afternoon, except the regular calls from the first officer that our berthing time had again been delayed.

At 21.15h, the crew finally got the order to haul up the anchor. Sitting in the crew-lounge with a music video playing in the background, I wondered if there was still a chance that my brother would come on board that evening. But no, five minutes later the news came that we were just going to drift until our supposed berth at 23.00h. I hoped very much that Arjen had checked back into the hotel.

We finally berthed at 00.15h. I was still awake and watched.

The agent came on board as soon as the gangway was dropped. He recognised me from before in early January, when we had been waiting together on a dark, windy quay, for the *Serenity* to berth, so that I could embark with my backpack and two boxes filled with things that I needed to write the guide-book. While we had waited, huddled behind some containers to try and stay out of the biting wind, the agent had taught me the right way to pronounce Gioia Tauro.

Now we met again and he asked me if my trip had been nice. Then he told me that he had had regular contact with my brother during the day and that Arjen had indeed done the smart thing and had gone back to the hotel.

I was relieved to hear this and trudged off to my cabin to get some sleep.

CHAPTER TWENTY-FOUR

'I have news for you.'

I watched as Arjen unzipped his backpack and started taking things from it, putting them on the low table - some cans of coke, a plastic bag with a couple of left-over raisin buns, a cd-wallet and a Stephen King book.

'News?'

'Yeah.' He sank down on one of the two couches in his cabin, the one next door to mine on deck 5, which had previously been occupied by Lukas. I sat down as well.

'Helma is pregnant,' he said.

'Really?'

'Yes.'

'Wow, that's great news. Congratulations.' My brother and sister-in-law had been married for more than three years and this was going to be their first child.

'When is it due?'

'In August.' With a metallic click, Arjen opened one of the tins of coke and drank from it. 'You know, you're the last person to know about it. You've been away for so long.'

'You could have told me when I phoned you from Port Kelang.'

'Yeah, I know. But I wanted to tell you in person.'

'It's appreciated.'

We sat in silence for a bit. Arjen looked as tired as I felt. He had walked up the gangway 30 minutes before. Mr Figueira had met him halfway and taken over his backpack. I had been waiting on the main deck near the gangway with Mr Morayta and Mr Reyes and as I greeted my brother, I overheard Mr Morayta whisper to Mr Reyes, 'six-footer. He's a six-footer.'

After I had briefly introduced Arjen to the first officer in the ship's office, and Rodel and Ramon in the galley, I took him to his cabin.

'The Filipinos have been looking forward to meeting you,' I said. 'I have been spending quite a bit of time with them since the last passengers left.'

'I am sure I will get to know them quite well in the next two weeks.'

I nodded. 'I bet you had a horrible day, yesterday, waiting for us to berth.'

'Don't remind me. It was terrible.' Arjen heaved a deep sigh. 'I could actually see the ship in the distance. It was so frustrating. I talked to the agent a few times during the day and at nine in the evening, he advised me to go back to the hotel for another night.'

'Yeah, the agent told me about it when we berthed last night. Anyway, you're here now. That's the most important thing.'

'When are we leaving La Spezia?'

'Not until tomorrow afternoon. We will have some time to go into town later on. I want to develop some pictures, have a haircut and check my email. Maybe we can go after lunch.' I looked at my watch. It was 10.30h.

'Do you want to have a tour of the ship?' I asked.

'Yes, please,' Arjen said. 'After that I will unpack. When is lunch?'

'Half past eleven.'

'Great.'

Out in the corridor we bumped into the captain. After the introductions were done, I showed Arjen my cabin. Then we walked to the mess and lounges on deck 1 and the laundry room second deck down. We walked back up to deck 5 via the outside stairs, past the empty swimming pool.

As Arjen unpacked, I decided to dash ashore and pop to the newsagent on the main road to buy some phone cards. That morning before Arjen had come on board, I met Mr Toribio in the corridor on deck 1.

'Are you waiting for your brother?' he asked.

'Yep, I assume he will arrive pretty soon.'

'That's great.' He looked a bit shyly at his feet, seemingly screwing up his courage to say something else.

'Can I ask you a question?' he finally asked.

I nodded.

'Are you going on shore leave today, by any chance?'

'Yes, I am. Why?'

'I was wondering if you could buy me a phone card ashore. I don't have time because of my shift and I really need a card to phone my wife.'

'Of course I can buy you a phone card, no problem.'

'That's great.' He turned towards the stairs. 'If you wait here, I will get you some money.'

'Cool.' I leant against the wall to wait. From the corner of my eye, I saw Rodel poke his head out of the pantry door.

'I couldn't help overhearing,' he said, 'but are you going to buy a phone card for Mr Toribio?'

'Yes,' I nodded.

'Could you buy one for me as well?'

'Of course I can.'

'Great. I will also get you some money.' He quickly dried his hands on a towel and rushed upstairs to his cabin on deck 2. I decided I might as well wait in the crew-mess, where I could take the weight off my feet.

I had only just sat down when Rodel came back and handed me his money.

'Here's ten US dollars. There is a small newsagent on the main road, left out of the gate. They take US dollars.' I took the money from him.

Mr Toribio returned as well, followed by Mr Morayta. As Mr Toribio handed me his money, Mr Morayta asked, 'could you buy me and Mr Reyes phone cards as well?' I nodded. He handed me 20 US dollars. Then Mr Figueira walked into the mess. He was clutching some US dollar bills. I smiled at him. 'Let me guess. You would like to have a phone card.'

'Yes, please,' he said. 'If it isn't too much trouble.'

'Not at all. Are there any more of you guys who want to have phone cards?'

'Very likely,' Mr Morayta said. 'I will go and find out.'

By the time he returned, Rodel had found a piece of paper on which I wrote down who wanted how many cards. Meanwhile the pile of dollar bills on the table kept growing.

Walking down the gangway two hours later, I checked if I had the list and the money with me. I had to buy 21 phone cards in total and had 150 dollars in my pocket. When I was halfway down the gangway, I noticed that the second officer had started to climb up.

'I found a present,' he shouted, waving a small box at me. We met and he opened the box. On some dark blue satin was fastened a pretty silver ring with a small diamond.

'Do you think she will like it?' he asked.

'I am sure she will,' I smiled. 'It's very pretty. When do you disembark?'

'Right this minute, actually. I just have to get my bags from upstairs. There is a taxi waiting for me at the gate to take me to the airport.'

'Well, I wish you a very good trip,' I said, shaking his hand.

'Thank you. It was nice meeting you.'

'And you. Bye.'

'Bye.'

I continued on my way down the gangway and wondered what the new second officer would be like.

When I returned to the ship, it was almost 11.30h. As I walked along the main deck towards the accommodation block, I kept an eye on the containers, which were flying over my head at regular intervals. Two gantry cranes positioned side by side were taking the containers off our deck. I preferred to wait and not walk by until the grapplers were going down towards the quay to deposit their loads on to the waiting trucks.

Stevedores and part of our deck crew were climbing up and down the ladders in between the stacked containers on our deck. Some of them were carrying long poles to unlock the twist-locks that kept the containers together while they were stacked. Others collected the locks once a container had been lifted off, and threw them in a large metal box. I always hoped none of the twist-locks would clatter down by accident and hit me in the head as I walked by.

As I had passed the most dangerous zone I saw Mr Morayta climbing down a short ladder and jump on to the main deck.

'I've got your phone cards,' I said.

He flashed his captivating smile and said, 'Thank you so much. My shift is nearly finished. Shall I take the cards and distribute them among the guys?'

'If you could that would be great. I don't really want my brother to have his first meal onboard by himself.'

219

'Of course not.' He took his work gloves off. 'You give me the list and the cards and run upstairs to have lunch with your brother. No problem.' I handed him the pile of phone cards and continued on my way to the mess.

After lunch, forty-five minutes later, I walked down the gangway again, this time with Arjen. We were heading towards La Spezia's city centre. At lunchtime, we had met the new second officer. He was a tall slim man in his early 40s, with short blonde hair and a hint of a beard. He seemed to take his job very seriously. Although he had only just arrived, he had told my brother he wanted to take him on a safety walk as soon as the *Serenity River* was back at sea.

The walk into the city centre from the container port was just a bit too far to be handy or comfortable, so we decided to take the bus. The bus stop was on the main road, about five minutes from the gate. By the time we got off the bus near the city centre it was almost 13.00h.

Walking into the largely pedestrianised main street, we noticed that the shopkeepers were taking their wares and signs in and locking the doors behind them.

'What's happing?' Arjen asked, looking around with some surprise. We were almost the only people left walking the streets.

'Oh no, I forgot...' I said, hitting my forehead with my hand. 'It's this stupid siesta thing they have. Everything will be closed between now and three o'clock. So annoying.'

'Then what are we going to do? I don't feel like walking around for two hours.'

'No, nor me.' I looked at the now completely deserted street. 'It looks like that cafe is still open. Let's check it out.'

Although there were no customers inside, the sign on the door said the cafe would be open until 18.00h without any breaks for siesta. We went inside and sat down at the window overlooking a small triangular square with a fountain in the middle. We drank our beverages and looked at the empty square.

After almost an hour, we both felt we had stretched our welcome to the limit and went back out on to the main street wondering where to go next.

'I think there is a chance the supermarket is open,' I said. 'It's between here and the container port. We passed it already by bus.'

'Let's go there then.'

At 15.00h, we returned from the supermarket and were back in La Spezia's main street. All the shops were opening up again. I dropped my role of film off at a photographers after which we went to an internet cafe. I checked my email and Arjen phoned his wife.

As we were waiting for my pictures to develop, we looked around the shops. Then we returned to the ship, where we arrived back in time for the evening meal.

My mission to get a haircut had not been successful. All the hairdressers we walked past had been very busy, and I hadn't felt like waiting an hour for my turn.

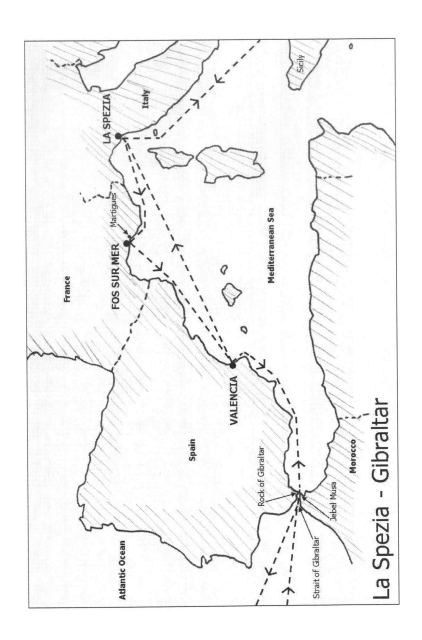

La Spezia - Gibraltar

CHAPTER TWENTY-FIVE

I woke up with a start and sat up straight in bed, slightly disorientated. I could feel the vibration of the engines in the distance, which could only mean we were about to depart. I looked at my alarm clock that stood on its little rubber mat on my nightstand. It was 14.30h and I had been asleep for almost an hour-and-a-half.

I jumped out of bed and pulling on some clothes, phoned Arjen.

'Yes...?' his voice came in my ear.

'The engines have just started. I think we will be leaving soon.'

'Really? I hadn't noticed that.'

'Can't you feel the ship tremble?'

'Now that you mention it, yes.'

'I think we should go down to the main deck.'

'Good idea.'

'I will knock on your door in two minutes.' I hung up the phone and started putting on my boots.

Earlier that day, Thursday 6th March, the day after Arjen had arrived on board, I had gone into La Spezia on my own to send some emails. When I had finished at the internet cafe, I dropped in at the railway station for a look at the times of the trains back home.

On my way over to La Spezia to embark the ship, I had come by train from the Netherlands – a 27-hour journey, in which I had to change trains in Zurich, Milan and Genova. Luckily I now discovered that for the journey back there seemed to be a direct train from La Spezia to Zurich, making the trip a lot easier.

When Arjen and I arrived on the main deck, the gangway was already up.

Arjen looked over the railings at the activity on the quay. The crew released our lines. The tug-boats started pulling and slowly the gap between the quay and the ship became larger and larger.

We watched for a while. The weather was nice. It was sunny and clear and the wind, which had been so cold two days earlier, when I had seen Mr Navaez fish, had completely died down. As I looked at the Apennine Mountains in the distance, I remembered that when I had seen them in January, they had been covered in snow.

At 15.15h, it was time for a cuppa with the guys in the crew-mess. Arjen came with me.

The mess seemed emptier than usual.

'Where is everyone?' I asked. We sat down at a table around which only the deck crew was gathered.

'The engine crew are keeping an eye on the engine,' Mr Reyes explained. 'Over the last two days they have been busy replacing one of the pistons. And now they have to fine-tune the engine. We will move more slowly than normal adding two knots to our speed every two hours, until we reach our usual speed of 19 knots.'

'I see,' I nodded, taking a careful sip of my hot tea.

'How much is 19 knots in kilometres per hour?' Arjen asked.

'One knot is the same as 1.8 km/h, so 19 knots is about 35 km/h,' Mr Reyes answered. 'But you can't really compare the speed something has on land to the speed something has at sea.'

'Why not?'

'Well, 35 km/h on land is pretty slow, but 19 knots at sea is a good speed. A ship our size usually has an average speed of between 19 and 22 knots. There are larger container ships that go faster, but even they don't usually exceed an average speed of between 25-27 knots.'

'I understand,' Arjen said. 'And what is the maximum speed a ship is allowed to have when it enters a port?'

'Maximum speed when entering or leaving a port is usually 5 knots.'

'Interesting. Thank you for the explanation.'

'My pleasure,' Mr Reyes smiled.

'By the way,' I said changing the subject, 'did we get a new washing machine in La Spezia?'

'Yeah, we did,' Mr Morayta answered.

'I am glad we are having two washing machines again,' Mr Figueira said. 'I was so sick of washing my working clothes by hand.'

'Yeah, me too,' nodded Mr Morayta. 'At least now everything is back to normal in the laundry room.'

After the tea break, the second officer came to pick Arjen up for his safety walk. I joined them for fun.

It soon became clear that the second officer loved talking and he regularly strayed from the subject of safety to reminisce about everything and anything that came into his mind. He only stopped when it was time for the evening meal, two hours later.

***

It took us less than 16 hours to get from La Spezia to our next port of call, Fos sur Mer in southern France.

As I woke up the next morning, Friday 7th March, I noticed the drone of the engines had stopped. Half expecting to see we had berthed already, I opened the curtains, but saw instead that we were drifting in sight of land. The scenery wasn't very spectacular. The coastline was very flat and covered in heavy industry. Tall slim chimneys were sticking up into the sky, belching nasty coloured smoke. Large factories were dotted about connected by pipes and conveyer belts. In front of several of the factories, jetties jutted out into the sea. General cargo ships were berthed along them, their hulls scooped empty by large cranes, the cargo of iron ore dumped on to conveyor belts that ran back to the shore.

To the left in the distance I could see the familiar silhouettes of gantry cranes, some with their arms down busy unloading container ships, some with their arms up, waiting for more ships to arrive.

It was a clear day with just a few clouds dotted about, but the coastline was covered in a yellowish haze that had come as smoke from the many chimneys, had mixed and now drifted above the land as an ominous polluting cloud.

So far, I had not been able to see any towns or villages, but looking at the coast through my binoculars, I spotted a few villages. Small white houses were situated between the steelworks and silos of the petroleum industry.

I dressed and knocked on my brother's door. He was awake and together we walked down for breakfast. The captain was sitting by himself in the officers' mess, munching away on his scrambled eggs and toast. No one else was there yet.

'Not much of a view outside,' he said, as Arjen and I sat down.

'No indeed,' I said. 'It all looks very dreary and drab. Are we waiting for a berth?'

The captain shook his head. 'Not a berth, the pilot. He will come around nine.'

Rodel came in and put two plates full of scrambled eggs, fried tomatoes and mushrooms in front of us.

'Is it known yet until what time shore leave will be?' I asked.

'Probably be until midnight,' the captain answered, 'but we will know more once we are berthed.'

'Looks like we will have some time to check out the scenery.'

'Yes, you will,' the captain smiled. 'Good luck with that.'

'Thanks, we'll need it.'

The pilot arrived at 08.45h and we berthed at 10.00h. The agent didn't arrive until 11.00h, a chubby man in his early 50s. He laboured up the stairs to the captain's office on deck 5, which he reached completely out of breath, muttering that every ship should have an elevator. After he had finished his business with the captain, he told me that the most interesting town in the neighbourhood was Martigues, a 30-minute drive by taxi.

'But I wouldn't go there if I were you.'

'Oh? Why not?' I asked somewhat surprised.

'Because it's very expensive to get there.'

'How expensive?'

'About 50 euros for a one way taxi ride.'

'Yes, that is expensive. What about buses or trains?'

He shook his head. 'No, nothing. Only taxis.' He handed me a card on which was printed the phone number of a taxi company.

'In case you decide to go.' I took the card and thanked him for his information.

Having decided at lunch we wanted to go to Martigues, we hitched a ride to the gate, where the attendant phoned a taxi. It arrived 10 minutes later.

The taxi driver was a jolly guy with a goatee beard, who told us with some pride that Fos sur Mer was the most polluted town in the whole of France. 'But we still attract a lot of tourists.'

'Really?' I tried to keep the scepticism out of my voice.

'Well... No. But people are visiting Martigues and the Camargue.'

The landscape was flat and empty, except for one hill with a church on top of it.

'That's the original village of Fos sur Mer,' the taxi driver said, pointing at the hill. 'The church was built in 900AD. There is also a castle up there. Until the 1960s, Fos sur Mer was a small fishing village. Then all the factories were built.'

'That must have changed a lot around here.'

'It did. My grandparents were fishermen and farmers. Now everyone either works in the petroleum factory, or at the steelworks.'

'And Martigues? Is that polluted as well?'

'Much less. Martigues is situated on a lake, a bit away from the industry. In the summer it is busy with people who come to the town in little boats from Marseille and Arles, but now at this time of the year it is very quiet.'

It took us about 30 minutes to reach the town of Martigues, where the taxi driver dropped us off near a shopping centre. I paid him 50 euros.

We entered the shopping centre and found a photo shop where Arjen dropped off some rolls of film to be developed. Then we went down to the centre of Martigues to have a look around the boulevard. It was very picturesque, but quiet as most of the shops were closed.

After having walked around for a bit, we took the bus back to the shopping mall, where we did some shopping and picked up the pictures. The owner of the photo shop was kind enough to phone a taxi for us.

We waited for it outside in the sun and after about 20 minutes, it came. It was the same driver that had taken us to Martigues. He drove us all the way back to the port and dropped us off at the bottom of the gangway. Again, I paid him 50 euros.

***

'Careful, watch out!' Rodel said, throwing out his arm in front of me, to stop me from stepping forward. A big crane on eight huge wheels suddenly roared past us from behind a stack of containers. It was carrying a bright red container in between its four high legs, the driver situated in his glass cabin right at the top.

'Thanks, mate,' I said to Rodel and carefully stuck my head around the containers to check if any more were coming. It was the evening of our day in Fos sur Mer and together with Arjen and Ramon, we were on our way to the other end of the port, to visit the seamen's mission.

The coast was clear and the four of us quickly walked across the road, reaching the relative safety of the containers stacked on the other side. As soon as we had crossed the road, another crane came - this one carrying a blue container.

'It's actually quite ridiculous that we are allowed to walk across the port like this,' Arjen remarked. 'It's not a very safe thing to do.'

'Everyone is doing it,' Rodel said casually. 'If you keep your eyes and ears open it is okay.' The crane roared past us, and then suddenly stopped. We watched as the driver turned his crane true 90 degrees and slowly moved the high legs in between the rows of containers carrying the blue container over the top of the ones already there, some of which were stacked two high. When the crane reached its destination, the driver slowly lowered the container on top of two other ones. Freed from its burden the crane carefully backed out, turned and roared off to get another load.

'Was anybody else reminded of Star Wars watching that?' Arjen asked.

'Yep, me,' I said. 'All these cranes of varying shapes and sizes have always reminded me of Star Wars. Especially those ones we just saw - they are exactly like the imperial walkers from the Empire Strikes Back.'

Arjen nodded. Geekieness confirmed, we walked on.

After ten more minutes dodging cranes and giant forklifts, we reached a large opening in the fence. The road went through and met up with a perimeter road outside the fence. After we had walked through the opening, we turned left and soon reached a small wooden building of temporary quality. Two phone booths were situated outside it, both occupied.

'This is where I can phone from?' Arjen asked.

Rodel nodded. 'You have a phone card, right? Otherwise you can buy one inside.'

'I have one.'

As Arjen waited for a phone to become available, Rodel, Ramon and I stepped inside. Via a short hallway, we entered the main room. It was occupied by a bar on one side along the wall, a pool table in the middle and several couches and lounge chairs along the other walls.

An older man behind the bar wished us good evening as we walked past him. We were not the only guests. One guy in a blue denim jacket was sitting at the bar reading a magazine. He had eastern European features; dark hair and a large moustache.

Two other men were playing pool. I guessed they were Filipino, which was confirmed when they greeted Rodel and Ramon in Tagalog.

We sat down.

'Have you been here before?' I asked Ramon.

'Yes,' he nodded. 'This is a nice place. I think they are planning to build a new larger mission a bit further down the road. This one is only temporary.'

Arjen had come in and sat down near us.

'It's too cold to wait outside,' he said looking around. 'What is this place?'

'A seamen's mission,' Rodel said. 'Most ports will have one.'

'Seamen's missions are places where everyone who is at sea can go for a drink, or play some pool and meet other people,' Ramon explained. 'They also have phones and often have a little shop.'

'And many of them have internet access these days,' Rodel said.

'So it is just a place for you to go and hang out,' Arjen said. 'To be off the ship for a while.'

'That's right. Especially now cargo operations get faster, we are in ports for less time. It gets more and more difficult to get shore leave and it's not good to be on board all the time.'

Listening to Ramon and Rodel explaining to Arjen about seamen's missions, I noticed a little pile of newspapers on the table beside me. I took one. It was the latest edition of *The Sea*, an international bi-monthly newspaper that was published by the Mission to Seafarers, and freely distributed to seafarers in ports all over the world. On each of the ships I had travelled, I had seen some issues of *The Sea* lying around.

Arjen had noticed through the window that one of the phones had become available and went outside to phone Helma. When he returned, we walked back to the ship. It was still light, but the sun was setting fast and all around the port huge lights came on. It felt even more unsafe to walk across the port than before. We dodged the cranes, and forklifts as well, as we could.

Back on the ship, we went to the crew-lounge for a little while. I played cards and Arjen chatted with some of the guys.

We departed Fos sur Mer at 01.00h that night. I didn't wait up for it. Our next port of call was Valencia in Spain.

CHAPTER TWENTY-SIX

The next morning, Saturday 8th March, I found Arjen on the sun-deck looking at the coastline through his binoculars. Although our course took us mostly in a straight line, we were never very far from land that morning and had been able to see the Spanish coast for a lot of the time. The weather was lovely. Hardly any wind, the sea flat like a mirror.

'Anything interesting to see?' I asked.

'Not that much. Just some small villages along the coast and a few boats.'

He looked for a bit more, then taking the binoculars from his eyes said, 'Is it time for lunch yet?'

I checked my watch. 'Almost.'

'Good, I'm hungry. Let's go down.'

When we arrived in the mess, the second officer was already there. We sat down and waited for Rodel to bring us our food.

'Have you heard about the strike?' the second officer asked, cutting a large chunk off the piece of chicken breast on his plate.

'Strike? No. What do you mean?'

'There is going to be a strike in the port of Valencia and it looks as if we might get caught in it.'

'Will that delay us?' Arjen asked, slightly worried.

'Possibly.'

I knew why Arjen was worried about delays. 'I am sure we will arrive in New York in time for you to meet up with your friend,' I said to him.

'Yeah, I am sure we will,' he sighed.

Rodel brought us our plates and we started eating. The second officer had finished his lunch and got up to get ready for his watch on the bridge. As he walked out the door, the captain walked in and sat down in his usual place. He nodded a good-afternoon at us.

'Nice quiet day today,' he said.

'Indeed, very nice,' I replied. 'The second officer told us just now there is going to be a strike in Valencia. Is that true?'

'Yes,' the captain nodded. 'The stevedores in Valencia will be on strike from Monday morning 08.00h. I don't think it will affect us too much. I want to leave Valencia before the strike starts, whether the loading is finished or not. If we don't leave, we might be caught for as many as four or five days and that would be unacceptable.'

'So we will arrive in New York on schedule?' Arjen asked.

'Probably.'

'That is good to hear.'

We continued eating.

In the afternoon, while Arjen visited the second officer on the bridge, I started on the Fos sur Mer chapter. I was planning to have Fos sur Mer and Valencia finished before we arrived in New York.

Later, after the evening meal, I dropped in at the crew-lounge for a game of tong-its. No one was playing cards, however. Instead, they were all standing around Mr Figueira, shaking his hands. He had a big grin on his face.

'What's happened?' I asked Mr Morayta, who stood closest to me.

'Mr Figueira just had a message from home,' he answered. 'He wife has given birth to their first child, a baby girl.'

'That's great news,' I said and shook Mr Figueira's hand. 'Congratulations, you must be very happy.'

'Thank you. I am,' he smiled.

At 20.00h, the call came from the bridge that we were on approach to Valencia and the crew that were on standby disappeared for berthing. I phoned Arjen and said I would meet him on the sun-deck to watch. It had become dark by now, but there was still more than enough to see.

We sat down on the edge of the empty swimming pool and watched as the port slowly drew near. The thing that really caught our eye was a large futuristic looking building on the edge of the city, not too far from the port. It was shaped like the upside down hull of a ship, its roof an elegant curve, made of a white material. Bright lights illuminated the building.

After we had berthed, I went up to the captain's office for my usual talk to the agent. As I came around the corner on deck 5, I could hear the voices of the captain and the agent coming out of the office. They were discussing the strike.

'I don't care if we haven't finished loading on Monday morning,' the captain said. 'We are leaving before the strike starts.'

'But you can't leave before all the containers are on board,' the agent said in a thick Spanish accent. He sounded aghast.

'I will, because arriving a week too late in New York would be worse.'

I heard some shuffling of papers. Someone gave a deep sigh.

'Let me make a calculation,' the agent said. More shuffling of papers followed, then a somewhat tense silence. In the corridor, out of sight of the two men, I waited.

After a while the agent said, 'it looks like the loading will be finished anyway before eight o'clock on Monday. Probably around seven in the morning.'

'Well, that is good news then,' the captain said.

'Yes, it is.'

As soon as I had spoken with the agent, I told Arjen that we would be avoiding the strike *and* that we would have the whole of the next day to explore Valencia.

'Shall we go as early as possible?' Arjen asked. We were standing on deck 5 watching the gantry cranes that came trundling up to start the cargo operations.

'Yeah, I think that's a good idea,' I answered. 'Right after breakfast. But we could set foot in Spain tonight if you want.'

'Do you want to go into the city now?' Arjen asked surprised.

'No, I meant walking down the gangway and jump on to the quay.'

'Ah... Good idea.'

We walked down to the main deck and under the watchful eyes of Mr Morayta and Mr Henarez, we both, for the first time in our lives, set foot in Spain.

***

Valencia is situated on the same longitudinal meridian as London, which meant that we were now in the western hemisphere. For some reason the eastern and western hemispheres don't seem to have the same connotation as the northern and southern hemispheres, but for the whole trip I had been in the eastern hemisphere, so I thought it worth noticing that we were now in the west.

To make the most of the day Arjen and I went into the city immediately after breakfast. The agent had told me that the best way into town was by taxi. Before we walked off the ship, we went into the ship's office on the main deck to let the first officer know we were going.

'How are you getting into the city?' he asked.

'By taxi.'

'Well, let me phone you one. I have the phone numbers of many taxi companies right here.' He pointed at some business cards on his desk. 'They should come to the bottom of the gangway.'

He took his mobile phone off the desk, dialled the number on the first card and waited for someone to answer.

'Yes... hello. I would like to have a taxi at the container port. The quay is called Principa Felipa,' he said in his heavy German accent.

He listened intently. A slight frown appeared on his forehead.

'No... container port... Principa Felipa,'

He listened again and then looked at his phone in surprise. Even from a distance, I could hear the soft beeping noise coming from it.

'They hung up on me! I will try another one.'

We watched as he dialled another number and waited for it to be answered.

'Yes... hello. Can I have a taxi at the container port? The quay is called Principa Felipa... No... wait...'

He looked at us. 'They hung up again! I can't believe it. They don't seem to be able to understand me. I have one more number.'

He dialled the last number and waited for an answer.

'Yes... hello...' he said deliberately slow and clear. 'I would like... a taxi... at the... container port... Principa Felipa.'

The phone spluttered something in his ear.

'Con...tai...ner port...' More splutters. 'No... Don't hang up!' Disgusted he threw his phone back on the desk.

'Unbelievable! I am sorry, but it seems I can't phone you a taxi... It might be best if you ask the foreman of the stevedores to order you one.'

'Yeah, we will,' I said. 'Thanks anyway.' He waved his hand and turned back to his loading schedules.

On the quay, the foreman called us a taxi, which arrived 20 minutes later.

On our way to the city centre, we came past the futuristic building we had seen from the ship the evening before. The taxi driver explained that it was one of the buildings of the new arts and science museum that would be built over the next few years. From close up it looked even more impressive.

The road from the port to the city was lined on both sides with tall five or six storey 19th century houses. But the city was much older than that.

Originally founded by the Romans, Valencia was at first a small fortified city. After the Romans had left the Visigoths moved in. Around the 8th century, internal fights between the Visigoth kings made it easy for the Muslims to invade and take the city. They ruled for 500 years, enlarging and modernising it. The population kept growing even after the Christians had taken over in 1238. They also enlarged the city and built the walls, of which parts can still be seen today.

It was Sunday morning 9th March, and relatively quiet in the city. The taxi dropped us off at the railway station, south of the city centre. From there we turned north and walked into the city along a wide street.

After a 15-minute walk, we arrived at a large rectangular square. Four-storey buildings enclosed it on three sides. In the middle was a park with grass and benches. At the far side of the square stood a large church, which no doubt was Valencia cathedral. Bells were pealing from the tower to the left of the entrance and people were entering the building for mass.

Star Wars in For sur Mer.

Berthed in Valencia.

A Storm in the Atlantic sends a big wave crashing over the containers in the front of the ship.

Rough seas during the wind force 11 storm in the Atlantic.

All assembled at the muster station for another safety drill. From the right: Ramon, Mr Navaez, Mr Orozco, Rodel, Mr Toribio, Mr Figueira and Arjen.

View from the bridge on a calm day at sea.

Approaching New York – the Verrazano-Narrows Bridge.

Clearing the Verrazano-Narrows Bridge.
The antennae are already pulled down in preparation for clearing the Bayonne Bridge.

The Rotterdam pilot is winched down from a helicopter to board the FTK Kowloon.

Passing through the centre of Savannah to reach the container port.

The Serenity River *berthed in Savannah, ready for departure.*

Dolphins playing in front of the ship in the mouth of the Savannah River.

Ramon and Rodel posing for the camera.

Approaching the Strait of Gibraltar from the Atlantic Ocean. Europe on the left and Africa on the right.

*The author and Rodel
on deck 1.*

*Group photo with the guys on deck one. Standing from the left:
Mr Morayta, Mr Navaez, Mr Orozco, Rodel, the author, Mr Lozada,
Mr Henarez. Sitting from the left: Mr Reyes, Mr Ibanez, Mr Toribio,
Mr Adega, Mr Pachero and Mr Figueira.*

Deciding we would visit the cathedral after mass, we wandered around a bit. At the other side of the cathedral, we came across an excavation, where archaeologists were digging up the remains of the Roman city. I bought an English newspaper at a newsagent (the Independent, that was imported all the way from the United Kingdom), after which we almost got lost in a maze of narrow streets. Eventually we made our way back to the cathedral square.

It was nearly 12.00h by now. We bought some sandwiches, which we ate sitting on a bench in the middle of the square. It was a lot busier than earlier, mostly with tourists. As we ate our sandwiches, the bells of the cathedral started ringing and again people walked into the cathedral.

'For sure there is not another mass,' I said, watching as more people entered the cathedral.

'I hope not,' Arjen said. 'Then we still wouldn't be able to go inside.'

'Maybe we should just go in and see what happens.'

We got up and walked to the cathedral. Noticing that tourists were still going in and out, we entered as well. The interior of the cathedral was divided into three huge areas by large pillars, light filtering through stained-glass windows.

A mass was held in the middle of the cathedral, while in the side aisles the tourists walked, looked, pointed at the stained-glass and took pictures. The priest and his congregation continued with mass, seemingly oblivious to what was happening around them.

'They're clearly used to having tourists walking around during their services,' I whispered to Arjen. He nodded.

We stuck to the side and slowly made our way to the back of the cathedral

There, some people were gathered around a wooden box with a pointed lid, almost like a roof. The front side of the box was made of glass. People were staring through the glass at an object in the box. As we came closer to have a look, a teenage girl turned to the woman next to her and said in a heavy American accent, 'Mum, this is so gross. I can't look at it.' She walked away, clearly disgusted. Her mother followed.

Stepping closer I could now see that in the box lay something that looked like a brown stick. Looking more closely I realised it was an arm. A mummified right arm and hand, the fingers thin and gnarled, but covered in rings.

'Great Scott,' I said. 'I wonder who that belonged to.'

'It says here St Vincent,' Arjen said reading the small sign screwed to the outside of the box.

More people had gathered around. A few women crossed themselves. They stared into the box with reverent looks on their faces. We stepped aside to give them some space.

We walked back to the main entrance via the other side. Mass had finished and we were able to walk through the middle and have a look up into the large dome that stood over the crossing. It was light and airy.

Back outside we decided to check out the northern part of the city centre where the city walls used to be. A large gateway had survived and still stood over the road going out of the city. We climbed to the top of one of its towers and looked out over the dried up river that used to run on the outside of the medieval walls, giving the fortified city an extra layer of protection. The old riverbed was covered in grass and trees. Paths criss-crossed it and people were walking their dogs.

After visiting two art museums, we were both very tired and decided to go back to the ship. It was almost 16.00h. Instead of having to walk all the way back to the taxi rank on the cathedral square, we managed to hail a taxi in the street. It took us all the way back to the bottom of the gangway. The day had become pretty warm and I was sticky and sweaty - wearing too many clothes. Back in my cabin, I took a quick shower and then read the newspaper.

By the time I had finished the paper it was time for the evening meal and I took the paper down to Ramon.

Walking into the mess, I noticed that Rodel had given us new seats. We were now at a table that was laid for three. Arjen had already arrived.

'A change in the seating, Rodel?' I asked as he came in from the pantry.

'We have another passenger,' he answered. 'The captain wanted to have you all at the same table.'

'Ah, I see. No problem.' I had already sat at many different places during the trip. Now I was back at the same table I had started at and where I had sat with Nick and Lukas.

'When did this passenger arrive?' I asked Rodel as he put a plateful of spaghetti in tomato sauce in front of me.

'He came last night. You missed him at breakfast this morning, because you left early.'

As we ate, Mr Navaez poked his head around the corner of the pantry door.

'Do you still want to have a haircut?' he asked me. 'I have some time now.'

'Yes, I do. I will be ready in ten minutes.'

'He's going to cut your hair?' Arjen asked when Mr Navaez had gone.

'Yeah, I never managed to get that haircut in La Spezia and it is getting far too long. I understand from Rodel that Mr Navaez cuts all the crew's hair.'

'Well... Good luck with that...' Arjen said with a somewhat sceptical look on his face.

'I am sure he will do a great job. Besides, I only need three centimetres off the bottom. I am not asking for a complete re-style...'

As I arrived in the sports room on second deck down, Mr Navaez was already waiting for me. With him were Mr Morayta and Mr Orozco, who claimed they had come down to play some table tennis. But as soon as Mr Navaez started cutting my hair, they stopped playing and watched, making jokes about how short my hair was getting. I grinned at them and said I didn't care, as I had brought a woolly hat with me, which I could always wear, in case it turned out disastrous.

But as I had expected, Mr Navaez did a great job. After we had brushed up all the hair that had fallen to the ground, we walked back up to the crew-lounge, where I saw that Arjen was being taught how to play tong-its. I joined him and with Mr Navaez, Mr Ibanez and Mr Toribio played a few games.

At one point Rodel sat down near us.

'Have you seen the new passenger yet?' he asked me.

'No, but I assume he is around.'

'Yes, he is. He was a bit late for dinner. I am sure you will meet him tomorrow at breakfast. He is going to New York.'

'No worries,' I nodded.

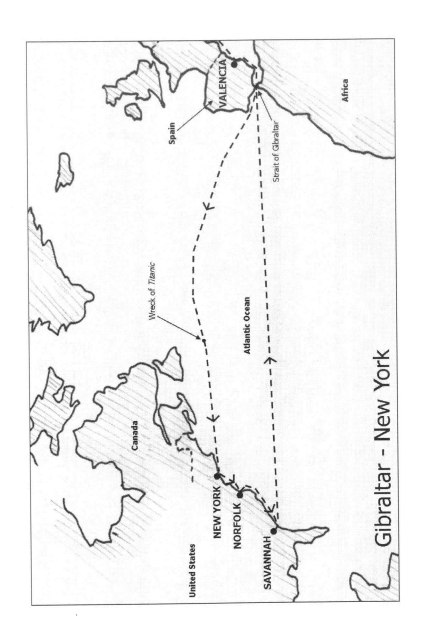

Gibraltar - New York

CHAPTER TWENTY-SEVEN

The next morning I woke up with a headache and a sore throat, and hoped I wasn't going to get a cold. We were still berthed in Valencia and it was Monday morning, the day that the strike would begin.

I walked into the mess for breakfast and saw that my brother was already there. He was talking to a guy I had never seen before and concluded he must be the new passenger. The man stood up when he saw me approach. He was younger than I had expected, mid-thirties, slim build with short dark hair. We shook hands.

'Hi, I am Randy,' he said with a German sounding accent.

'Nice to meet you. My name is Maria'. I sat down. 'Where are you from?'

'Switzerland.'

'I understand you are going to New York.'

'Yes. I must say that I am a bit nervous about the trip. I have never travelled on a container ship before.'

'I am sure you will be fine,' I said while tucking into my fried eggs. 'This is a really cool way of travelling.'

The last container was loaded on to our deck at 07.55h, just before the strike began.

I sat with Arjen on the sun-deck waiting for our departure, as an eerie silence came over the port. The gantries swung their arms back up and moved off to come to a halt at the end of the quay. Cranes and forklifts stopped moving. Stevedores and other port workers clambered into waiting vans and drove off. The port was deserted; the strike had begun.

'Are the pilots on strike as well?' Arjen asked.

'I don't think so. Otherwise the captain would have insisted we leave before it started.'

We waited and looked out over Valencia. I could see the cathedral in the distance. At 08.20h, two cars drove on to the quay. One stopped at the bottom of our gangway. A man got out and started to climb up.

The other car had driven all the way to the front of the ship. There a number of lines came down from our fo'c'sle that had been fastened around bollards on the quay when we berthed. Two men, one of whom was carrying a two-way radio, got out of the car. It then drove all the way back to our aft deck and stopped. Two more men stepped out and walked to the bollards that held our lines from the aft deck.

A tremble went through the ship as our engines started.

'Looks like we're going,' I said. 'I wonder if Randy knows about it.'

'I think he does,' Arjen said, pointing at the wing of the bridge. Randy was up there, talking to the captain. The man who had climbed our gangway now appeared on the wing and shook the captain's hand. It was the pilot. Randy discretely stepped back, out of the way.

In the meantime, two tug-boats had arrived. They had fastened themselves to the ship, fore and aft.

We watched from up high, as the second officer slackened one of the lines on the aft deck. The slack enabled the men on the quay to release the line from the bollard. It then slipped into the water with a soft splash. A winch on our deck hauled up the line, the end of which left a wet trail across the deck where it had been dragged.

The second line was released as well and the tug-boats started pulling us away from the quay. After three or four minutes we were far enough away from the quay to go under our own steam. The tug-boats released us and moved away.

As we slowly sailed away, I watched the deserted port glide past. Two smaller container ships were still berthed at the quay we had just left.

Our next stop was New York.

After our departure, I went back to my cabin. I still didn't feel very well and on top of my sore throat and headache, I had now also developed a muscle ache all over my body. Huddled on the couch, I finished reading the newspapers I had bought in La Spezia and flicked through *The Sea*, which I had taken from the seaman's mission in Fos sur Mer.

Just before lunch, I managed to climb up to the bridge and asked Mr Adega when we would be going through the Strait of Gibraltar.

'Tomorrow morning at six,' he answered. 'But as we have to turn the clock back tonight, it will actually be at five.'

I sighed. 'Not a great time to do some Rock spotting.'

'No, not really.'

In the evening, I felt slightly better and went down to the crew-lounge for a while. I didn't feel like playing cards, but instead struck up a conversation with Ramon.

'Did you happen to read that article in the newspaper, about America's plans to invade Iraq?' I asked him.

'Yes, I did,' Ramon nodded. 'It was interesting. I know you are not in favour of an invasion, but it's different for us, Filipinos. For us it is not about the war.'

'What do you mean?'

'Well, for the last one hundred years the United States has helped our country. They gave us money and helped when we had floods or other natural disasters. In exchange, we let the Americans build naval and air force bases in our country, which in turn gave us employment.

'Many Filipinos are very thankful for what the Americans have done for us and will support them no matter what. You see... They are afraid that America will stop helping us, if we are against them. We can't do without their support. For many people the help America gives us might be the only thing that feeds them on a daily basis.'

'So what you are saying is that, if you are against the invasion, your children might starve?'

'Yes, that is correct.'

'I had no idea that things were like this in your country, Ramon.'

'That's okay. Privately I am against an invasion, just like you. Many Filipinos are.' He shrugged his shoulders. 'We just can't express it.'

'Yes, I understand that now,' I nodded. 'Thanks for explaining it.'

'You're welcome.'

Before I went to bed that night, I turned back the clock one hour. We had been in the same time zone since leaving the Suez Canal, but were now in for another stint of time changing.

***

The next day, Tuesday 11ᵗʰ March, my alarm clock went off at 04.30h. Ridiculously early, but Arjen and I had decided we didn't want to miss seeing a glimpse of the Rock of Gibraltar. I got up and looked out of the window. It was still dark, but I could see the Spanish coast, dotted by lights. The Rock was silhouetted against them and remarkably well visible.

I dressed and phoned Arjen to wake him up. Together we walked up to the wing of the bridge. It was freezing cold. The second officer saw us and waved us in. It was past his watch, but he was still on the bridge, as was the first officer.

Looking through the large windows, we could see the lights of the African coast on our left and Gibraltar on our right. Arjen studied it through a pair of binoculars.

Randy appeared on the wing of the bridge. He was carrying his camera and took a picture of the Rock. It flashed and I wondered how the picture would turn out.

Having past Gibraltar, we went back to our respective cabins and beds. I fell asleep almost immediately.

I woke up again at 07.15h. The ship was pitching heavily. It was light now and I looked out of my window. The sea was rough. The waves were large and had white foamy heads. I gathered from this that we were in a storm; I guessed a wind force 8.

At breakfast, the captain told us we were following a northerly route across the Atlantic Ocean.

'It's called the Great circle,' he said. 'It will make our route across 500 nautical miles shorter than if we were to follow a more southerly route. We are about 18 hours behind schedule and it would be nice to make up the time.'

He looked at us and smiled. 'The problem, of course is that the weather is always a bit worse on this route, especially at this time of the year.'

All during the captain's story the ship shook occasionally from heavy waves crashing into the hull, and the pitching was still very bad.

Rodel walked in with our breakfasts. He had some trouble keeping on his feet. The tea in my cup moved backwards and forwards to the rhythm of the pitching, at times almost going over the rim.

'Captain, the passenger just called,' Rodel said, standing at the captain's table, his hands holding on to the back of a chair. 'He said he was seasick and couldn't come down for breakfast.'

'Okay, thank you,' the captain nodded and then looked at us. 'Have you two got any problems?'

'No, not at all,' Arjen said. I also shook my head.

'Good. There are seasickness pills at the dispensary. Don't hesitate to ask for them.'

Later in the day, the wind died down to force 4, but the swell remained. We were still pitching heavily. Although I wasn't seasick, I did experience some problems when I sat behind my computer. Within 15 minutes, I would be slightly dizzy, with a headache. From previous experience, I recognised the symptoms as the early stages of seasickness. That day it never got any worse however and stopped as soon as I did something other than staring at the computer screen.

It came at a bad time, as I had hoped to make some headway with the guide-book, but that was out of the question. So I just hung around, read a book and drank tea with the crew. At least my cold had gone, which was a relief.

In the evening we had to turn the clock back another hour.

***

In the next two days, Wednesday and Thursday, the wind disappeared completely, but the swell lingered on. I still wasn't able to sit behind the computer and instead spent some time on the bridge with Mr Adega. He told me the captain had decided on a course change, which would not take us so far north and therefore out of the swell. It did mean that we would take a bit longer to reach New York.

The effect of the course change became clear on Thursday. The swell had gone and I was able to work on the guide-book the whole day. Randy was also feeling a lot better, but preferred to spend most of the time in his cabin. We only saw him in the mess at meal times, although one evening he hung out with the officers in the officers' lounge.

Boredom was already setting in among the officers and crew, and none of them looked forward to five more days at sea. Arjen and I were spending our evenings in the crew-lounge, where we watched a movie or played cards. We felt it was time for some diversion to perk everyone up a bit.

'It's a tradition, you know, that the passengers buy some beer for the officers and crew,' I said to Arjen on Thursday evening. We were the only ones left in the crew-lounge, as most of the Filipinos had retired to their cabins early.

'You mean just buy a case of beer and give it to them?'

'Well, it is usually done during a barbecue, but I am quite sure we're not going to have one during our Atlantic crossing. The weather is far too bad for that.'

'Then how can I give them the beer?'

'We could organise some indoor thing.'

'Like what?'

'I have no idea...'

At that moment, Rodel and Ramon walked in. They had just finished their shifts.

'Not many people here tonight,' Rodel remarked.

'They've all gone to bed,' Arjen said.

'Shall we play some cards?' Rodel asked, taking a deck of cards off the table. Arjen, who had been looking bored, perked up at this.

'What if I teach you a Dutch card game?' he said enthusiastically. 'After all, I have been learning tong-its.'

'Okay.'

Rodel, Arjen and I gathered round a table. Ramon decided to watch.

Arjen shuffled two decks of cards together and dealt all the cards out between us.

'This game is called black eights,' Arjen said. 'Hold the pile in your hand, without looking at them. Now one by one we will put a card open on the table. When a black eight appears on the table, try to grab it as quickly as you can. The person who has all the cards in the end wins.'

'Sounds rather violent,' I said.

'Yeah... It's best not to wear any rings or other jewellery.'

We started playing and soon got the hang of it. It was a fast game where loads of grabbing was involved, with many chances to get scratched. Rodel enjoyed it a lot and was in stitches most of the time.

We played for a while.

The evening seemed long, as we had to turn the clock an hour back again.

On Friday morning, there was another fire drill. Apparently, the US coastguard is very strict and can even ask captains to have a drill, while the coastguard watch if everything is done according to the rules.

It was clear that the second officer was nervous about it. He had seen in the log that our last drill had been in the South China Sea, over a month ago, and he wanted to be prepared for the coastguard, just in case they decided to come on board.

Together Arjen and I walked down to the muster station with our life-jackets as soon as the alarm went off. It was cold outside and everyone hoped it would soon be over. The heat suit came out again and I took some pictures of it in action.

At lunchtime, it became clear that Arjen had done some thinking.

'What if we organise a card evening tonight? With Dutch card games,' he said as he ate his tomato soup.

'Like a party, you mean?'

'Yes, against the boredom. I could donate a crate of beer.'

'That's a great idea. Then I will get a bottle of rum. Let's make a poster this afternoon.'

At teatime, everything was organised and the posters distributed around the ship. They didn't reveal much; just that everyone on board was invited to an evening of Dutch card games, which would be held in the crew-lounge at 19.00h that evening.

The guys were very curious and asked many questions when I went down for tea in the crew-mess. I couldn't explain much, however, as Arjen was in charge of the games and I didn't know much about them.

After the evening meal we helped the second officer (who was now in charge of the ship's store) carry up two large cases of beer (with 24 bottles each) and a bottle of rum to the crew-lounge. A crowd had already gathered and everyone was in high spirits.

We started the games at 19.00h, when Rodel and Ramon came off duty. Ramon had spent part of his afternoon deep-frying prawn crackers, which he carried with him in a huge bowl as he entered the lounge.

Black eights was the first game we played. It turned out that Mr Ibanez was the one with lightning fast reflexes and he managed to grab most of the cards and win nearly all the games.

Randy arrived and shyly stepped into the crew-lounge. He had never been there before, but was soon chatting away, clearly enjoying himself.

As Arjen explained the rules for the next game, the first and second officers walked in. We couldn't persuade them to play, but they watched and drank beer.

After two-and-a-half hours of cards, we were sick of it and played some loud music. It wasn't long before people started dancing. Arjen had centre stage with his Blues Brothers act and Michael Jackson moonwalk.

The party finished at 00.30h. It had been a great success.

Before I turned off the light on my nightstand, I remembered to turn back the clock one hour.

CHAPTER TWENTY-EIGHT

For the second time that week I woke up from the pitching of the ship, but this time it was even worse than a couple of days before. It was Saturday morning, 15th March, the day after the card evening and I looked at my alarm clock to check the time - 07.30h. A giant wave crashed into the *Serenity* with a terrific bang and the whole ship shuddered.

I got out of bed and walked to the window. The sea was wild. I had never seen waves like that. I walked to the living room and looked out to the front. A huge wave crashed over the fo'c'sle, splashing up higher than the containers on our deck. The wind then picked up the spray from the crashing wave and with enormous speed and force splattered it against my window several seconds later.

'Whoa, this is bad,' I mumbled. I grabbed the phone to ring Arjen to find out if he was awake.

'Did you see that giant wave just now,' he shouted as soon as he answered.

'Yes, I did.'

'This is so cool! I am going to take loads of pictures.'

Another wave crashed over our bow with a loud bang. I watched as the force literally pushed the front end of the ship down. It bounced back up with a shudder and I grabbed on to the window sill to keep upright. Again, the spray splattered against my window.

Down in the mess everything was in uproar. Cups, saucers and plates bounced up and down with a loud clatter; tea and coffee spilled out on to the white tablecloths (I envisaged a lot of extra washing for Rodel); from the galley came the sounds of pots bouncing around on the stove and in the background was the overall noise of waves thumping into our hull.

Despite the mayhem the captain was drinking his coffee and trying to butter some toast.

He smiled as I walked in.

'Wind force 10?' I asked him by way of greeting.

'Eleven,' he answered.

As if to confirm this, another wave crashed into our hull with a loud bang, shaking the whole ship.

Arjen walked into the mess and sat down, putting his camera down on the table.

'I have just been to the bridge.' His eyes were bright with excitement. 'Wow, this is fantastic.'

'You took some pictures?' I asked.

'Yes, I took one of a big wave splashing over the containers.'

Randy also walked in. In stark contrast to Arjen, he looked far from happy. His cheeks were pasty and on the brink of turning green.

'I think I am going to be seasick again,' he said.

'Try to eat something, it might help,' I suggested and gestured for him to sit down.

The ship shuddered and pitched wildly. One of the cups rolled off its saucer and on to the table. Arjen caught it and put it back on the saucer.

Randy had followed the cup with his eyes and now really turned green.

'I think I better go back to bed.' He turned and stumbled to the door.

On the bridge later in the morning, Mr Adega told me that Randy wasn't the only casualty. Mr Orozco and Mr Pachero, down in the engine-room, also showed signs of seasickness.

'Or maybe it was the amount of beer that I heard they consumed during the card evening last night that is catching up with them now.'

I smiled at him. 'Who knows...?' I peered down at the chart. Our course was plotted on it with a pencil line. Every hour the officer on watch would mark our position, which in general was on or close to the pencil line. This morning however, I noticed that our position marks were erratic and had hardly moved forward.

'It looks like we're not going anywhere,' I remarked.

'That's correct. We are pushed around a bit by the waves and as we can only have a speed of 13 knots, we don't move forward very much.'

An extra big wave crashed over the fo'c'sle and Mr Adega and I looked up in time to see the spray hit the large windows of the bridge with a loud clatter. Five sets of windscreen wipers worked furiously to drain the water away.

'That spray is called green water,' Mr Adega said. 'It gets blown up so high that it reaches the bridge.'

'How long do you think this storm will last?' I asked.

'Probably not that long. It came up very suddenly and then they usually don't last long.'

Mr Adega was right. In the afternoon, the storm died down and in the evening, it was only a wind force 8. Four days before wind force 8 had felt like a substantial storm, but now it just felt like a gentle breeze. The swell remained, however, but to my surprise, I was able to sit behind the computer and work.

I was very tired in the evening. This might have been the result of having to brace myself against the sudden movements of the ship all day long, but I also had the feeling that ship lag was catching up with me again.

I went to bed at 21.30h, and then still had to turn the clock back another hour.

The next morning I woke up at 06.00h; I had slept for nine-and-a-half hours. Before breakfast, I went outside for a quick look at the weather. The swell had now completely disappeared, but there was a bitterly cold wind, that made me go back inside really fast.

It was Sunday and as I walked into the mess, I dropped in on a conversation the captain was having with Arjen and Randy.

'I hope you feel a bit better this morning?' the captain asked Randy.

'Yes,' Randy nodded. 'Much better, thank you.'

'Good.' The captain took a sip of his coffee. 'You know... Yesterday's storm was a typical example of a storm that can suddenly develop out of a low-pressure area. It lasted only 13 hours, not long enough to create a large swell. To create a swell, a storm must rage for at least 24 hours. That's why today, the sea is calm.'

'Well anyhow, our meals are a lot quieter today,' Arjen remarked.

'Yes, they are,' the captain smiled. 'Oh, by the way, you are all invited for drinks in the officers' lounge at eleven o'clock.'

Later on the bridge, I had a somewhat surreal conversation with Mr Adega. He showed me that night's logbook entry, in which the second officer had noted down temperature and wind force.

'Look,' he said, 'it says here that last night it was *below* zero.'

'That's pretty cold,' I said, not exactly knowing where he was going with this.

'But it didn't snow!'

'Yeah... and?'

'It can only be below zero if it snows. So it can't have been below zero. It didn't snow.'

I blinked at Mr Adega, wondering if he was pulling my leg, but he looked at me in all earnest.

'Actually,' I said, 'it *can* be below zero without snow.'

'Really?'

'Yes. Like in my country we have not much snow, but in winter it often freezes.'

'So, being below zero doesn't need to mean snow.'

'That is correct.'

'Ah... I never knew that...'

Back in my cabin, I heard a knock on my door. It was Rodel. Sunday morning was normally his time to clean my cabin and I had been slightly surprised on my return to find he hadn't been yet.

'I am going to clean your cabin tomorrow,' he said. 'I hope that is okay with you.' He looked a bit out of sorts.

'Yes, of course that's okay,' I said. 'Are you not feeling well?'

'No, I am not. I am a bit depressed.'

'How come?'

He sighed. 'I always get a bit homesick in the Atlantic Ocean as we are then the furthest away from my country as we can be. I also still have almost five months left on my contract, which is a long time. Every day is just the same...'

Again, he sighed, then continued. 'On top of that I don't like it when the sea is rough like yesterday and I hate the cold.' He looked very miserable now. It was totally out of character for him.

'I am sorry to hear all that, but I am afraid I can't help you.'

'I know, but it helps to talk about it.' He smiled a weak smile. 'I will see you later in the mess.'

'Yes, you will. Oh... the captain is having drinks in the lounge, so we will probably be later for lunch.'

'No problem.' He waved a goodbye and slouched off.

As I closed the door, I thought that it wasn't fair that the Filipinos had nine-month contracts, while the Germans only had to do six months at the time. Nine months away from family and friends was just too long.

***

'I have a bottle of red wine here, especially for you,' the captain said, pointing at a bottle that was standing on the bar. 'I know you don't drink beer, so I hope you will enjoy this.'

I looked at the bottle and said, 'thank you, that is very thoughtful of you.'

The officers' lounge was filled with people, most of them drinking beer, or, as I discovered later, beer mixed with champagne. Arjen just stuck to champagne and was handed a glass by the second officer, who was playing barkeeper.

'A glass of wine for you, then?' the second officer asked me, removing the seal from the bottle and grabbing the corkscrew that was lying on the bar.

'Yes, thank you.'

The captain raised his voice. 'Now that everyone is here, I would like to present the passengers with the mile certificates for their journeys.' From a plastic folder he took two A4-sized papers, and handed one to Randy and one to Arjen. I looked at Arjen's certificate over his shoulder. At the top was a map of the world, with the route that the *Serenity* had taken since Arjen had been on board. Below that were printed the ports that had been visited and the nautical miles between each port. At the bottom, the mileage was totalled up to, in Arjen's case, 4246 nautical miles.

'Cool,' Arjen said. 'How far is that in kilometres?'

I did a quick calculation. 'Well, times one point eight, so... um... close to 8000.'

'Great.' He turned to the captain. 'Thank you, I will put this in my scrapbook when I get home.'

The first officer appeared next to me. 'I wonder how many miles you will have done at the end of your trip.'

I nodded. 'Yeah, me too...'

He took a sip of his beer/champagne mix. 'The captain brought it to my attention that your cabin is very cold,' he continued.

'Er... yes... that is correct. I mentioned something to him this morning.'

'I have an electric fan heater in my cabin that I don't use. You can borrow it if you like.'

'That would great. My cabin can become very cold as it is on the corner, especially with a cold wind.'

The first officer smiled. 'I understand. I will leave the heater outside your cabin after lunch.'

'Thank you. It would make life a bit more comfortable for me.'

After three glasses of red wine and two handfuls of peanuts, Arjen and I made our way to the mess for lunch. Randy joined us, but the Germans all stayed behind in the lounge to drink.

'I was a bit disappointed that I became seasick again,' Randy said after we had sat down. 'Someone told me that you only get seasick once.'

269

'Ah... yes... The famous seasickness myth,' I said. 'As you have seen it is not true. You *can* get seasick more than once.'

'Unfortunately.'

'But besides having been seasick twice, are you having a good time?' Arjen asked.

'Yes, definitely. This is a great way to travel, isn't it?'

'Absolutely,' Arjen smiled.

When lunch was finished, Arjen went for a session in the sauna on the second deck down. Before we had joined the officers in the lounge at 11.00h, he had already turned the sauna on, so that it would be nice and warm after lunch.

I went to my cabin and to my great delight found an electric fan heater in front of my door. Now I was finally able to heat my cabin properly. The general heating of the ship just didn't seem to be able to make it warm enough.

Later in the afternoon Arjen knocked on my door.

'I have to show you something on the bridge,' he said as I opened the door.

'Okay.'

We walked upstairs and entered the bridge. It was the end of the second officer's watch.

'Look,' Arjen said, pointing to the chart. I squinted down and saw a dark blue cross printed on it accompanied by the comment: 'Wreck of the Titanic, 1912'.

Our course indicated by a pencil line, showed that we were sailing over the *Titanic* right at that moment.

Involuntarily I looked out of the window, to see if I could get a glimpse of the famous ship, but all I saw was grey water.

'Isn't this cool?' Arjen said enthusiastically.

'Very cool, even though there is actually nothing to see.'

Back in my cabin, I wondered if we, like the *Titanic,* were in any danger of an encounter with an iceberg. I didn't think so, as it wasn't wintertime anymore and we weren't in the arctic region.

I suddenly had to think back to my trip on the *FTK Kowloon,* when, on our way back from San Francisco to Tokyo across the Pacific Ocean, we entered the Bering Sea. It had been early summer, which is why we were able to go safely into the Bering Sea. In wintertime, it would have been far too dangerous, with many storms and chances of rogue icebergs.

Most of the one-and-a-half days we had spent in the Bering Sea it was misty with poor visibility. But as we turned south back into the Pacific Ocean, the mist disappeared giving us a spectacular view over Attu Island, one of the dozens of islands in the Aleutian Island chain. Its landscape was wild and empty with snow covered mountains that steeply rose up out of the sea to a thousand metres high. Watching it, I had wondered if anyone actually lived on these remote Alaskan islands.

CHAPTER TWENTY-NINE

We were nearing the United States and everyone seemed to be relieved that our ocean crossing was nearly over - anxious to go ashore and phone family and friends.

It was Monday 17ᵗʰ March, and during the day, I listened to the BBC World Service a number of times. America's pending invasion of Iraq had been looming over our time on the Atlantic, and as I listened to the World Service broadcasts during the day, I kept Ramon up to date with the news, as he was especially interested.

Rodel had perked up a bit since my conversation with him the day before. He came to clean my cabin in the morning and told me how Mr Adega had advised him to change his routine.

'A change in routine, will make my boredom go away,' he said from my bedroom, as he changed my bedding.

I was sitting behind my computer putting the final touches to my chapter about Valencia. 'How are you going to do that?' I asked.

'Well... right after my evening shift is finished I will go to bed for an hour-and-a-half, waking up at eight. Then I will go down and spend some time in the crew-lounge.' He came into the living room and chucked a pile of dirty bedding on the floor. 'I hope it will work. In any case, we will be in New York tomorrow and I will be able to phone my family and girlfriend. I am looking forward to that a lot.'

Later in the day, the first officer told me that we were scheduled to berth at Newark's Port Elizabeth Container Terminal, at 20.00h the next day. This would probably mean that Arjen would stay an extra night on board, before disembarking on Wednesday.

That evening just before 21.00h, Ramon, Arjen and I walked up to the bridge to listen to the live broadcast of President Bush's

273

Address to the Nation. It was all dark on the bridge, except for some little lights and the radar screen that gave off a ghostly green light.

In his speech, Bush said that the United States would invade Iraq in two days time if Sadam Hussain had not left the country by then.

In two days time we would be in New York.

Before I went to bed that night, I turned back my clock for the last time on the trip. From now on, we would only put the clock forward again.

***

The world was white when I woke up the next morning. The *Serenity River* was moving forward through a thick mist that obscured almost everything. From my cabin, I had difficulty seeing our mast, which meant visibility couldn't be more than 150 metres. On the bridge, I discovered that we were close to land and in a busy shipping lane. Mr Adega had to keep all his wits about him to make sure we weren't going to collide with other ships in the mist. He kept a constant eye on the radar screen and when necessary made slight adjustments to our course.

Arjen had been given the green light by the captain about spending another night on the ship. It would make things a lot easier for him, as it meant that he didn't have to go into Manhattan late in the evening looking for the hotel he and his friend had booked.

At 15.30h, we went for anchorage off the Long Island coast. The mist had gone. Unfortunately, a haze obscured the land. We were not sure if the coastguard would come and pick us for a random drill, but the second officer was nervously walking around, as if he was expecting them to come on board at any moment. In the end, they never showed up.

At 16.30h the pilot came onboard, that is to say, six pilots came on board. One of them was the real pilot, one was a teacher and the rest were apprentice pilots. They were on a field trip and arrived by boat. Pilots arriving by boat seemed to be the norm at most ports I had been to, except for Rotterdam where, on the *FTK Kowloon*, a helicopter had dropped off the pilot. The poor man was let down via a winch on a cable, while we were holding on to our hats.

It was very busy on the bridge and Arjen, Randy and I were standing on the wing, trying to avoid the crowd.

Slowly the *Serenity* made its way along the coast of Long Island. After a while, the silhouette of an enormous suspension bridge loomed up behind the tiny houses on the shore. It looked a bit like the Golden Gate Bridge in San Francisco, but this one was painted grey instead of red.

One of the apprentices walked towards us and pointed at the bridge.

'That is the Verrazano-Narrows Bridge and it connects the west point of Long Island with Staten Island.'

'It is huge,' Randy remarked.

'It is. It's more than a mile long.'

'That would be one point six kilometre,' Randy said with a smile.

The apprentice smiled back. 'Yeah, I guess so...'

'When was it built?' I asked, as I focused my binoculars on one of the two huge pylons.

'It was finished in 1964.'

'Are we going to go under it?' Arjen asked.

'Yes, we are.'

There was a chill in the air and I stamped my feet as I had become really cold from standing around. The apprentice returned to the bridge and Randy followed him in.

'I think I am going indoors for a bit to warm up and have something to eat,' I said.

'What time is it?' Arjen asked.

'Almost half past five.'

'I will go with you. As long as we are back in time to see us go under the bridge.'

Fifteen minutes later, we returned to the wing. Randy was still on the bridge, talking to two other apprentices. We were now much closer to Long Island and as we glided past, I could see rows of semi-detached houses, made of red brick, with steep roofs.

Then the Verrazano-Narrows Bridge, with its enormous pylons and high bridge deck, loomed over us. Slowly we past under it. The bridge deck came pretty close and gave the illusion we would be able to touch it. In reality however, we cleared it by at least five metres. Arjen was impressed.

Having passed the bridge, we now sailed into the Upper Bay, staying close to Staten Island. In the distance, I could see the skyline of Manhattan and the Statue of Liberty.

We followed the shore of Staten Island into a side arm to the north of the island. Here the teacher and apprentice pilots left the ship and only the main pilot remained.

It was getting dark, but there was more than enough to see and the pilot was eager to point out the sights.

On Staten Island, some guys played a baseball game on a large triangular green field. They were dressed in light grey uniforms and a crowd was watching them from concrete stands that enfolded the field on two sides. Everything was lit up by large spotlights.

The north side of the river was reserved for a large oil and petroleum refinery.

'It has been a very cold winter this year,' the pilot told us. 'We still had snow last week. Everyone is hoping spring will come soon.'

After a while, another bridge appeared; its arch all lit up in red, white and blue lights.

'Do we have to go under that bridge?' Arjen asked the pilot.

'Yes, we do,' he nodded. 'That is the Bayonne Bridge and it is a bit of a challenge for us.'

Arjen looked at it. 'Why?'

'Because it is very low.' The pilot pointed to our monkey-deck, where the normally upright antennae were now lying almost flat down. 'If your captain hadn't pulled down the antennae, we wouldn't be able to go under it.'

'Wow,' Arjen said.

A large dredger glided past us, spewing out the silt it had collected from the bottom of the river.

'The harbour authorities have to constantly dredge this part of the river so that large ships like yours can come here,' the pilot explained.

We passed under the bridge. The top of the little mast on our monkey-deck, on which now flew the American flag, almost grazed the bottom of the bridge deck as there was a clearance of less than a metre.

Having cleared the bridge, we turned right, into another bay. In the distance, I could see the container port. We would be berthing soon. It was 19.15h and I was almost frozen.

'I'm going inside to have a hot cup of tea and warm up,' I said to Arjen.

'Okay. I am staying here to watch us berth.'

After I got myself a cup of tea from the machine in the pantry, I wandered into the crew-lounge. It was deserted as all of the crew were outside waiting for us to berth. Rodel was the only person inside. His eyes were on the tv.

'Anything interesting to watch?' I asked, sitting down on a couch.

'No.' He shook his head. 'Just a programme about what America is planning to do in Iraq.'

We watched for a while in silence, then switched to a different channel.

Immigration came on board as soon as we berthed. In most ports, the immigration procedure was pretty laid back, but not so in the United States. Instead of the captain handing all the passports of the crew to a lone immigration officer or the ship's agent, he now handed each of us our passport, after which we had to wait our turn until the immigration officers called us in to see each of us individually.

The whole crew lined up outside the captain's office on deck 5. Clutching my passport, I joined the queue. Then it was my turn to go in. Three large men with crew cuts and dark blue uniforms were sitting around the table. None of them smiled. One of them invited me to sit down. The room felt smaller than it had ever done before.

I handed my passport to one of the men. He checked my name and passport number with the ones on the crew-list, compared the photograph with my face and then flicked through it, until he came to the page that held my US visa.

'You're Dutch, right?' he asked.

'Yes, sir.'

'Then why do you have a visa? A visa is not necessary for someone from the Netherlands.'

I quietly thanked him for calling my country Netherlands instead of Holland.

'I needed a visa last year, when I travelled on another container ship to the west coast of the United States.'

'They told you to get a visa for that?'

'Yes, sir.'

'How long did you stay in the United States on that trip?'

'About five days, sir.'

'And how long are you planning to stay on this trip?'

I did a quick calculation. 'Also about five days, sir.'

'Okay, no problem.' He grabbed a stamp from the table and with a thump stamped my passport.

'Do you realise that your visa is valid until 2012?' he asked.

'Er... no. I didn't realise it was valid for that long.'

'Well, it is.' He handed me my passport back.

For some reason, I felt relieved to get out of the office.

Then the captain waved Arjen in. He got his passport stamped without a problem.

By now it was 21.00h and I decided to try to get some sleep before our midnight expedition to the port canteen, where Arjen wanted to phone his wife and I our parents. Due to the time difference that was best done at 01.00h.

I went to bed and set my alarm for 00.30h.

It wasn't easy to wake up three-and-a-half hours later, but we managed it and walked down the gangway and across the port to the canteen, both still half asleep.

Opening the door of the canteen, I noticed a poster that was stuck to the glass with sticky tape. 'Boycott the loading and unloading of French ships!' it read. I wondered what it was that the French had done to upset the stevedores.

After the phone calls, we walked back to the *Serenity River*.

CHAPTER THIRTY

The next day was Wednesday 19th March and in the morning at breakfast, Rodel told me what the poster on the canteen door had been about.

'France is against the invasion, so now everyone in the United States is boycotting French products,' he said, as he brought me my breakfast. 'Apparently French fries and French bread are now called Freedom fries and Freedom bread.'

'Seriously?'

He nodded.

'But that is totally ridiculous.'

Rodel shrugged his shoulders and disappeared into the pantry.

Arjen and Randy came in. They each carried a large backpack that they dumped in a corner.

'Ready to go, I see...' I said as they sat down for their last meal on board the *Serenity*. Randy had asked Arjen and me if he could accompany us into the city. He was on his way to friends in Pittsburgh, but had decided he wanted to stay in Manhattan for one night. He hoped the hotel that Arjen had booked would have some vacancies for the coming night.

At 08.00h, we took the shuttle bus to the gate, where the attendant phoned a taxi for us. One of the apprentice pilots of the evening before had told us that the cheapest way to get to Manhattan would be to take a taxi to Newark Airport and from there a bus into Manhattan.

'A taxi into Manhattan from the port is very expensive. That will easily cost you over 100 dollars. Much better to go by bus.'

Newark Airport wasn't far away from the port. From the ship, we could see the planes land and take off. As we arrived, the bus to Manhattan was about to leave.

It was a nice sunny day and from the freeway, we had a magnificent view over the water towards Manhattan and Brooklyn. Then we entered the Lincoln Tunnel, which connects New Jersey with Manhattan and emerges above ground a little south of Central Park. As soon as we came out of the tunnel, we had reached the bus terminal and exited the bus. Arjen's hotel was not very far away, but too far to walk with heavy luggage, so we took the subway.

The lady in the ticket booth was kind enough to explain that the little brass coins she had sold us were actually our subway tickets. She also pointed us in the right direction for the Lexington Avenue subway.

We found the right platform, boarded and surfaced across town about 10 minutes later. From there it was another ten-minute walk to Arjen's hotel.

As we walked, we were completely surrounded by skyscrapers and although I had been in cities with skyscrapers before, it was somehow special to be in New York. Particularly the tall, slim Chrysler Building had me awestruck as I had always had a soft spot for 1930s architecture.

Checking into the hotel Arjen discovered that his friend Rolf had arrived the evening before. He came down to meet us. Randy also checked in and after we said goodbye to him, I walked with Arjen and Rolf into a Starbucks next door to the hotel. We got something to drink and sat down at a table.

Arjen and Rolf had plans to make for their 5-day visit to New York and started looking at brochures for things to see. I soon concluded that it might be better if our ways parted. Unlike them, my main reason for visiting Manhattan was to find a tourist information and an internet cafe.

Half an hour later, after I had bought some packed sandwiches for lunch, we said goodbye on the corner of Park Avenue and 57th Street. As I walked off, I realised it was a bit strange to be on my own again.

The first thing I found was an internet cafe and I spent 10 minutes checking my mail. Then I walked to 7th Avenue where the tourist information was. I realised that even though on my map everything looked pretty close, the distances between the streets were further than I thought. After I had found the tourist information and got the brochures I needed, I suddenly felt really tired. At first I thought this was because of the broken night I had had, but then I realised it was more likely that I was still ship lagged.

I sat for a while in a chair inside the tourist information, wondering what to do next. I didn't feel like sightseeing much, but didn't want to go back to the ship right away. I was after all in New York.

Feeling a bit less tired I walked out on to the street again and after having wandered around for a bit I found myself at one of the most recognisable places in the world, Times Square.

It was crawling with tourists.

From Times Square, I walked into a large bookstore where I spent half an hour browsing the shelves and in the end, I bought four books. I was now totally knackered and decided I just wanted to go back to the ship.

At 15.00h, I returned to Newark Airport. I got out at arrivals as I reckoned it would be easier to get a taxi from there. Before taking a taxi though, I quickly went into the airport terminal. I had forgotten to buy a newspaper in Manhattan before I boarded the bus, but now I had another chance to buy a New York Times. To my shame, I have to admit I had not expected much of this newspaper. I was pleasantly surprised however, that it turned out to be a very informative, unbiased newspaper and I became an instant fan.

The taxi dropped me off at the gate at 16.00h.

***

'So, we have two new passengers?' I said to Rodel as we were walking towards the port canteen together. I had just finished my evening meal where I had met Christina and Brian, an elderly Canadian couple, who were on their way to Valencia.

'Actually, we will have three new passengers, but one hasn't arrived yet,' Rodel remarked. 'It's a German man. He's going to be in your brother's cabin.'

'He'd better hurry up then,' I said. 'Aren't we supposed to leave at midnight?'

'Yes, but he still has five hours to embark.'

We arrived at the canteen at 19.30h. It was busier than it had been the night before. Stevedores on their breaks were sitting around the tables and ship crews were hanging around the phones that lined the wall. A tv, volume on full, was mounted high on a wall. Everyone ignored it.

I spotted Mr Ibanez, Mr Morayta and Mr Navaez sitting around the end of a long table and then saw Mr Lozada making a phone call. He waved as he recognised me.

Rodel walked to the phones to wait for his turn. He was going to phone his girlfriend. I joined the other guys at the table. The loudness of the tv made it difficult to have a conversation, so everyone just sat. Mr Morayta flicked through a magazine with a bored face and I picked up a two-day old newspaper. I skimmed the headlines without much enthusiasm. On the tv, the commercial break was over and the programme started again. It was a home improvement show. The presenter, with a big smile and a serious looking tool belt, demonstrated the best way to replace shingles on a roof.

Rodel had finished his call and joined us.

'Interesting programme?' he asked.

'No, not at all.'

We kept watching. When another commercial break came on, one of the stevedores reached up and manually changed the channel.

A news anchor-woman appeared and suddenly the atmosphere in the canteen changed. Where before it had been reasonably calm and relaxed (if that were possible with the tv at its loudest), the tension now rose and everyone fell silent and gawked at the tv.

'What's happening?' I asked Rodel.

'I don't know.'

'What time is it?'

Rodel checked his watch. 'Almost eight o'clock.'

'It's the ultimatum, isn't it?' I said. Rodel looked at me blankly.

'Bush's ultimatum for Iraq! It was ending tonight at eight. The invasion is about to begin!'

As if on cue a new programme started. It was called 'Attacking Iraq' and the opening credits were accompanied by some serious action-movie music. The anchor-woman returned and explained that Bush's ultimatum had expired and that 'We are now at war'. She disappeared and instead we got a grainy picture of a desert, where, as of now, nothing was happening.

I felt ridiculous staring at the tv waiting for something to happen. I wondered if it was real. Was I really here in New York, in this canteen, watching a war start? Couldn't be! I got up.

'I'm going back to the ship,' I said to Rodel. 'I am not going to stare at a tv and watch how a war starts. This is crazy.'

'Yeah, you're right,' Rodel said and got up as well. 'I will walk back with you.'

We exited through the door on which there were now three more posters calling on people to boycott French ships and goods.

I went to bed early. We left New York for Norfolk at 01.00h that night. I didn't wake up for it.

CHAPTER THIRTY-ONE

The taxi was driving quite fast through a quiet Norfolk suburb of detached and semi-detached houses. Most of them were mid-19th century two storey wooden buildings with gables and verandas. The suburb didn't look very prosperous. The houses were in desperate need of some paint, the gardens ill kept and rusty old cars blocked the driveways.

The taxi turned left, then right. I had the distinct feeling we had been in this street before. I glanced at the taxi driver and saw a frown on his forehead. He turned his head as if searching for something familiar. My heart sank; it seemed we were lost.

I glanced at my watch for the hundredth time since getting in the taxi, hoping the driver wouldn't notice. It wasn't a good time to get lost. I should have been back on the *Serenity* more than half an hour ago and the drive back from downtown Norfolk had already taken 15 minutes longer than the drive to Norfolk had done.

Finally, the taxi turned into a road that looked more as if it would lead to the port. I could feel the driver's relief. Within four minutes, we arrived at the gate.

We were stopped and I handed over my passport for the officer to check. He gave it back and waved us through.

'I can't take you all the way to the ship,' the taxi driver said. He was sweating profusely.

'That's okay,' I said. 'Just get me as close as you can.' I looked out of the window. In the distance, I could see the ship. An enormous amount of stacked containers separated me from it.

All too soon the taxi stopped.

'This is it,' the driver said. 'That will be 15 dollars.' I handed him the money.

I got out of the car and slung my bag over my shoulders. It was heavy from all the leaflets I had collected and the two copies of the New York Times I had bought. As the taxi drove away, I looked at the ship again. It looked different than it had done in the morning.

Suddenly I realised why and a cold dread came over me. The gantries had moved away. The loading had stopped!

I started running, hoping the gangway would still be down. I thought of all the times before I had taken risks to go ashore, but always making it back in time, because the loading had been delayed. This time it hadn't. In fact, it had finished early.

I crossed one of the large roads in between the stacks of containers. Luckily, the Star Wars cranes and forklifts were busy on the other side of the port. I kept running. My heart was beating rapidly, my throat burned from breathing too fast and I had a stitch in my side. Running was not my strong point.

Then I reached the end of the containers and had, for the first time, full view of the ship that had been my home for almost three months. The gangway was still down! I slowed down a bit. As I came closer, I could see that the safety netting, which was normally fastened around the gangway when the ship was berthed, had already been taken in. For sure, it wasn't long before departure.

I noticed two figures standing at the top of the gangway and recognised Mr Morayta and Mr Reyes. I waved at them and they waved back.

When I came into earshot, I shouted at them, 'I hope you weren't waiting for me?'

'No,' Mr Morayta shouted down, 'for the pilot.'

I climbed the gangway. It was weird as the handrails and netting were missing. Totally exhausted and out of breath I arrived on the main deck.

'Welcome back,' Mr Reyes said with a smile.

'Thanks,' I smiled back weakly. 'When is the pilot coming?'
'In about 15 minutes.'
I realised that this time, I had cut it really short.
It was 11.15h and almost time for lunch.

Norfolk, Virginia, situated on the shores of Chesapeake Bay, is a large city further down the east coast from New York.

We had arrived at the entrance to Chesapeake Bay at 18.00h on Thursday 20th March, 17 hours after we had left New York. The day had been uneventful. At breakfast, the first officer told me that the invasion of Iraq had now begun.

The question of the day was what had happened to the German passenger. He had not arrived before we departed New York and the agent hadn't heard or seen anything of him. It was a bit of a mystery.

Christina and Brian, the new passengers who had embarked in New York, were very nice. It was their first time on a container ship and they were relishing the experience.

It was dark by the time the pilot arrived to guide us into Chesapeake Bay. I watched our approach to Norfolk from the sundeck. Lights dotted the shorelines on both sides. Two lighthouses shone their intermittent beams across the water of the bay. Norfolk Naval Base was fully lit up.

Shore leave was expected to be short in Norfolk, most likely not longer than part of the next morning. However, I *had* to try to get into the city, even if it was only for an hour. To my horror, I had discovered that I had forgotten to take my research on Norfolk with me from home and if I wasn't able to go ashore, the guide-book would be without a chapter about Norfolk.

We berthed at 21.00h.

'Did you have a nice time in Norfolk,' Christina asked me as we sat down for lunch.

'Yes. Very short, but it was okay' I answered.

'Did you manage to do all you wanted?'

'Just. I was lucky to come across a tourist information after only 10 minutes of wandering around, so now I, at least, have the information I needed about Norfolk.' We had finished our soup and Rodel brought out the main course: mashed potatoes, steak, peas and carrots.

'You were back only just in time,' Brian remarked. 'We saw you running up, from the sun-deck.'

'I wanted to buy a New York Times, but I just couldn't find a newsagent anywhere. In the end, I walked into an hotel and bought one there. By that time it was almost 10.30h, the time I was supposed to have been back. I took a taxi and it all would have been okay if he hadn't got lost.'

'It's a good thing I didn't go with you,' Christina said. 'I would have slowed you down horribly.'

'I am sure you wouldn't have.' I smiled at her.

Just after lunch, the *Serenity River* departed from Norfolk. We made our way back through Chesapeake Bay and into the Atlantic Ocean. This time I was watching from deck 1 with Rodel.

We passed the Naval Base again. It was all but deserted.

'Last time I was here, there were many more ships over there,' Rodel said, pointing to the base. I saw that a few smaller naval ships were berthed for maintenance. A submarine was out of the water, captured in a dry dock. Even from where we were, we could see the bright pinpoint lights from welding torches that were doing repairs to its hull.

The Bay widened out. Another city lay on its north shore and in the distance, I could see the water of the Atlantic Ocean.

'Are you already thinking about leaving the *Serenity*?' Rodel suddenly asked.

'You mean when we arrive back in La Spezia?'

He nodded. 'It is only 15 days from now.'

'I know, but I am not thinking about that yet.' I watched as we silently glided past Fort Monroe, a large Civil War fort situated on the north side of the bay.

'I have far too much to do, before I can start packing,' I continued. 'I have to finish the guide-book and then print out six copies. Besides, I don't like thinking about leaving. I prefer to pretend I stay on board forever. That makes it easier, you know.'

'Perhaps.' He looked at me with a sad face. 'We will miss you.'

I gave him a quick hug. 'I know. I will miss you guys too.'

Our next port of call was Savannah in Georgia, even further down the east coast of the United States.

***

The next day, Saturday 22th March, at 16.00h I looked out over a shallow bay at the mouth of the Savannah River. We were just drifting around, waiting for the pilot who was to guide us along the river to Savannah, 25 kilometres inland. It was a quiet, warm and sunny day and on the bay wind surfers and small sailing boats tried to catch what little wind there was to propel them forward.

I was lazing around on the sun-deck with Christina and Brian and looked through my binoculars at the beach resort that was situated on the south side of the river mouth. Most of the day, while the *Serenity* was sailing down the coast, I had been working on the guide-book, the Norfolk chapter in particular. We had already heard that the chance of going on shore leave in Savannah was small.

The pilot arrived at 17.30h and our two-and-a-half hour journey along the river began, passing its beautiful delta, covered in marshy tidal swamps with shrubs and trees.

Savannah used to be a trading port and even today, a large part of the city is focused on the river, which still passes right through it.

The container port was situated beyond downtown Savannah and as we were gliding through the city, we looked down from up high, on the people who were relaxing around the boulevard. The light was fading, but the waterfront was well lit and many people were enjoying an evening stroll in the warm air. Old warehouses, five storeys high, lined the boulevard; their ground floors turned into little cafes and restaurants, their upper storeys now apartments. Some people waved as they spotted us, and we waved back.

After we had past a large bridge, we could see containers and gantries, and knew we were getting close. Around 20.00h we berthed. Christina and Brian went back to their cabin and I walked down to the main deck where some of the engine crew were hanging around.

As the gangway was let down I noticed an older man with a long white beard walking towards the ship. He was dragging a suitcase behind him.

'Who's that?' Mr Orozco asked, pointing to the man, who was now climbing the gangway, even before the safety netting was placed round it. Mr Morayta sprinted down to take the man's case.

'I don't know,' I said. 'I didn't think we were getting any more passengers.'

'I bet it's that missing passenger from New York,' Mr Navaez remarked.

'Yeah, you could be right.'

It was now totally dark and against the bright lights of the port I saw a large swarm of mosquitoes that hovered lazily nearby. One of them landed on my arm and tried to bite me. I slapped at it and then saw another huge mosquito launching an attack on me.

'I am getting out of here, guys,' I said. 'Mosquitoes love me and I don't want to be eaten alive.'

Later I bumped into Rodel in the corridor on deck 5. He looked harassed.

'Two more passengers have come on board,' he whispered, carrying some large towels.

'Two?'

'Yeah. One is the German guy who should have boarded in New York. He had apparently arranged with Ariel Rügen that he could board here in Savannah instead of in New York. But they never told us... The captain is a bit annoyed.'

'And the other new passenger?'

'A lady from France. She's over 80 and doesn't speak a word of English. If you ask me she is getting a bit...' He made a circular motion with his index finger near his temple.

I smiled.

'Where are they going?'

'The lady goes to Valencia, the guy to La Spezia.' Rodel sighed deeply. 'I better go and give him his towels.'

'Good luck with it, Rodel.'

'Thanks, I need it...'

The next morning it was confirmed that there wasn't enough time to go on shore leave. I was a bit disappointed, but there wasn't much we could do about it. I did however, want to set foot on Savannah soil, so after breakfast I walked down the gangway to find a phone on the quay to phone my parents. Arjen had also phoned them and told them that he and Rolf were having a great time exploring The Big Apple.

Loading was complete at 11.00h and I went down to the quay for the second time that day, to take some nice pictures of the *Serenity River* without the gantry cranes. Mr Reyes was standing at the top of the gangway, keeping an eye out for the pilot and I told him not to haul up the gangway, before I was back on board.

After I had taken the pictures, it was time for lunch.

There had been another alteration in the mess. Christina, Brian and I had now moved to the largest table in the far corner, where all the passengers could sit together. I had never sat at that table before.

Lunch was utter chaos. I felt so sorry for Rodel.

He just wasn't able to explain to Cecile, the French lady, that the soup was the starter after which would follow the main course. She kept asking for things that were not on the menu. Christina tried to help out with translating, but her French, although the best of everyone on board, was only school French, and unfortunately it didn't help much to clear things up.

Georg, the German guy, was nice enough, but loved talking and was holding long monologues which no-one was listening to, as we were all trying to explain to Cecile about the menu.

I was glad when lunch was over and escaped to the wing of the bridge for a bit of peace and quiet, and see us depart and go down the river again.

After I had taken a last wistful look at downtown Savannah, the ship went past an oil refinery, next to which was another Civil War fort, like the one I had seen in Norfolk a few days before, but smaller.

Urbanisation disappeared and the swamps took over again. I looked down at the muddy riverbank and hoped I would see some alligators. I didn't see any, but as I looked up, I saw a huge bald eagle sitting in a tree, right in front of my eyes. It was dark brown with a white head and it was watching the ship go by. It was the only time I ever saw one of those magnificent birds in the wild.

As the ship neared the river mouth, I decided to walk to the fo'c'sle.

Christina had beaten me to it. She sat on one of the bollards and watched as the riverbank went past. I sat down as well and we chatted for a while.

Suddenly I heard familiar splish-splash sounds coming from the bow of the ship. I ran towards the pointed end of the fo'c'sle and looked down over the bulkhead at the bulbous nose far below me in the water. Three dolphins, two large ones and a small one, were jumping in and out of the water in front of the nose. I was ecstatic. I had seen dolphins from the fo'c'sle before, but never had I seen them jump in front of a ship, as I had seen them do on tv.

Hanging over the bulkhead Christina and I shouted in delight every time the graceful animals jumped out of the water. They stayed with us for ten minutes, then moved off to find another ship.

In the evening we put the clock forward one hour. I wondered if Cecile had understood what Christina meant when she told her about it during the evening meal.

CHAPTER THIRTY-TWO

I stared at the screen of my computer at the list I had just made of all the things I still needed to do before we reached Valencia. It was huge.

I sighed deeply. So much still to do and only nine days to get it done.

There was a knock on my door and Rodel came in carrying a vacuum cleaner and a bucket full of bottles with cleaning aids. He was now cleaning my cabin on Mondays.

'What are you doing today?' he asked as he pulled the electrical cord out of the vacuum cleaner.

'I will be writing the whole day,' I answered. 'Norfolk and Savannah.'

'Pity you couldn't go ashore in Savannah yesterday.' He walked to the wall socket to plug in the vacuum cleaner. 'I have heard some interesting gossip.'

'Tell me...'

'The chief engineer has been nagging the captain the whole morning about having a barbecue on our way back to Europe. But the captain doesn't want it. He says the weather is too bad to have a barbecue out in the open. So now the chief is really angry with the captain and has gone down to the engine-room very grumpy.'

'The captain is right. The weather is too bad to have a barbecue. What is the chief thinking of?'

'Well... you remember what I have said before: the chief is only interested in free beer.'

I nodded. 'Yeah, I remember.'

Rodel plugged the vacuum cleaner into the wall socket and switched the machine on with his foot.

'Talking about parties,' I said loudly. 'I am going to give a farewell party soon. Probably before we reach the Mediterranean.'

Rodel switched the vacuum cleaner off.

'That's great! Did you know it is Mr Morayta's and Mr Lozada's birthdays soon as well?'

'No, I didn't know that. Maybe we could organise something together.'

'My thoughts exactly,' Rodel said and he switched the vacuum cleaner back on, leaving me pondering options.

Lunch was chaotic again. Cecile still didn't understand how the meals worked and I started to think she probably never would.

Georg had arrived a bit late that morning for lunch and he explained to us that he didn't live by watch or clock.

'But how do you know when it is time to eat?' I asked him.

'I totally rely on my internal clock,' Georg answered. 'It tells me when it is time to eat, and when it is time to sleep. No problem.'

'But we will have to put the clocks forward on an almost daily basis during our Atlantic crossing. For sure your internal clock will get confused after a while.'

'I don't think so.' He sounded very sure. 'I will be fine.'

I thought to myself that it would be interesting to see if he would be affected by the ship lag that was inevitably going to affect most of the people on board in the week to come.

We had to catch up on an extra hour as well. On our way from Europe to the United States we had to change the clocks six times to get to US time, but now, on our way back, we had seven changes to look forward to. Europe would go to summer time before we reached Valencia, putting its clocks forward one hour, thereby leaving us to catch up an extra hour.

Two days later, Wednesday 26th March, I was hanging up posters for the combined birthday/farewell party Mr Morayta, Mr Lozada and I had organised when I bumped into Ramon in the corridor on deck 1.

'That is a nice poster,' Ramon remarked as I taped one of the posters to the wall near the galley. 'Everybody is looking forward to tonight.'

'Yeah, me too,' I nodded yawning.

'I'm sorry, Ramon. I am not yawning because I am talking to you, but because of all the clock changing. I am very tired.'

I had woken up that morning still feeling as if it was the middle of the night. The ship lag had kicked in earlier and more severely than ever before.

'I understand,' Ramon smiled. 'We are all tired. But tonight we will have fun!'

'Absolutely.'

I walked to the mess to hang up a poster in there. The last two days I had managed to finish all the writing for the guide-book. Christina had volunteered to read everything I had written and take out any spelling and grammatical mistakes. Although my English was good enough, it was always good to have a native English speaker check things out.

I wasn't able to spend as much time with the passengers as I wanted, but that was mainly due to the guide-book and the need to finish it before we reached Valencia. Of the four passengers Christina and Brian were the ones who spent several hours a day in the officers' lounge reading books, or playing cards. Georg and Cecile mostly stayed in their cabins and we usually only saw them during meal times.

I hung up a poster on the door of the officers' lounge and one on the notice board in the stairwell. I was happy to see that there wasn't a clock-changing announcement on the notice board. Tonight at least we didn't need to change the clocks.

The last poster I hung up in the crew-mess, next to the daily telex printouts of the world news and piracy alerts. I hadn't heard much news in the last few days, so had little idea of what was happening in the world.

***

'I am afraid that Christina can't come to the party tonight,' Brian said as he sat down next to me on the couch in the crew-lounge.

'Oh..? I hope she isn't ill?'

'She has a bit of a cold and really didn't feel up to going. She's really sorry she can't be here, as she was looking forward to it.'

I nodded. 'Yes, she told me. I hope she will feel better soon.'

Almost everyone on board had gathered in the lounge for the party. I had never seen the room so full. The captain was sitting near the tv and was talking to some of the Filipinos. The second officer and Georg were standing at the bar and were having a good natured discussion with Mr Navaez and Mr Orozco, who were behind the bar, handing out drinks. I was sitting near Mr Morayta and Rodel – we nibbled some Pringles crisps.

To get the party going, Mr Lozada switched on the karaoke machine and started singing the first song of the evening. When his song was finished, it was Mr Morayta's turn.

'Is it typical of a Filipino party that the birthday boys start off the singing?' I asked Rodel.

'Yes,' he nodded. 'Soon it will be your turn.'

'But it is not my birthday, so I don't have to sing,' I said, glad that Cecile had chosen that moment to step into the lounge. Several of the guys jumped up to give her a seat.

After most of the guys had sung, Brian and Ramon sang a duet. The crowd cheered them on.

Brian's enthusiasm infected the second officer who also volunteered to sing. His voice was beautiful and he was asked for several encores.

True to a typical party on a container ship, dancing followed the singing. By this time, Cecile and some of the Germans had gone back to their cabins, but Brian and the captain were still there, as were the second officer and the ship-mechanics. Some of us danced together in the space in front of the tv. Brian joined in as well.

After the dancing, more singing followed. It was a great evening.

When the party was finished at 01.00h, I told Rodel not to expect me for breakfast.

I had planned to have a lie in the next morning and I was doing well until the phone rang and woke me up at 08.30h. It was the first officer.

'Good morning. I am phoning you to warn you that the disk I lent you with the pictures of the ship might have a virus on it. So you better check your computer to make sure the virus hasn't infected that as well.'

'A virus... okay... I will check it...' was all I could bring out and hang up again. I fell back asleep immediately.

At 10.00h, a ringing phone woke me up again. As I answered, I thought that it was typical that normally no one ever phoned me and *now* that I wanted to sleep in, I was phoned twice.

It was Rodel. 'Good morning! I am ringing you to wake you up. It is ten in the morning.'

'I didn't tell you to wake me up at ten.'

'No? I could have sworn...'

'I said not to expect me for breakfast... I want to sleep until eleven.'

'Ah... Well, in that case you can sleep for another hour...' It sounded like he was smiling.

'Yeah, I know... I will...' I hung up and fell back asleep.

The next time I woke up it was 11.10h. For some reason my alarm hadn't gone off at 11.00h as planned, but at least I was awake. I had a shower and then went down to the mess, where I was nicely in time for lunch.

CHAPTER THIRTY-THREE

It was Friday 28th March, and I was busy doing the final edit of the guide-book. Christina was feeling a lot better and was now at top speed reading the chapters.

At 10.00h, there was a knock on my door. It was Brian.

'Here's the first bit that Christina has checked,' he said handing me a pile of papers. 'The rest will come a bit later.'

'Thank you. Now I can start printing the first lot.' I flicked through the pages that Christina had checked and saw she had found some weird mistakes.

After I had made the changes, I got ready to start the printing. The guide-book had a total of 61 pages, which all had to be printed out separately, before being put in see-through pockets that were going to be collected in a large ring binder. I had to print a total of three copies with the name *Serenity River*, and another three copies, each with a different name of the sister ships. The printing didn't only require a lot of patience, but also concentration, as I had to make sure the print-outs for the different ships didn't get mixed up.

In the evening, I escaped the printing for a while and spent some time with the guys in the crew-lounge. Mr Reyes played his guitar, while others played cards or chatted. The evening was short as for the fifth time since leaving Savannah we had to put the clocks forward an hour. I tried to go to bed at a normal hour, but couldn't sleep for a long time.

At breakfast the next day Christina handed me another batch of edited chapters.

'The last ones will come this afternoon,' she smiled.

I smiled back. 'Thank you. I really appreciate you checking everything. Otherwise the books would have been printed with some very bad mistakes.'

'You're welcome. I enjoy reading it.'

I continued printing during the day and just before it was time for the evening meal, Christina brought me the last pages she had checked. Now I could finish off printing the guide-books. It was exciting finally to see the finished product. I planned to hand the first book to the captain the next day.

Before I continued printing in the evening, I had another haircut by Mr Navaez. While he cut my hair, he complained about the severity of the ship lag during this crossing.

'Everyone is terribly affected,' he remarked. 'Far more than before.'

'Yeah, I have noticed that myself. The passengers are feeling it as well. I don't know why it should be so bad this time.'

'Well, we can only hope we don't have to change much more.'

'Only two more left, I think.'

***

The captain was flicking through the guide-book I had just officially handed to him.

The passengers were all gathered together in the captain's cabin for a Sunday morning drink before lunch and I had thought this the perfect time to hand him the finished book.

'This is looking really good,' the captain said. 'There is lots of information in here that the passengers might need during their stay on board. Well done.' He handed the book to Georg, who looked through it.

'Have you finished your printing now?' Christina asked.

'No, I still have to do the ones for the sister ships and my own personal copy. I will be printing for a lot longer.'

'I thought printing was easy,' Georg said.

'It can be,' I answered. 'But this guide-book is saved in loads of different files, which all have many pictures. They take a long time to print.'

'I believe you,' he smiled and handed the book to Cecile.

'When are we going to be in Valencia, captain?' Brain asked.

'Probably on Wednesday.'

'And will we be able to see the Rock of Gibraltar?'

'That depends on the weather, but I do think we will pass through the Strait during the day.'

I pretended to listen to the conversation, but as soon as the captain had mentioned arriving in Valencia on Wednesday, I had started to calculate how many more days I had left to finish the printing. I was planning to send my printer and scanner back home from Valencia and any printing would have to be finished before then.

I spent the rest of the day printing and after the evening meal joined the guys in the crew-lounge, where I showed them the finished guide-book.

As I went to bed that night I put the clock forward another hour.

The next day I did still *more* printing. However, I also started sorting out all the stuff that had accumulated in my cabin over the last three months. I had realised it would be impossible for me to take it all back on the train myself, so I was going to send some things back with the printer from Valencia.

On the way over two boxes, one with my printer and scanner and one full of supplies like paper, ink cartridges, see-through pockets, ring binders etc. had been flown over to La Spezia to meet me on onboard the *Serenity River*. Now I estimated I could probably fill three boxes, what with all the brochures and other souvenirs I had collected.

As the printer rattled away on the pages of the guide-book, I stood and surveyed the stuff I had spread out on the floor of the living room. There were three piles: one of stuff that could be chucked out, one of items I wanted to send home in Valencia and one of the things I would take with me on the train.

Ramon had given me a spare cardboard box for the extra things I wanted to send back.

While looking through all the cupboards and drawers for things to send home I had come across one small item, that I had absent mindedly put in my night-stand drawer a few days earlier, but that was actually really important to me.

It was a small bone hanger in the form of a stylised fishhook fastened to a piece of black string. I had put it on the pile to-take-home-myself. I picked it up and put it around my neck thinking back at how the hanger had become mine.

Two years before my trip on the *Serenity River*, I was in Auckland, New Zealand, where I had already boarded the *Galactic Star* for my journey back to Europe. We were to set sail in the afternoon and in the morning, I took my chance and went ashore for some last minute shopping. During my six months in New Zealand, I had been looking for a nice bone hanger, a typical Kiwi souvenir, in the form of a dolphin, but I had never been able to find one that I liked.

As I walked up the steep main street in downtown Auckland, I saw on the pavement a stand behind which a lady was selling souvenirs, many of which were bone hangers. I stopped to see if she had any dolphins that I liked.

'Are you looking for a hanger?' she asked as she saw me checking out the animal shaped hangers.

'Yes, I have been looking for a dolphin.' I took one of the hangers of the rack. It was a dolphin and I really liked it.

'Why do you want a dolphin?' the lady asked. She pointed at another rack, which had hangers in the more traditional Maori shapes. 'These hangers have the traditional symbols of my people.'

I looked at the hangers she pointed out. 'I would love to have a hanger like that as well,' I said, 'but this is my last day in New Zealand and I have only a few New Zealand dollars left.'

'You are leaving today?'

'Yes, this afternoon.' I looked again at the dolphin hanger in my hand. It was very pretty, although not traditional Maori.

I handed the hanger to her. 'I just love dolphins, so I am afraid I will take this one. I am sorry if I don't choose one that is a Maori symbol.'

'That is okay, darling. Don't worry. Dolphins are very special animals.' She wrapped the hanger in some paper and handed it to me. I paid her and as I turned to leave, she called me back.

'Just wait a second, darling.' I turned round and saw her looking through the Maori hangers on the rack, and take one off. 'This hanger is in the shape of a fishhook,' she said holding it up. 'The fishhook is the Maori symbol for safe-journey-over-water.' She handed me the hanger. 'Here, you take it.'

'But... I don't have any money left.'

'Take it. You are going to travel over water, aren't you?' I nodded. The hairs on the back of neck had started to tingle. 'Then it is for you. It will keep you safe.'

'Thank you.' I suddenly felt very emotional. I hadn't told the woman I was going to spend the next two months on a ship, and yet she had given me this special hanger.

I thanked her again and as I walked back to the ship I put the fishhook around my neck, where it stayed for two months and where was consequently was on all my later journeys on ships.

That evening on the *Serenity River,* I managed to get all the Filipinos together outside on deck 1, where one of the ship-mechanics took a group photo of us.

In the evening, the clock was put forward for the last time. We were finally back on European time and could try to shake off our ship lag. Over the last week, Georg hadn't managed to change his internal clock in sync with the changing of the clocks. To be honest, I had not expected he could. After each time change, he had showed up later for breakfast until one morning Rodel had found him in the mess at 11.00h, expecting to be in time for breakfast. It didn't seem to worry him that he missed out on meals.

I wondered if it was better to keep with the changing of the clocks and try to stick to the new time, or to ignore it like Georg had. He surely seemed to get more sleep and was less tired, but eventually he would *have* to catch up on the time. I concluded that his method was more like jet lag, while the rest of us were all suffering from ship lag. However, Georg was lucky he was a passenger. Had he been a crew-member, he wouldn't have had a choice but to follow ships time.

The next day I finally finished printing after which I packed the boxes that were to be sent home from Valencia.

At 16.30h, we neared the Strait of Gibraltar. I went to the bridge and found that Christina and Brian were already there. Land was in sight, Europe on the left and Africa on the right, with a narrow opening in the middle for the Strait.

Due to the shipping lanes, we had to stay closer to the African coast this time. The weather on the European side wasn't very good. It was misty and rainy and it was impossible to see the Rock. That was a bit disappointing for Christina and Brian, but at least the weather on the African side was good. We could see Jebel Musa, a mountain on Morocco's north coast that sometimes, together with the Rock of Gibraltar, is referred to as the 'two pillars of Hercules', the end of the known world in Grecian times.

The Strait was busy and many ships were traversing it, but there were also numerous ferries crossing the shipping lanes from Africa to Europe and back. With Brian, I walked on to the wing of the bridge to have a view straight down into the water. The moment we looked down, a small pod of pilot whales swam past the ship. It was magnificent to see these huge animals moving through the water.

Christina came running up at Brian's shouts and was able to catch a glimpse of them. They both thought that seeing the whales made up a lot for missing out on the Rock.

In the evening, I went to their cabin for a few farewell drinks. Even though I had not spent that much time with them, we had become friends. They showed me pictures of their house in Canada and I showed them pictures of the earlier part of the trip on board the *Serenity*.

It was quite late when I went to bed.

CHAPTER THIRTY-FOUR

We berthed at Valencia at 14.00h the next day, Wednesday 2nd April. The city still looked the same from the sun-deck. The strike was over. I hoped the port workers had achieved whatever they had wanted to achieve.

I decided I wanted to go into the city in the afternoon, mainly to develop some pictures. I was particularly curious about the group photo with the guys.

When the agent came, I arranged with him to send my boxes back to the Netherlands by courier. I had to fill in a customs declaration form and the agent told me he would pick the boxes up the next morning before we departed Valencia.

Christina and Brian disembarked in Valencia, as did Cecile. Rodel was secretly happy she was going.

Two taxis came to the bottom of the gangway at 16.00h to pick everyone up. Georg was riding with Cecile to give her a hand with her luggage at the railway station and Christina and Brian had offered me a lift into the city.

'How long will you be staying in Valencia?' I asked as we drove through the suburbs on our way to the city centre.

'We will be here for three days and then take the train to Barcelona,' Christina answered.

'Valencia is a beautiful city,' I said. 'Don't forget to take a look at the withered arm of St Vincent in the cathedral.'

'We won't.'

We arrived at the station and I got out. 'I wish you both a very nice continuation of your trip,' I smiled.

'Yes, you too,' Christina said. 'And have a good journey home.'

'Thank you.' The taxi drove off and I waved. Then I spotted the other taxi. Georg was helping Cecile out of the car. I said goodbye to Cecile and then walked into the city centre, looking for a photographers. I found one in a side street.

Waiting for my pictures to be ready, I walked further into the city and ended up at the cathedral square. The weather was nice and warm and the square was packed with tourists. I bought some newspapers and sandwiches. I wasn't going to make it back to the ship in time for the evening meal.

I sat on a bench in the square for a while flicking through the newspapers. I was a bit shocked to find that almost all the articles in the paper were about Iraq and the war. Being on the ship, I hadn't heard much news, and I was actually glad about that.

I ate my sandwiches and then walked into the cathedral for another quick look at St Vincent's arm. It was still lying in its pretty box with a gaggle of tourists goggling at it.

After I had picked up the pictures, I took a taxi back to the ship, where I was dropped off at the bottom of the gangway at 19.00h.

The day after, a Thursday, we were still in Valencia when I woke up. Officially, shore leave was until 10.00h, but I didn't feel like going into the city again. Instead, I walked on to the quay and took some pictures of the ship.

Mr Figueira had taken my three boxes down to the ship's office on the main deck, from where they were to be picked up by the agent.

Our departure was delayed by a couple of hours, but at 13.30h, we left.

Just before the gangway was hauled up, the agent came onboard for a quick talk to the captain and the removal of my boxes. Mr Morayta helped carry them down to the quay and then sprinted back up to haul in the gangway. As I walked to the fo'c'sle to see us go, I saw the agent stuffing my boxes into the boot of his car. It was warm and sunny, and sweaty spots had appeared on the back of his shirt. He wiped his forehead with his arm.

The fo'c'sle was a haven of tranquillity. The captain hadn't given the order to release the lines yet and Mr Adega and the deck crew were hanging around, lazily sitting on bollards and looking out over the port. I joined them. Then they were set to work releasing the lines. As always being on the fo'c'sle made me feel detached from the rest of the ship and as we glided out of the port, I stayed for a while and looked out over the calm Mediterranean Sea.

In the evening, I spent some time with the guys in the crew-lounge playing cards. I was still tired from the ship lag and couldn't concentrate very well. At 20.30h, I retired to my cabin where I read the last bits of the newspaper I had bought in Valencia.

I went to bed at 21.30h, but woke up two hours later from the sound of a big wave crashing into our hull. A storm had apparently come up. I fell back asleep, but woke up again two hours later. The *Serenity* was pitching and rolling like mad, waves crashed into our hull that sent shudders through the ship.

I switched on the light and saw that my alarm clock and book had tumbled to the floor despite them being on a rubber anti-slip mat. I got out of bed and walked to the living room, worried that my laptop might have crashed to the floor as well. It hadn't yet, so I put it on the floor where it was safe. Then I went back to bed and fell asleep again.

The next day, the storm was still raging - a force 12 hurricane that had come up out of nowhere. Our speed was a measly seven knots.

In the morning, I spent some time on the bridge and looked at the waves as they crashed into our hull, sending large sprays of green water all the way up to the bridge.

The captain was on the bridge as well. He didn't seem worried.

'This is not going to last long,' he said, looking as more green water splattered with force against the windows. He turned to me. 'This is your last day at sea, isn't it?'

'Yep,' I nodded.

'Then this storm is Neptune's way of saying goodbye to you.'

'I like that,' I smiled at him.

The storm died down in the afternoon and then completely disappeared. At 15.00h, I went down to the crew-mess for a cup of tea with the guys. They asked me how many words I had learned in Tagalog and ticking them of my fingers, named them all. There were more than I thought.

During the evening meal, the captain gave me my mile certificate. In my three months on the *Serenity River,* I had travelled an astonishing 29,592 nautical miles, which equals 54,804 kilometres, close to one-and-a-half times around the world along the equator.

After the meal, I went to the crew-lounge. I was now very well aware that it was almost time for me to leave the ship. Mr Reyes sang and played his guitar and asked me what my favourite songs were. Together we looked through his songbook and he played them for me.

I couldn't sleep and at 22.30h, I went to the bridge for a chat with Mr Adega. The bridge was dark, but as before the radar screen and some other little lights illuminated the interior. I sat down in the second chair.

'So, this is your last night on board,' Mr Adega said.

'That depends,' I replied. 'I will probably take the train back home on Sunday. I hope that if the *Serenity* is scheduled to stay in port until Sunday morning the captain will allow me to stay on board for another night.'

'I am sure he will allow that. We're not expecting any passengers, so your cabin will be free.'

'When will we be arriving in La Spezia?'

'Tomorrow morning. I am sure we won't leave until Sunday, so you can stay on board for another night. I give you permission for that!'

I smiled at him. 'Thank you. I will let the captain know...'

I looked out over the water. The clouds had gone and a faint moon was shining on the waves. They were calm again. It was hard to believe we had been in a hurricane earlier in the day.

'Are you looking forward to going home?' Mr Adega asked.

'Yes, of course. But I know I will get homesick for the ship as well.'

'You must keep in touch with us.'

'I will.'

***

The next morning, Saturday 5th April, we arrived in the Bay of La Spezia around 07.00h. I looked out of the window and saw the city in the distance, bathed in the sunlight. We were waiting for a pilot, but at that moment, we were going nowhere. There wasn't space for us at the quay yet.

After breakfast, I started sorting out the stuff I hadn't sent home. Most of it were clothes. At 09.00h, I went up to the bridge.

'Still no space at the quay?' I asked Mr Adega, who was looking through his binoculars at the port.

'No, not yet.' He handed me the binoculars. 'We're supposed to go where that large dark blue ship is on the right.'

I looked and saw that the gantry cranes had moved away from it. 'Looks like they've stopped loading.'

'Yeah, they have,' Mr Adega nodded. 'I am sure they will depart any minute.'

I walked back down to my cabin, but didn't feel like packing. Instead, I went to the sun-deck for a while. When I got there, I saw that the container ship that occupied our berth, had started to move, and a small pilot boat was coming towards us to drop off the pilot.

At 09.30h, we berthed in La Spezia. My days at sea were now officially over.

But my work wasn't done yet. I still had three guide-books on my desk that needed to be taken to *Serenity's* sister ships. As these ships would be arriving in the future, I had organised with the La Spezia agent that he would take the books to the respective ships when they arrived. To that end, I met the agent in the captain's office soon after he had arrived upstairs.

'So you have finished your job,' the agent said as I handed him the books.

'Yep, I have. I hope you will make sure these books get to the other ships when they berth here.'

'Of course I will, no problem.' He put the books on the table in front of him. 'Did your brother have a nice time on the ship?'

'He did, very much.'

'I am glad to hear it.'

Even though I am European and had arrived in a European port, I couldn't just go ashore. Like everyone else on board, I had to wait until customs and immigration had cleared us and gave me an official shore leave pass.

I was eager to go ashore, because I wanted to develop my last rolls of film and do reprints of the group photo for the guys. At 12.00h, we were finally cleared and I made my way down the gangway. I hadn't eaten anything yet. It was Saturday and eintopf was on the menu.

I found a small photographer's shop and handed in my requests. Then I wandered over to the supermarket where I bumped into the first officer.

Back on the ship, I tried to sleep for a while. This time I had remembered that the shops were to close between 13.00h and 15.00h and that the city had gone on siesta. I had to wait until after 15.00h to buy a train ticket. The captain had given me permission to stay on board one more night.

I couldn't sleep however, and at 14.00h went down to the crew-mess to see if there was anything left to eat.

Ramon had just returned from making a phone call ashore. Like me, he was hungry and quickly warmed up a bit of leftover eintopf, which we ate together in the mess. It didn't actually taste too bad.

At 14.30h, I walked down the gangway again and caught the bus to the railway station. By the time I got there, the shops were open again and I managed to buy a ticket for the train back to the Netherlands leaving the next morning. After that, I bought two newspapers, one for Ramon, and phoned my parents. I told them to expect me back home somewhere around midday on Monday.

On the way back to the ship, I picked up the pictures from the photographers. I returned to the ship at 17.20h, where I ate my last evening meal on board alone. Georg had disembarked and all the officers were at work, but Rodel kept me company.

In the evening, I went down to the crew-lounge for a while, and handed out reprints of the group photo to the guys who were there. It was quiet in the lounge as many of them were either working or sleeping. Rhythm of life on board always changed when we arrived in a port.

I played a few games of tong-its and then went upstairs to pack my bags. As all my belongings slowly disappeared into the depths of my backpack, my cabin changed back from being mine to being an empty shell, waiting for its next occupant.

I didn't sleep well my last night on board. Even though I knew that the loading would take until at least the afternoon of the next day, I kept waking up thinking we had already set sail and were back on the Mediterranean. Several times during the night, I got out of bed to check if we were still berthed.

The last time I woke up was at 04.30h. A tremble from loading a container had gone through the ship and in my dream, I mistook it for the tremble of the engines starting. I jumped out of bed and ran to the window, but the loading was still going on. The bright lights on the gantries lit up the scene. I watched for a while as Mr Reyes and Mr Morayta scampered along the containers on the deck unlocking twist locks.

They didn't notice me.

CHAPTER THIRTY-FIVE

It took me 28 hours to get back home from La Spezia by train. The boxes that had been sent from Valencia had already arrived.

The train left La Spezia at 10.44h. It was Sunday morning 6th April, and there were only a few buses to get me to the station from the port. I could obviously have taken a taxi, but I was so used to taking public transport that the thought didn't even cross my mind.

Rodel escorted me to the bus stop. Even though I had sent a lot of stuff home, my backpack was still ridiculously heavy. I hadn't been able to fit everything in, so on top of a small daypack, I also carried an extra plastic bag.

With Rodel's permission, I had prepared a packed lunch from the bread and buns we had for breakfast that morning. It was quiet at breakfast, even the captain was still asleep. At least I had managed to say goodbye to him and the first and second officers the evening before.

Now all that remained after breakfast was saying goodbye to the guys. As Rodel took my luggage down to the main deck, I walked around the ship for the last time. Here and there, I met crew-members and said goodbye to them. I even went into the engine-room to say goodbye to the guys that were working in there.

Then I went into the crew-mess where Rodel, Ramon, Mr Toribio and Mr Reyes were waiting. It was 09.00h and I needed to leave in order to catch the bus to the railway station. Single file, we walked to the gangway; the guys were carrying my luggage. Mr Adega was waiting at the top of the gangway.

I gave Ramon a hug and told him to keep up his high spirits and great cooking. Then I hugged Mr Adega who said that he would miss our chats on the bridge.

Rodel was the first person down the gangway. He carried my big backpack. I followed him, carrying my folded up trolley. Behind me came Mr Reyes carrying my daypack. He was followed by Mr Toribio with the plastic bag. There was something surreal and slightly comical about the whole situation.

On the quay, I fastened my big backpack to the trolley. Rodel carried the daypack and plastic bag. After saying goodbye to Mr Reyes and Mr Toribio, we walked towards the gate. I looked back every now and then to wave at the guys, who were still standing at the top of the gangway.

'You will write, won't you?' Rodel asked as we walked along the main road to the bus stop.

'Yes, I will. I promise.'

'Life on board will be boring now,' Rodel sighed.

I tried a smile. 'I am sure you will have some new exiting passengers soon.'

We reached the bus stop. It didn't take long for the bus to arrive. I hugged Rodel and said I would miss him dreadfully. He helped me get my luggage on board. The bus drove off and I waved to him through the window.

Gathering my bags around me as well as I could, I sat down in an empty seat. The bus wasn't very full.

One of my rules is never to look back when leaving a place where I had a good time, but in the bus I couldn't help myself. In the bend towards the city, an opening appeared in between the industrial buildings of the port. I looked through it and saw the top of the *Serenity's* accommodation block, the bridge and monkey-deck, sticking out above the containers. The Italian flag on the little mast swayed limply in the breeze.

Then the bus turned a corner and everything disappeared from sight.

MORE STORIES OF TIME ZONES
AND CONTAINERS

A chemical spill out of a container and a collision with another ship - the adventures of life on the high seas continue in More Stories of Time Zones and Containers.

A collection of 16 previously untold short stories More Stories *is a fitting sequel to* Time Zones, Containers and Three Square Meals a Day. *The authors recalls further adventures on board the* Serenity River, FTK Kowloon *and* Galactic Star, *as these large container ships travel the around world.*

So how quickly does one become seasick in a lifeboat?

Curious about Maria's further adventures on the *Serenity River, FTK Kowloon* and *Galactic Star*? Then grab a copy of *More Stories of Time Zones and Containers*, which contains 16 untold short stories of life on board the container ships, and is available as paperback.

Read on for one of the short stories of *More Stories of Time Zones and Containers*

FOCUSED ON FOOD

I knew something wasn't right as soon as I stepped out of the taxi. It wasn't actually hard to guess something was wrong as the whole area in front of the gate was full of police cars and fire engines, all with silently flashing blue lights.

I had come back from a day's shore leave, visiting some friends in Geelong, when I returned to the gate at Melbourne's Swanson Dock.

A group of people stood behind some yellow tape on which was printed in black letters 'Danger - Do Not Cross'. They were looking towards the port, possibly to find out what was happening, but nothing much was to be seen.

I heard my stomach rumble as I made my way towards the gate building. It was almost time for the evening meal and I felt as if I could eat a lot.

I reached the gate building from where a security officer looked down on me through a little window with a sliding pane of glass. His brown hair was pasted to his forehead in straggly strands, from under which the sweat dripped down his brow. He looked at me with a bored face.

'Can I help you?'

'Yes, I was wondering what is happening here?'

'Do you belong to any of the ships that are currently berthed in the port?' He now looked bored and annoyed, probably thinking I was a thrill seeker.

'I do. I am a passenger on the *Galactic Star*.'

'No worries. I can't let you in, though.'

'What has happened?'

He sighed. Clearly, he had told the story before. 'A container standing on the quay has leaked some stuff and until we know if it's toxic or not, all cargo operations have been suspended and all people evacuated. No one is allowed in.'

'But I don't want to miss the evening meal.' My stomach rumbled, as if to concur.

'Sorry, but I can't help you there. You're not allowed to go in.'

I turned to walk away, disheartened. I had been looking forward to the evening meal as I knew the cook had been preparing fried potatoes with onions and veggies, which I loved.

Then I saw the first officer of the *Galactic Star* get out of a taxi and walk towards me.

'What's going on here?' he said in his strong German accent, looking at the fire engines and police cars.

'A leaking container. We're not allowed to go in.'

He looked at his watch. 'But my shift starts in 15 minutes! I will talk to the guy.'

Together we walked to the gate. Again, the man looked down with a bored face.

'I need to get to my ship,' the first officer said. 'My shift starts in 15 minutes and I still need something to eat.'

The man slowly turned his head to look from the first officer to me, and then back. I could almost hear him thinking that the only thoughts on our minds seemed to be about food.

'No one is working at the moment as all cargo operations have been suspended, so the good news is that you won't be too late for your shift,' the man said with a hint of the dry Australian humour I had learned to recognise during my stay in the country.

'Bad news is, I can't let you in,' the man continued, 'so I suggest you get the weight of your feet somewhere, in anticipation of the all-clear.'

The first officer realised that there was no arguing with the man and sighed deeply. We turned around and saw that the little shop outside the gate had some chairs and tables. We sat down and waited.

More taxis arrived delivering people to the gate. They were all, one by one, turned down by the security officer.

At some point a few firemen appeared from behind the gate, wearing white hazmat suits. Nothing more seemed to happen and we continued waiting. The first officer looked at his watch every five minutes and my stomach rumbled more and more ominously.

Then after 35 minutes of waiting, more firemen and policemen came sauntering back from behind the gate. One of the policemen started taking down the yellow tape, while the firemen disappeared into their fire engines and drove off. When all the tape was rolled up, the policemen got into their vehicles as well and drove away.

The first officer and I got up from our chairs and walked back towards the gate. The security officer had stepped outside his office and was now waving people through. Clearly, the emergency had past.

We joined some other men in the shuttle bus which took us across the port to the *Galactic Star*, where the first officer and I got off. We climbed the gangway and made our way to the mess. The steward had saved us some fried potatoes and veggies, which the first officer started to wolf down. I ate a bit slower.

We never did find out what the stuff was that had leaked out of the container on the quay, but clearly, it hadn't been too dangerous. Otherwise, our exile would have lasted longer than just the 35 minutes we had had to wait.

###

ACKNOWLEDGEMENTS

Many people helped me getting this book ready for publication and I am grateful for all their help.

In particular, I would like to thank Anita Nicholson, Carla Jol, Yvonne Klein-Wildeboer, Ria van Loenen and Jonny Todd for reading early copies of the manuscript and giving me helpful tips on how to improve it.

I especially want to mention and thank my friend Graeme Robertson for his ongoing willingness to read my manuscripts and his advice about grammar, spelling and punctuation. I also like to thank his wife Ann for providing a lovely lunch, while Graeme and I were slaving over the computer, ironing out my grammar.

I would also like to thank Linda Elder for critiquing my manuscript and advising me to make some very important last-minute adjustments.

I would like to thank the officers, crew and passengers of all the ships I have travelled on, for their companionship during the long hours at sea, and the fun times during shore leave. I also like to thank the Ariel Rügen Shipping Company, for giving me the chance to take these wonderful journeys in the first place.

Rodel deserves a special mention. He graciously allowed letting me use his real name. After spending three months with Rodel on the *Serenity River*, we became lifelong friends and I am glad that he was able to move his career up from steward to chief cook.

Finally, I would like to thank my brother Arjen and his wife Helma, Nick and my brother's friend Rolf, who besides Rodel, let me use their real names. Consequently, all the other names mentioned in this book, including those of the ships and shipping company, have been changed.

PICTURE ACKNOWLEDGEMENTS

All the pictures in the book were taken by the author except:
Shanghai skyline, taken by Mr Chavira; Author lying on the deck of the fo'c'sle, taken by Alec; Author hanging around on fo'c'sle in Valencia, taken by Mr Adega; Star Wars in Fos sur Mer and the two pictures of the storm in the Atlantic, taken by Arjen Staal; Author and Rodel taken by Mr Reyes.

All the maps in this book were made by the author.

ABOUT THE AUTHOR

Author, Traveller and Mad about Architecture, Maria Staal was born in the Netherlands where she studied construction engineering and became a specialist in architectural history. Her love of travel led her to embark on not one, but two ocean crossings on container ships, which in turn led to an impromptu job working for a shipping company writing guidebooks for their passengers.

She also spent four years living in the medieval town of York in the United Kingdom, where she wrote two books about the history and architecture of that unique city.

Maria blogs about her experiences as a writer at www.mariastaal.com.

Follow Maria on Twitter at @mariastaal and Facebook at Maria-Staal-Author

28776397R00180

Made in the USA
Lexington, KY
02 January 2014